DODGING EVIL

A Yaqui Girl's Shocking Education from Society, Religion, and Spirituality

PC FIELD

© 2021 P.C. Field

All rights reserved.

No part of this publication in print or in electronic format may be reproduced, stored in a retrieval system, or transmitted in any form or by any means, electronic, mechanical, photocopying, recording, or otherwise without the prior written permission of the publisher.

The scanning, uploading, and distribution of this book without permission is a theft of the author's intellectual property. If you would like permission to use material from the book (other than for review purposes), please contact info@bublish.com. Thank you for your support of the author's rights.

Editing, Design and Distribution by Bublish, Inc.

Paperback ISBN: 978-1-64704-190-8
eBook ISBN: 978-1-64704-191-5

To all who are seeking a spiritual connection
with God that is real and personal.

To those who are lost in the wastelands of religion and spirituality.

To those who are confused and looking for answers to the
questions, "Who am I?" "Where did I come from?" "What
am I doing here?" "Where am I going?" and "Why?"

Table of Contents

Foreword ix
Acknowledgements xi
Introduction xiii

ACT 1: THE BEGINNING

Chapter 1　The Joy of Innocence 1
Chapter 2　Our First Trip North 21
Chapter 3　Back Home 30
Chapter 4　A New Life & New Lessons 37
Chapter 5　More Death Rituals 44

ACT 2: DODGING EVIL

Chapter 6　School Daze 51
Chapter 7　Church Dogma 59
Chapter 8　Responsibility & Dependence 67
Chapter 9　Dreams, Visions & Nightmares 75
Chapter 10　Temper Tantrums & Lies 81
Chapter 11　A Long Walk on the Dark Side 93
Chapter 12　A Life for a Life 99
Chapter 13　Love? and Marriage 115

ACT 3: SURRENDERING

Chapter 14 Awakening 131
Chapter 15 On the Fence 154
Chapter 16 Finding Brian 164
Chapter 17 Overflowing 183
Chapter 18 Church Dogma vs. Spirituality 193
Chapter 19 More Spiritual Lessons 224
Chapter 20 True Love and Marriage 233
Chapter 21 Everything Takes Time 249

Epilogue 255
About the Author 257

Foreword

There is a thing biblical theologians call "positional" sanctification, and then there is that which they call "experiential" sanctification. When a person receives Christ as Lord and Savior, he is "sanctified" unto the Lord at that moment. He is the Lord's redeemed, saved, eternal child and nothing less than that forever. That's his "positional" sanctification. However, there is a process we go through in life in which we grow "experientially" in that sanctification. That's spiritual growth, and that's what Paul is talking about when he says in Philippians 3 that he has not attained yet, but forgetting those things that are behind, he presses forward for the prize of the upward call of God in Christ Jesus. We are all on that path, aren't we? Not there yet, but pressing ahead.

Dodging Evil is a very interesting and insightful book on the spiritual reality that constitutes the essential element of our existence. And best of all, it points to Jesus!

Brian Larson, Calvary Chapel Truckee, September 12, 2017

Acknowledgements

This memoir never would have been completed without the generous assistance of Writer's Digest Books, agents in their awesome workshops, and boot camps. Marion Roach-Smith, Danielle Barthel, Gina Panettieri, Mark Malatesta, Paula Munier, Alexa Bigwarfe, Mr. Geoffrey Stone, and Jerry Jenkins, masters of editing, you all were "special helpers." I am forever in your debt. Michael and Kathie Giorgio of AllWriters' Workplace and Workshop and dear friend Angela Hughes, I value all your guidance and every critique more than you will ever know. Ryan Davenport, Kayce Henderson, and The Deb, my indispensable technical support team, without you, I would still be sitting at my computer, wondering what in the world to do next.

Brian Larson, you helped me find Christ Jesus and my way back to God. Without you, I wouldn't have a story to share. My husband and son, your encouragement to write and reassuring reviews were priceless. Last, but certainly not least, my many clients who insisted I write this book in the first place, thank you, one and all. You were right. I needed to do this.

Introduction

Long before we became flesh and blood, we existed solely in spirit. We shared an open relationship with our Creator and worked out, in detail, what our physical lives would be while here on Earth. We each came for a specific purpose with lessons to learn along the way, a goal to reach, and the gifts and abilities to do so. I believe no one is here by accident. I know I am not.

We are one with all creation, made from the same energy and spirit. We come from God, we are of Him, and we have free will to choose whether to walk with Him or fall into the darkness of self. When I surrender all of my *self* to Him, I am made whole; I neither need nor desire anything in this world of flesh. Staying surrendered is the hard part.

From the moment we are born, we are bombarded with distractions and diversions designed to prevent us from following our destiny. Our physical, fleshly, self-minded selves are more than happy to be misled. Our worlds, both physical and spiritual, are filled with imposters, false gods, liars, and corruptors of truth and light. All are wolves in sheep's clothing looking to lead us away from the truth and devour us spiritually.

Our physical selves are flawed. We have egos that get bruised easily. We are selfish, prideful, judgmental, and covetous. We can be very emotional, but those pesky temper tantrums are the worst! We begin to veer away from our chosen path and commitment. We forget where we have come from and why we came.

We learn behaviors and tactics from those around us. We learn to lie, cheat, steal, hate, and love. We forsake the spiritual path because we can't touch, smell, or taste it physically. But you can spiritually touch, smell, and taste by becoming *one* with everything.

Though we miss the spiritual mark more often than we would like, we can still find our way back. We can continue the spiritual journey we were born to experience. Our spiritual side, with its divine connection to our Creator, works within us, reminding us of where our path lies and how to get back on track. Still, our free will definitely determines how it all turns out in the end. Historically, we choose poorly.

No matter where you started or what your challenges have been in life, once you learn to listen and follow the right voice, you can start again and finish well. The spiritual path is the most rewarding, but following it can only be accomplished with the help of God's Holy Spirit and Christ Jesus. Of all the reasons we came here, the most important is to learn and live love.

Dodging Evil gives examples to help you learn these things. The experiences within this book can help you avoid many pitfalls. In this book, I share my amazing, supernatural, spiritual experiences. I will share lessons learned through the good, bad, and ugly parts of my journey. All of these experiences have solidified my belief that we are all spirit beings. My faith in God and Christ is real because they are real.

I'm not a theologian, and this is not about organized religion. In fact, I have had many adverse experiences with some organized religions and their dogmas. This is about my personal, philosophical, and spiritual relationship with God and my Savior, Jesus. It is also about my relationship with evil. It is about my ongoing battle between the flesh and spirit—some fights I have won, and others I have lost. All of these battles start with a thought. What happens next is what I choose to do about that thought. I have overcome many of the obstacles we all face and have attained great love, peace, and joy in my life. I wish this for each and every one of you.

I have used different names throughout the book to shield the innocent. Sadly, this also serves to conceal the guilty. Of course, no one is hidden from the eyes and ears of God. Vengeance and justice belong in God's hands, not mine. I leave Him to deal with those who have and will wrong me. I choose to follow the path of forgiveness and the freedom it brings.

Come, join me on this journey. You will laugh, you will cry, and you will definitely be shocked. There is much to be learned by examining the choices I have made in my life and the consequences I have experienced as a result.

Before we can move forward, we must look all the way back to the beginning:

In a dimension not of Earth, a young spirit saw a group of elder spirits looking over a balcony. Something below seemed to be of interest to them. The young spirit saw they were filled with sorrow, shaking their heads in dismay, and it decided to see why. It was shocked by the scene below.

"Why are they doing such horrible things to one another?" the young spirit asked with disgust. "We have given them everything they need to live in peace and love. They keep choosing the way of evil!"

An older, wiser spirit asked the younger, "Do you think you could do better if you were in their place?"

"Of course!" bragged the younger spirit.

"Then let's go ask The One Who Knows if you can go there." The younger spirit, filled with anticipation, agreed.

The One Who Knows allowed the young one to go prove itself in the dangerous and troublesome Earth dimension. The elder spirits prepared the young spirit for the important journey. They warned it that the Earth realm was both beautiful and evil. "There are many things to distract you from your goal, to make you forget from where you have come. The flesh and the spirit will be at war against each other. Evil and those who follow it will be at war against you.

"We and The One Who Knows will be watching over you. Call upon us for help and don't forget where you have come from. Now, sleep!" the elder spirit commanded. The young spirit fell instantly into a deep sleep…

Jeremiah 1:5 (TLB)
I knew you before I formed you in your mother's womb…

Romans 8:29 (NKJV)
*For whom he did foreknow, he also did predestinate
to be conformed to the image of his Son, that he might
be the first born among many brethren.*

Psalm 71:5-6 (NIV)
*For you have been my hope, Sovereign Lord, my confidence
since my youth. From birth I have relied on you; you brought
me forth from my mother's womb. I will ever praise you.*

ACT I

THE BEGINNING

THE JOY OF INNOCENCE

SPRING 1982.

As I lay on the hospital bed, attached to a machine tracking my contractions, I worried about my unborn son. *Will he have the same gifts and knowledge I was born with? Will he want these gifts, and will he use them? Will I be able to teach and guide him?*

I dreaded going through another horrible birthing experience. To make matters worse, I had just been told my son was breech! I cried out to God for mercy to please not let this birth be like my first, begging him to do something.

He did.

My young doctor came into the room. "Pam, I hope you will let me do a cesarean. I have never delivered a breech baby. With a cesarean, you will be sedated and won't feel a thing." God proved faithful once more. He answered my plea for help instantly! I marveled at His love and forgiveness toward me despite all I had done to ruin our relationship. As the medications took hold and darkness enveloped me, I thought about my life journey, which started in 1947.

I was born aware of a powerful energy. It was everywhere and felt natural. The energy flowed into and through me, and it made me a smiling, laughing baby. I could feel the energy flowing through my hands and body. It felt so wonderful that I would rub my hands together to feel the energy whenever I could not touch or feel other things around me, and I would bounce it back and forth between my hands. Even today, this energy comforts me and fills me with happiness and peace. It has always flowed throughout my whole being, especially in and out of my hands.

By age two, I was able to talk about the things I felt and saw. I discovered that besides the main energy to which I was connected, I could also see the life force or energy of every living thing. The energies seemed to be the same, yet they were separate and looked different physically.

As a two-year-old, I was eager to play with and learn more about the powerful energy. I would relax and feel or imagine the energy flowing in and all around me. I could feel the same energy in people, water, plants—everything. Best of all, the Spirit energy and I talked to each other.

I could hear a voice in my mind. This voice came as thoughts, not sounds, and I replied aloud to the voice. At two, it was not unusual to talk to the voice or see spirits passing by. It wasn't at all frightening; I thought it was perfectly normal.

Most of my family believed my gifts came from someone called God, but others were not so sure. I felt people's pain and reached out to touch them where they hurt, but I didn't always get to actually touch them. My gifts include "the touch," a healing touch that causes energy to constantly flow in and out of my hands. Since birth, I have been compelled to reach out to those in pain. I was intended to become a healer.

My dad was troubled by my gifts. He had stopped believing in God after his experiences during World War II and the Korean War, including losing his only brother and close friends. He felt that a God of love would not have allowed such a tragic loss of life to happen. We didn't talk about religious or spiritual things in our immediate family because of Dad's feelings. We went to a Catholic church twice a year—Easter and Christmas—because his mother demanded we all go. Dad was not a Catholic who went to church every Sunday or confessed his sins to a priest.

Mom was the one who talked to me about God and my gifts, explaining I had inherited them from my grandmother, her mother, and these gifts had been passed down from generation to generation, usually to the first-born child. Grandmother was a full-blooded Yaqui, and Grandfather was half Yaqui and half Italian, but Mom and I had not been raised on a reservation or near other Yaqui people, so I was never taught about the secret traditions handed down within the community. The main belief of the Yaqui people is that all things are made of Spirit energy, thus making us one with the Creator and all creation.

The Yaqui lived and migrated from northwestern Mexico (Sonora), where they were brutally chased from their homeland by the Mexican and Spanish rulers who wanted their fertile land and minerals. They also migrated to the Southern California coast and southwestern Arizona. Many live in Arizona and California today.

My mom's mother, being full-blooded Yaqui, was considered a "bruja" or witch—instead of a "curandera" one who heals with the power of God—because she used her gifts for the dark side to secure extra personal power. Grandmother was supposed to teach me the traditional way to use my gifts, but she passed over before I was of age.

Mom told me the energy or Spirit I felt and talked with was called God, Our Father, the Creator of All Things—and He loved us. It made sense to me as the energy or feeling of love and God were one and the same in my mind. God's love felt like my parents' love for me, just a lot bigger. But I couldn't see God like I could my parents or other spirits. His presence was overwhelming and all-consuming.

I saw spirits every day. The spirits would pass by me, just like other people. They all seemed to be going somewhere important. Some I could see through. They were like thin, floating clouds. Some were solid-looking, like regular people, and others were dark shadows.

I thought everyone was aware of these things. When I discovered my mom couldn't see them, I was surprised. She told me not to speak of the things I felt or saw to anyone outside of our family. It was dangerous, she warned me; I could be taken away by someone called "They."

Mom never said who "They" were. She just warned that if I was found out, I would be taken away, never to be seen again. "They" would do tests on me like a lab rat. I didn't know what she meant back then, but it sounded horrifying from the tone of her voice and her energy. Fear surged deep within me, taking my breath away. I wondered if someone in the family or tribe had been taken away in the past and that was why I needed to keep my gifts secret.

Every day, I would have more revelations by and through the Spirit and my gifts. Mom and I were in a store one day when a woman passed us. An odd greenish-brown light surrounded her, and her energy was extremely low. Tuning into her with my Spirit energy, I felt pain on the right side of my body, which also made my stomach feel upset.

Mother saw me reaching out to the woman. Quickly and quietly, she told me the woman was a drunk and I didn't need to pay any attention to her. I felt sorry for the woman because I also sensed a deep sadness in her. Besides physical pain, sadness was something I also felt in animals.

The eyes and energy of both animals and people say more than their mouths. At the age of three, I didn't know what all the emotions actually were, but I did know happiness, sadness, and anger. Those energies, I had experienced myself, just like pain. Pain is pain, no matter what level it is or the age of the sufferer. All these revelations made Mom uneasy because she had been frightened of the things her mother had done with her gifts.

Mom had seen her mother do many bizarre things she couldn't explain. My grandmother had used spirits and mystical tools to read fortunes and heal those who had come to her for help. She had also helped people get even with others who had put spells or curses on them. She would send tenfold spells or curses back upon those people.

I thought the reason "They" didn't come to get her was because she had been a mean, powerful witch whom no one had wanted to mess with. For a split second, I felt excited; someday I would be able to do that, too. I would be strong like Grandma and be able to heal people and send curses or spells to bad people.

At that particular time, however, I was still innocent. I felt the wonderful energy of love everywhere. I was visually and physically enthralled by everything. I asked questions of God. I wanted to know everything about this world. How had He made colors? How had He come up with all the flowers, animals, and insects? The list was endless. God answered, "I saw it in my mind and felt it in my heart. I willed it to be, and then I spoke, commanding it to be." This sounded easy to me, but as hard as I tried, I couldn't do it.

One day while I was exploring in the backyard, a new, very different energy came upon me. It was extremely dark and heavy, hovering over my head, blocking the sunlight and pushing me down to the ground, yet I saw nothing. For the second time in my life, I felt fear. Just as I was going to run away, a yellow butterfly flew close to my face, touching my nose. It distracted me from the dark energy, and I focused on chasing the butterfly.

I forgot about the dark, heavy energy until later that night. I woke to Mom screaming, a bunch of loud thumps, and Dad yelling directions. The first thing I noticed was the dark energy I had felt earlier. It hung in the air of the bedroom I shared with my older sister, Allie, and my younger sister, Lily, and I sensed it throughout the rest of the house. As I came out of the bedroom, I saw Mom chasing a huge rat with a broom, and Dad was telling her to sweep it out a propped-open door.

The rat was black and flat like a sheet of paper. Its legs were on each corner. It actually waddled side to side, not like a regular rat running on all four legs. Mom hit it many times, but she never seemed to harm it because it was already flat. She finally swept it out and Dad quickly shut the door. We had never seen a creature like it before and haven't seen anything like it since.

I wondered what kind of energy it was, whether it had come from the creature or something else. Being three years old, I quickly dismissed the incident and the energy. I didn't feel or sense it again for two years.

A few months later, my sisters and I were again awakened in the middle of the night. Lily and I were wrapped up in blankets and put into the backseat of the car, while Allie, in her PJs, walked on her own. Great-Grandma, our dad's grandmother, was dying. We needed to go to her house right away. I didn't understand what my parents were talking about, so I fell back to sleep.

When we reached Great-Grandma's house, Lily and I were carried in, set down in the hallway in front of Great-Grandma's bedroom door along with Allie, and told to pray for her. We were left there while our parents went into another room to be with other adults.

How do you pray for the dying? What is dying? I wondered. This was my first introduction to death and the strange customs and rituals concerning it.

Being closer to the doorway than my sisters, I looked inside. The only light came from a few candles. I saw Great-Grandma lying in her bed. A woman dressed in black kneeled on the floor, sobbing, asking God to show mercy to Great-Grandma. I thought this must be the kind of prayer they wanted from us kids. I wondered what mercy was.

The energy of the room was one I hadn't experienced before. It was a feeling of great apprehension, like looking down from a high cliff, knowing you have to jump into the ocean below. It was both exciting and scary.

Suddenly we heard women screaming from the bedroom. The noise startled Allie and me and caused Lily to cry. Allie tended to Lily while my attention went to the sounds. In the darkest corner of the room, I saw women in black dresses and veils, wailing at the top of their lungs. They were moaning and rocking, saying things I didn't understand.

One of them screamed loudly, "He is taking her! He is taking her!" I looked back at the bed to see who was taking Great-Grandmother. I saw no one. Great-Grandma was still lying in the bed. Then I noticed she was floating in the air, too! *This must be dying*, I thought. *When your energy or spirit leaves the body and returns to where it came from, back to God.*

Being three, it made sense to me. There was nothing to fear, nor any reason to scream, wail, or cause such a commotion. She wasn't gone; her spirit was simply entering the spirit world from where we all come and will return. I knew this because God told me and because I could feel His Spirit and see everyone else's. We are all one in God's Spirit, no matter what we look like, male or female, young or old, in this dimension or another.

There was another loud outpouring of wailing and moaning. Then the same loud voice said, "He has sent her back to us. She is coming back!" They all cried out with joy. I looked back toward the bed and watched Great-Grandma slowly float down from the ceiling back into her body. A few minutes later, she was talking and drinking soup. All was well.

Lily and I were scooped up. Allie followed us as we were wrapped up into our blankets and put back into the car. I was happy those women could see what I saw, or at least, the one who had spoken could.

I'm not alone, I thought. *Everyone could see. They just want to keep it a secret, too. Everyone must know about "They."*

Such is the innocence of a three-year-old. Things are simple. Long explanations, interpretations, or theories are not needed. The experience made me feel secure in the knowledge that we are all spirit beings as well as physical beings.

I was exposed to three more events concerning death that year. Each taught me that we are spirit beings in a physical body and our spirit returns to God when the body dies.

Every other day, a kind, elderly neighbor would walk past our yard on his way to the corner market. He would always bring a treat for us kids and Mom. My sisters and I would anxiously wait for him to return, giggling in anticipation.

One day, as the elderly neighbor passed our driveway, another neighbor backed her car into him, knocking him down. I heard an odd popping sound when he hit the pavement.

I rushed over and was surprised to see his brain exposed. His skull literally had split open. I could see the pastel colors of his spirit glowing, full of life. I thought he was fine. He just needed to have his skull pushed back together and to get some rest.

Meanwhile, the other neighbor was angry at the man for being old and slow. She acted like it was all his fault. When the police and ambulance came, she kept saying it wasn't her fault. Being naive, I thought he would be back because his body was very much alive and his spirit hadn't left him.

We never saw him again. I missed his kind smile, gentle spirit, and, of course, his treats. I felt his spirit every once in a while. I thought it odd that I couldn't see him.

One day, we went shopping at a big neighborhood market. When we pulled into a parking space, we saw children inside the car next to us. Two older boys were in the front, and a little girl was in the back. She was between two and three years old, just like I was. She was beautiful, with blonde hair and big blue eyes. Her skin and spirit glowed brightly all around her. She was full of life.

She bounced up and down on the back seat while clinging to the window frame. We all gasped as she came close to falling out of the open window.

"That child is too beautiful for this earth," my mom said. "Her life will be hard or privileged. Either way, it will destroy her."

Mom turned to the two boys and warned them not to let the little girl bounce so close to the open window. They should roll the window up partway so the girl wouldn't fall. They mocked Mom, telling her they knew what they were doing. They said they were watching their sister closely, even though they both were in the front seat.

It was common in those days for kids to be left in cars alone when parents went shopping. Kids were also allowed to roam their own neighborhoods. People looked after each other's children, pets, and property. Neighborhoods were like an extended family.

While Mom and Dad went into the store, Allie sat in the front seat. Lily and I stayed in the back. Our windows were down, too, because it was hot. We passed the time playing with the little girl, saying hi, laughing, and bouncing up and down together.

Lily and I bounced, but away from the window. At one point, the girl reached out across to us and almost fell. One of her brothers grabbed her pants just in time and pulled her back into the car.

"That was a close one!" he said, laughing. His brother laughed, too, and the little girl squealed with delight.

"Roll up the window like my mom told you!" I shouted. Allie agreed, but they ignored us.

A few minutes later, the little girl started yelling, "Mommy, Mommy!" Filled with joy, she jumped up and down. A woman with a full cart of food approached the cars, passing between our car and theirs. She yelled impatiently at the little girl to shut up and get back while continuing past us to the trunk of their car.

I wondered how she could be so mean to her little girl. Why not give her a hug or touch her hand to let her know she was happy to see her, too? As the mother passed the window in a huff, the little girl reached out to her. Missing her mother, she fell out the window, landing head first on the pavement.

Once more, I heard an odd popping sound, but this time, it was muffled. We all gasped. The two brothers started yelling, each blaming the other for not watching, while the mother's loud, urgent cries for help filled the air. She screamed at her oldest to run into the store and call for an ambulance.

Allie closed the windows and didn't allow us younger ones to look, but we could hear the cries of the mother. I could feel her pain and sorrow. She was very concerned for her daughter, even though she had just shunned the girl not a minute ago. I made a mental note to never treat my children or any other child in such a way.

When our parents came out, Dad moved our car to make room for the ambulance and police. He loaded our groceries while Mom told us to close our eyes and lie down on the back seat. Allie's face and energy told me everything. She was pale, horrified at what she saw. The energy from everyone else was a mix of fear and sadness. I knew the little girl was alive in spirit, going back to God. My eyes were closed, but I could see her spirit face, smiling. One hand was waving goodbye as she was led away by someone.

My third exposure to death happened at night in the apartment complex crosswise from our house. While playing outside before bedtime, I smelled smoke. It smelled like the fire pit in our backyard after pouring water on hot coals. I asked Dad if he smelled it, too, but the smell seemed to have disappeared.

Later I heard sirens coming close and stopping outside. I went to the front door. I was overcome by many energies I had not previously experienced. Those energies were together yet separate, mixed with extreme fear, anger, pain, and hopelessness, all with a sense of urgency. I was confused and overwhelmed.

People were outside, crying. Firemen and police yelled for everyone to vacate the area. The apartment complex was engulfed in a full, raging fire. Flames and sparks flew high into the night sky. It was both beautiful and frightening.

I ran to my parents' side. The wind shifted and brought with it an awful odor that stuck to the inside of my nose, throat, and lungs. I gagged and asked Dad what the smell was. He told me it was the smell of burnt human flesh. He knew this because, as a Marine during World War II and the Korean War, he had smelled it many times.

It was a couple of days before all the people who died in the fire were found. The sweet, sickening smell of burnt, rotting flesh hung in the air. I learned that the physical body does indeed die and it isn't as clean and scent-free as when the spirit leaves it. Death is a reality for the flesh body.

We moved away from that neighborhood because of those lingering smells. I was also glad to move because I had disobeyed my parents, which meant the Boogeyman knew where I lived and would be looking for me.

My parents had told me tales of what happened to both good and bad children. They went through great lengths to prove the existence of the Boogeyman, Santa Claus, and the Easter Bunny much more than they did that of God.

I learned about the Boogeyman, Santa, and the Easter Bunny when I was about two years old. I also learned about God then, but He taught me about Himself. I was eager to learn as much as I could. After all, Mom told me to ask Him about everything. Oddly, I never asked Him about those three creatures. I trusted my parents. I learned that disobeying your parents would cause trouble with the Boogeyman. He would search for you and eat you for supper. In my case, I would be just a snack.

My troubles with the Boogeyman started when I left my tricycle out in the yard. The rule was *all* bicycles were to be left on the porch or inside the house. Well, one night, I was called in for supper. I was so hungry I jumped off the trike and ran straight inside.

The next morning, I went outside to ride my trike, but it was nowhere to be found. I couldn't feel its energy anywhere. A deep emptiness was in my chest; it flowed down into the ground. Dad told me the Boogeyman had taken it to his lair to build a big fire to cook me and other naughty children. I felt heavy with guilt because I had supplied fuel for his fire to cook children, even me. A part of me didn't want to believe in such a creature.

I challenged Dad on the existence of this scary, evil Boogeyman, but he wanted me to believe the Boogeyman was real, so he took me to its lair. We drove a long time to get there. It was dark, and I was scared. As we approached the lair, we saw a massive fire. At the top was my tricycle, or something that looked just like it. Luckily, there was no sign of the Boogeyman.

Dad suggested we get home fast before the Boogeyman came back; he might be able to sense me nearby and come after me. I felt terribly afraid. I swore never to disobey my parents again. Dad made a believer out of me, even though I never saw the actual Boogeyman. I didn't think about talking to God about it. This was between my parents and me.

Besides the Boogeyman, my parents did their best to prove the existence of Santa and the Easter Bunny. On Christmas Eve, we were sent to bed early because Santa wouldn't come if any children were awake. We were tucked in and told to go to sleep. Not long after, we would be woken by the sounds of sleigh bells, snorts, and hooves stomping on the roof.

Giggling with joy and excitement, we would wait until Santa left, and then we would run into the living room to see all the gifts he had brought. We would also look to see if he had eaten the cookies and drunk the milk or hot chocolate we had set out for him. He always finished both.

We would beg to open just one of the presents. I never saw Santa in our house, but he was everywhere during Christmastime, and each year, I would hear him, the sleigh bells, and the reindeer on our roof. I believed.

Easter was similar. We would be awakened by whispers from Mom and Dad. "Come quick, be very quiet, and you might be able to see the Easter Bunny!" They would lead us into the living room, and along the way, we would see many Easter eggs all over the floor, counters, and furniture.

Peeking into the living room from behind the sofa, we would see big, tall Easter baskets, candy, and more eggs. One year, amid the baskets, we saw the Easter Bunny! Its white fur looked so soft and smooth. Its pink ears flopped, and its pink nose twitched while it hop-hop-hopped around the living room. Then the real, live Easter Bunny, hearing us giggle with glee, hopped out of sight.

We weren't lucky enough to see him or her ever again, but I knew for sure the Easter Bunny was real, just like God, the Boogeyman, and Santa. I heard Santa on our roof, visited the lair of the Boogeyman, and saw the Easter Bunny with my own two eyes…and I spoke to God every day. I believed in them all. As a result, I was exceptionally good for a very long time.

I loved the freedom of being a child. I explored the world around me and felt safe, confident, and loved. After I turned five, Mom told me I was old enough to go to school. She tried to make it sound like a big deal, something I would really want to do.

"You will have so much fun in kindergarten. You will meet other children who might become good friends. You'll learn to write your name, read, and color pictures."

Then, in a somber voice, she said, "Remember, Pam, you must never, ever tell anyone about your gifts: the spirits you can see, or how you and God talk to each other. You must promise me you will be quiet about these things. 'They' will come and take you away from us. We will never see you again. Promise me!"

"I promise, Mommy, I promise!" I still had no idea who "They" were, but I was sure I didn't want to meet them or the Boogeyman. I also didn't like the idea of not talking to God. I asked God about this forced kindergarten. It was the law. My sister Allie didn't look like she enjoyed going to her school, so I wondered what I should do.

"Do not worry, little one; we can still talk, just not out loud. We can talk with our minds. Just like you hear me in your mind, you can also talk to me with your mind. Like when you are thinking about something, you talk to yourself. Talking with me works the same way. No one can hear us." God's Spirit chased away all the fear and anger. It filled me with peace. I was ready for kindergarten.

To my surprise, I actually enjoyed kindergarten. Mom was glad I liked it, too. I enjoyed learning my ABCs, counting to ten, coloring, and playing with clay. I asked a lot of questions. I was the kid who always asked why, how, and why again. It seemed to annoy the teachers.

They smiled through gritted teeth as they answered me. They tried not to show their annoyance, but I saw the energy around them, and I saw the truth of how they felt in their eyes. I stopped asking questions and enjoyed the short time with my classmates. I was grateful it wasn't a full day like Allie had to do.

She went to a Catholic school where nuns and priests taught regular school classes and God classes. I looked forward to getting older so I could go there and learn more about God from the experts. My mom told me the nuns and priests were holy people who knew everything about God. They loved God so much that they gave up everything to serve Him, and the nuns were actually married to God or Jesus. I wasn't clear about which. I figured I would learn more when I grew up and went there for school.

In the meantime, kindergarten was where I spent part of my day. After school, I sometimes got to visit my new friends. Anna was my best friend. She lived closer than the other kids, and Mother trusted her parents. I went to her house, or she visited mine. Anna and I both had overactive imaginations; her imaginary friend Tom played with us.

One weekend, I thought I was grown-up enough to walk to Anna's on my own. I knew the way by heart. Other kids roamed the neighborhood alone, and some were very young. I begged Mother to let me go. At first, she resisted, but she eventually gave in to my constant pleas. She warned me not to get close to or talk with strangers and definitely not to get into any cars. She told me that if I thought I was in danger, I should run home or to a trusted neighbor's house as fast as I could. She also told me to be back home by one o'clock or I wouldn't be able to walk to Anna's again.

I didn't know how to tell time very well, but I knew where one was on a clock. I thought Anna's mother would help me tell time, too. I started out walking confidently toward Anna's house. After a while, I became aware my timing was off. Traveling by car had been deceiving. It was a lot further than I remembered because I hadn't yet reached my landmark tree, the halfway point to Anna's. Was I lost?

The dark, heavy energy I had felt years ago when I had been playing outside suddenly came toward me. My heart raced. I wanted to run, but God's Spirit fell upon me, telling me to look to my right and not to be afraid; He was with me. I did as I was told. On my right, a block away, stood my landmark, the Spirit Tree.

I called it the Spirit Tree because it was huge, old, and wise-looking. It glowed with a peaceful energy that was very comforting. People always stood or sat near it. I ran quickly to the tree. It held and covered me in its spirit. A breeze came by and swept away the leftover residue of the dark, heavy energy. I walked faster so I wouldn't be late.

I finally made it to Anna's. We had a great time playing make-believe with her dollhouse, dolls, and imaginary friend Tom. I could actually see him, but I wasn't supposed to admit I could see anything called "imaginary". He didn't like that I was friends with Anna. He told me to go away, but I pretended not to hear him.

After a while, Anna's mother told me it was time for me to go home. Anna needed a nap, and if I didn't get going, I would miss my curfew. Anna started crying and making a big fuss. Her mother was getting upset, too, so I gladly left. I didn't want to share their yucky energy.

Outside, a light breeze swept away any lingering bad energy. As I briskly walked back home, I came upon a familiar street. I remembered Mom had driven down that street from Anna's before; it seemed to be a faster way home. The street went in a loop to our house. The thought that I should go this way came to my mind, but God said urgently, "Do not go that way. Danger is there. Go back the same way!"

I told him it was faster and I knew the way. The word "danger" went through one ear and out the other. This new road was very steep to walk down. I walked faster because it felt like I was being pulled along.

I felt the dark, heavy energy again, like it was right behind me. I turned around and saw a man following me! I had seen him earlier in his yard. He had strange-looking eyes and an ugly, dark, heavy energy about him. I ignored his questions and invitation into his house to call my parents, but he wasn't deterred. Continuing to ignore him, I started walking faster. He walked faster. My heart pounded so hard I thought it was going to come out of my chest.

Turning toward him, I stomped my foot on the sidewalk and said, "Stop following me. I'm not lost!" At the same time, a car pulled to the curb and stopped. The man inside asked if I was alright and whether the other man was bothering me. He offered to give me a ride.

When the two men started talking, God told me to run as fast as I could. Even as I ran, the dark energy seemed to be right upon me. Running out of breath, hairs standing on end, feeling he would grab me at any second, I saw Mom getting into our car. "Wait for me!" I yelled, running faster. I jumped into the backseat just in time. When I looked back, the man was standing next to our house. Our dog, Val, a Sheltie, was barking and lunging at him from behind the fence.

Mom asked if I'd had a good time at Anna's, and I told her I had. She told me she was headed for the store and was going to look for me on her way home, but I had come home early. If I hadn't run when God had told me, I would've been left alone with the scary man. Mom would have been looking for me in the wrong area.

I waited in the car when we arrived at the store. I was tired from all the walking and running. I wanted to rest and talk with God about what had happened. I didn't even think about telling Mom. This was between God and me.

Since going to school, God and I talked in our minds almost constantly. I hardly ever spoke to Him out loud. I said in my mind, "I'm sorry I didn't listen to you. You've never lied to me. I didn't even think about danger. What is that heavy, dark energy?"

"That energy is why I told you not to go down that road. It is called evil. It enters into people's hearts and minds, and yes, even children's, corrupting them to do evil things and to think only of their own needs and desires, forsaking all others, even me. They are filled with pride, arrogance, and selfishness."

"I don't like evil. It is a horrible feeling, so dark and heavy. Why did you make it?"

"I did not make it, but I did create the one who manifested it in his mind and heart. Lucifer is his name. He spreads it to others who are weak, easy to manipulate into selfness. He believes all humans are not worthy of my love or attention. He has sworn to prove to me that evil, not love, dwells in the minds and hearts of mankind.

"I believe all beings I created, even Lucifer, to be capable of great love. Lucifer chose not to love. Some will overcome temptations of evil because evil can be overcome and someday destroyed, but for now, little one, remember I am with you always. Do not fear. As you get older and experience more of this world, you will learn more about love, evil, and the choices one must make. You are learning even now to choose to listen to me or to go your own way."

"I will never leave you! You promised to be by my side always. I could never go anywhere you aren't, right?"

"Even though you will leave my side, I will always be near, watching over you for when you are ready to come back."

"I can't see my leaving your side ever."

"Time will tell. In the meantime, you will now have to be careful and aware of who comes close to you. Listen to my voice. The man who followed you home will be back and will try to get you and your sisters to go with him. Do not allow him to get close to any of you.

"I sent the man in the car to distract him, allowing you to run home before your mother left. You must pay close attention whenever you feel the dark energy or a spirit of evil coming toward you. Call upon me whenever this happens, and I will help you."

"Okay, I will. I wish evil had never been manifested." I didn't know what this word meant, but God used it, and He knew everything. "I hope everyone who has been captured by evil will be set free and their minds and hearts will be filled with you and your love."

I spoke with all the determination of a five-year-old. I was going to be obedient and do as I was told by both God and my parents. I wanted nothing to do with evil or the Boogeyman. I was so lucky to have dodged evil.

My sisters and I were bothered by the evil man every week. He would come by and try to get us to take candy or cupcakes or help him look for a lost puppy or kitten. I remembered what God and Mom had told me, and I made sure my sisters didn't go near the fence or take anything from him. Our dog, Val, would charge at him, barking ferociously.

The noise would bring Mom outside to see what was causing all the commotion. The evil man complained that Val was very vicious, a menace to the neighborhood, and should be put down. Val tried to attack him every time he walked by our house.

Mom told the man to walk on the other side of the street and to stay away from our fence. I still hadn't told Mom or my sisters about my first encounter with him. I kept us safe, with Val's help, just like God had told me to do.

About a week after Mom told him to stay away, I returned home from a visit with Anna. Ever since my earlier mistake of not listening to God, I had always traveled the original, safer route home. I had learned that ignoring God caused consequences not only for me, but also for others.

When I arrived home, police and men from animal control were talking with Mom and our neighbors. Val was tied to the porch, curled in a ball, shivering from head to paws. I asked, "What's going on? Why is Val tied up?"

I ran to him, hugged him, and told him he would be okay. I used my special touch to calm him. Mom explained someone had made a complaint about Val being a danger to the neighborhood and the officers were investigating. I knew it had to have been the evil man. Filled with anger, I blurted out, "The evil man did it, didn't he?"

One of the policemen and Mother came over and asked, "What evil man?" Sobbing, I told them of the first time, and all the other times, the evil man had bothered us and how Val had always protected us. I was careful not to mention my conversation with God.

"Val may bark or charge at strangers when they get too close, but he never bothers the mailman or milkman. You can ask anyone in our neighborhood," I explained.

The policeman nodded in agreement. "Yes, we have asked all your neighbors. So, tell me more about the evil man. Do you know where he lives?"

I didn't know the address, but I offered to show him. He drove me in the police car, and I showed him where the evil man lived. We learned that he was told to stay away from us and our part of the neighborhood or he would be arrested. Everyone would be on the lookout for him now. Mom told me I should have told her about him right away.

I thought God and I had it under control. When I think about it now, I'm sure I didn't say anything because I thought Mom wouldn't let me go to Anna's by myself ever again. I was glad it all was behind us, and I looked forward to summer break. I could hardly wait.

We were going to go camping in the Sierra-Nevada Mountains for the whole summer. I had never been to high mountains or a big forest, and this would be my first time fishing for freshwater fish. God told me

I would be able to hear and feel Him even more because of the quiet in the mountains.

I looked forward to less noise and pain. It was hard to filter out the energies, smells, and sounds flowing all around and through me in the big city. The emotion and pain energies I felt made me want to reach out to everyone, but I couldn't because of "They." I hadn't yet realized I was meant to help heal people, especially with my "special touch."

Sometimes I would sneak a quick touch physically or spiritually to someone in great pain or sadness and ask God to heal them. I would feel a surge of energy flow through me and into the person, and in return, their pain and emotions flowed into me. I would carry it all in my body. Many years later, I learned I didn't have to carry those emotions and pain until they faded away. I could, instead, give them to God right away by taking a deep breath and letting go of them.

Our First Trip North

As we prepared for the trip up north, I learned my grandparents on Dad's side were coming, too. It would take two days and a night to drive to the campground. I overheard Dad and Grandpa talking about the trip and how they needed to take plenty of water for the drive through the Mojave Desert. They had been told many cars overheat in the desert. We could become stranded.

The Mojave Desert sounded dangerous. It was full of poisonous snakes and other critters. Even so, it was worth the risk to get to the campground. I felt safe because God was with us.

Mom fried chicken so we could eat it cold later along with the cold potato salad. Those were our family favorites for all outings. Finally, everything was ready. At first light, we were going to hit the road. I wanted to take Val, but there was no room on this trip. Val would have to stay with my only real uncle, Mom's brother, Max. He had just moved in with us and had to work. "Maybe next year," my parents said. Next year? I was really excited to hear this news. Really? There was going to be a next year!

Long-distance traveling in a car wasn't as exciting as I had expected.

I was soon snoozing. Then I was thirsty and hungry, but worst of all, I had to go to the bathroom! There weren't many bathrooms along the way, and gas stations were far apart. When we had to *go*, it meant going on the side of the road.

The rhythm of the motor and the tires on the road put me to sleep. Suddenly a hissing sound woke me. I looked around and saw a big cloud of white smoke coming from the front of the car. It was so thick I couldn't see through it. I wondered whether it was fog and if we were back by the ocean.

"Has the radiator blown?" Mom asked.

"No, it just overheated," Dad answered. "We'll have to let it cool down. It's late, so we might as well stay the night. The sun will set soon; we can get an early start in the morning."

Jumping out of the car, Dad lifted the hood to allow more steam to escape and cool the engine. Grandfather, who was following us in his fully loaded truck, stopped to help. We all piled out of the hot car into an even hotter desert.

There were scattered patches of tall grass, bushes of some kind, tumbleweeds, cacti, and a lot of sand. I had a stare-down with a lizard until it ran under a large rock. While Dad and Grandpa tended to the car, Mom and Grandma fed us kids. There's nothing like cold fried chicken and potato salad to cool you down in the desert heat.

Dad and Grandpa told us about the dangerous animals that lived in the desert and why we had to stay inside the cars when it got dark. The desert definitely had an energy of its own, but it didn't feel dangerous to me. It gave me a gentle, ticklish feeling throughout my whole being.

We all watched the sunset; it was beautiful. I felt a peaceful energy. A hush fell over the desert. At first, it was very loud; then it settled down to a soothing hum. Everything came to life. The cacti, grass, and bushes all swayed to some mystical, musical vibration and soothing energy I could feel and see but not hear.

There was a halo around everything. Even the sand seemed to move as it glistened in the fading sunlight. It was like a dream in which everything seems real yet different. The twilight-hour colors and energy swirled throughout my whole being, the desert, and the night sky. I felt as one with this desert as with any other familiar place. I felt God, too. I soon fell into a deep sleep.

I woke to a voice calling my name. It was a strange voice—definitely no one I knew—yet it felt familiar. I thought I must be dreaming, so I ignored it. Again it called to me. I tried to open my eyes, but I couldn't. Again the voice softly called, "Paaaamm."

"What?" I asked. This time, I felt a surge of energy rush through my body, like when God's Spirit fills me. I thought it was Him calling. I finally opened my eyes and looked up at the open window from which the voice had come.

I saw what looked like a limb of a tree leaning against the car door and window. It moved as if it were swaying in the wind or dancing to the mystical desert music. I wondered how a limb from a tree could be there when I hadn't seen any trees in this desert and there wasn't any wind.

I rubbed my eyes and looked again. In front of me was a huge, scary, yet beautiful black snake! It had a dark blue halo all around it that sparkled like diamonds. White lights shot out from it like shooting stars or fireworks. It was beautifully mesmerizing. It was swaying with the desert, as was I, and I felt as though we were one. This time, it clearly hissed my name, "Paaaamm," and slowly came through the window.

Suddenly I remembered everything Dad had told me about poisonous snakes. Even though I didn't sense any evil or danger, I screamed and covered my head with my pillow. "It's trying to get me!" I repeatedly screamed until I woke up everyone.

"What is it?" Dad asked.

I told him a giant snake had come in through the window. He looked everywhere with a big flashlight and his handgun, but he didn't see a trace of it.

"Well, it's gone," he sighed with relief, and rolled up the windows, leaving a small opening for airflow. "Try to get some more sleep. We'll be leaving this desert soon."

I was filled with confusion over the snake. I had clearly felt safe, yet I had panicked. Why? I decided to ask God. "Father, what was the snake going to do?"

"It was going to share the wisdom of the desert and its peoples with you, especially since you were denied learning of your heritage of the desert. I sent my Spirit so you would not be afraid and you could understand.

"Lucifer will always try to make you and others fear, mistrust, and doubt all truth and knowledge of the Spirit in all its forms and ways. To keep you and others from accepting my Spirit, Lucifer used the memory of your dad's words against you. Those words took over your mind, causing you to fear.

"Do not worry. You will learn more as you get older and experience more of this world and the spirit world. Pay attention, learn, and grow, little one. All will be revealed in time." This statement was enough for me at five; I had no more questions concerning the snake.

I made up my mind right then that I wouldn't fear when I felt the presence of God. I would trust and stand firm on His words to me: "Do not fear. I am with you always." I had a lot to learn about the spiritual and earthly worlds. Sighing deeply, I fell back asleep.

Sometime later, eyes still closed, I faintly heard the car and truck engines start and felt the car moving. I could still feel and smell the desert as I drifted back to sleep. Mom's voice woke me: "Pam, wake up. It's time to wash up and eat." I sat up and looked around. We were at a truck stop.

The rest of the trip passed quickly. As we left the high desert, we drove by many pastures filled with cattle, horses, or sheep. We drove up and down mountains and down into canyons, some of which had raging rivers. Dad pointed out deep fishing holes where big fish could be waiting.

The air smelled different than any other place I'd been. I was told it was the combination of pine and cedar trees, wild grass, and flowers. Then there was just the fresh, clean air, no damp fog or salty-smell like near the ocean.

After a while, we drove down a mountain into a massive valley. We stopped in a small town. It had one stoplight and two gas stations. Dad had brought a map and asked Mom to find the small town that was near our campsite.

A bit later, we pulled up to an even smaller town and parked near an old store. The building was painted in barn-red paint that was fading and chipping. The words "Cash and Carry," in faded and chipped white letters, were over the store entrance. The store doubled as the local post office. We waited there for someone to take us to the campground. Shortly, a man in a pickup truck parked next to Dad's side of the car and told us to follow him.

We drove up a steep mountain road and went around two bends; on our right was a big meadow, and on the left a smaller meadow. We turned left on a dirt road and parked in the smaller meadow. We all piled out of the vehicles.

Cedar, pine, aspen, and willow trees were scattered everywhere. It smelled wonderful. A small creek flowed nearby. It was ice cold and so clear that I could see the bottom. The man told us it was artesian-spring-fed and good to drink. Wildflowers and tall green grass grew everywhere. Chipmunks and squirrels chirped at us, as well as many birds. We saw small rabbits. Dad told us they were called cottontails and were good to eat. This was news to me. Peter Cottontail was the Easter Bunny's helper. We couldn't eat him!

The man and my parents talked for a long time while I ran around, looking at and touching everything. My sisters and I helped unload the camping gear. We then watched Dad and Grandpa set up our large four-room tent and make a fire pit for cooking. All of us slept inside the tent. There was a bedroom for our grandparents, another for our parents, and one for us three kids.

The remaining room was like a living room with a picnic table. We had a chair at each end of the table for Grandpa and Dad. It was custom to reserve the heads of the table for the men of the family. The living room had a large lantern centered in the middle of the table that we used at night and when it rained, which wasn't very often. When we were stuck inside, we colored, read books, and played cards and other table games.

God was everywhere and in everything. His presence overwhelmed me. I was floating in the air. I was spirit, no longer in my body. I was one with everything. When God spoke, it felt like I was inside Him and He in me. His voice vibrated through me instead of just speaking in my mind like before. This wonderful place God had made was so stimulating to all my senses that I don't remember falling asleep.

Dad and Grandpa had all of us collect a lot of firewood that summer. We explored all around the camp area and went on overnight camping trips to nearby lakes and rivers to fish for trout. It was the best summer vacation ever. I never wanted to leave. During that time, God revealed that everything, no matter how big or small, seen or unseen, has a purpose. I wasn't certain exactly how I fit into it all, but I felt proud and grateful to be a part of God's creation.

I liked the slow-paced life in the mountains. My ability to feel the energies of everything was an amazing experience. I felt sunrises, sunsets, and moonrises; they gave me wonderful tickling sensations. I could see the halos of the trees at night easier than in the day. The night sky was so close; it looked like I could reach out and touch the stars. Summer ended too soon for me.

I didn't want to go back to the city, and I was in a gloomy mood while I helped to pack. However, I did enjoy making sure the fire was out by stirring the coals with icy creek water until no more smoke or heat came from the pit. Putting out the fire helped me put out the disappointment and anger in my heart.

God told me, "Don't worry. You will return." He used Mother to reinforce His promise. She also told me not to be sad, because we were going to return next summer and, if things worked out, we would be moving there for good. Those words gave me hope. I looked forward to next year.

The journey back to the city seemed to go much quicker than on the way to the mountains. Dad told me it was because we were driving downhill. I believed him, but in reality, it was probably because I slept most of the way. I looked forward to seeing Val and Anna. School was a distant third.

That school year, while waiting for the return of summer, I learned another valuable lesson. My family made weekend trips to the ocean shore to fish and dive for abalone. Dad showed us where we could play safely on some flat rocks.

The rocks were partially in the ocean and partially onshore; big waves would fill up the cracks between the rocks, and the water would overflow into the pools on top of the rocks. We could see the water rise and fall in the cracks. The rocks were close together, so we could avoid falling into the cracks.

Still, Dad gave us a stern warning: "You kids can play in the pools of water on top of the rocks, but don't jump in, hang your feet, or put them into the cracks between the rocks. You can get hurt."

"Okay, Daddy," we all said at once. He set up a couple of fishing poles for Mom and Allie and then dove into the ocean to hunt for abalone.

I was splashing in one of the rock pools when a starfish popped up between the rocks a few feet away. I ran over to see if I could catch or at least touch the beautiful creature. It was sticking to the side of the rock. I couldn't pull it free, but I could touch it.

A thought came into my mind. The starfish was in the water in the crack between the rocks, and it wasn't getting hurt. Since it was bigger than my feet, why couldn't I play in the water, too? Anyway, Lily had taken over my pool.

I wasn't going to *jump* between the rocks, just put my feet in the water. After talking myself into doing it, I sat down and put my left foot in the water. As I slid my right foot over to put it in, a huge wave hit the rocks hard. It caused my left foot to be pushed out and then sucked back into the crack. I was thrown onto my back. Afraid I was going to be sucked into the crack, I quickly pulled my foot out and ran back to my pool.

When I sat down, I noticed a stinging in my left foot, but it quickly stopped. Lily jumped out of the pool and ran over to Mom. I saw her saying something while pointing at me. Mom looked worried as she ran over to me. When she saw my foot, she turned pale and started screaming for Dad. I didn't understand why all the fuss until I looked down at my foot. To my surprise, I was sitting in a pool of blood.

Mother grabbed my foot to get a closer look. Between my heel and little toe, a jagged piece of flesh hung down, and blood gushed from the wound. She ran to get a beach towel. When she got back, she wrapped the towel around my foot, picked me up, and scrambled up the steep path to our car. Dad caught up to us with my sisters in tow. He took me from Mom and carried me and the fishing poles to the car.

Because of shock and blood loss, I felt strange, drowsy, and cold. God comforted me. I felt his arms around me, and a golden light kept me warm. Dad put me back in Mom's arms and told her to squeeze my foot as hard as she could while he drove us to the hospital. We were rushed into a small room, where a doctor told me I needed stitches right away. He also told me he was sorry but that what he needed to do was going to hurt.

He was right. It did hurt terribly when he began to stitch my foot back together. I screamed at him to stop hurting me. I called him a bad doctor and said I hated him and the nurses who were holding me down. I didn't think I would live through it!

When I recall the incident now, I think about the look in their eyes. They looked so sorry and sad as I screamed how much I hated them. This all happened because I chose not to obey my dad. I not only hurt myself, my parents, and sisters, but also the doctor and nurses. I hurt them terribly, in the worst way, emotionally and spiritually, with my words. I learned once more that whatever I choose to do will affect others.

Back Home

Finally, school was over, and we were heading back to the mountains. I had looked forward to summer break all through my first-grade school year. Next year, I would be going to the Catholic school with Allie, but after the first day of introduction, we would be in different classes.

I was thrilled to get away from the city and all those energies. Everyone was in a hurry, and hardly anyone smiled. A heavy energy seemed to suck the joy and life out of people in the city. I was thrilled to get away from the city and all those energies. This time, the trip up north seemed quicker, and Val was able to come. My grandparents brought a camping trailer, too. They didn't want to rough it anymore.

As soon as the campsite was set up, Val and I ran across the street to play in the big meadow. Tired, I made a bed to lie on from a circle of bent grass, just like the deer make. Val and I lay down to rest and soak up the sun's rays. I thanked God for making all this possible.

The bugs in the grass reminded me of the people in the city, running to and fro, doing whatever it was they were always doing. My bed in their pathway didn't stop them at all. It tickled as they climbed up and over my fingers. It felt like they had licked me before climbing over them. Their tiny legs had tiny claws that enabled them to climb up and down the creases in my skin.

I watched bees find flowers full of pollen and then rub it on their legs. I watched grasshoppers chew something and then spit out a dark liquid. A worm popped its head out and then dove back down into the black dirt. The dirt felt wonderful and smelled good. It all amazed me. God had created everything perfectly for the environment to flourish.

We had another wonderful summer. Val and I hunted squirrels, chipmunks, lizards, and rabbits every day. We tried to catch anything we came across. Val herded them, and I caught them by hand and used my special touch to calm them. More escaped than were captured, and everyone was surprised I wasn't bitten.

The hunting and chores were a very dirty business. This, of course, led to one necessary but uncomfortable task. It was the only downside to all this fantastic camping. We had to take baths in the ice-cold creek. The water was so cold that it gave us all headaches.

My parents came up with a solution. They found or bought large metal tubs that the local ranchers used to water or feed their cattle. We used small metal buckets to heat the water over the fire and then poured it into the big bathtubs. Then we poured cold water into the tubs to make a wonderfully warm bath for us—no more headaches.

Speaking of headaches, that summer was the first time I used my "touch" to heal a family member. It was Mom. I felt a terrible pain in her head. I could actually see the pain in her eyes and energy field. It made me a bit dizzy, causing me to squint. I asked her, "What's wrong?"

"I'm having a terrible migraine headache."

"Can I help you, Mom?" I reached out to touch her. She didn't answer one way or another.

I was led by the Spirit to put my hands on her neck at the base of her skull. I then placed one finger on each side of her upper neck and was told to push up under her skull. The pain was excruciating. I asked Mom if she knew what I should do next besides breathe.

"This kind of stuff always frightened me," she reminded me. "I wouldn't learn any of it from my mother, but you can always ask God what to do. He will guide you. What you are doing is already helping a lot."

God reminded me that I needed to let Him take the pain instead of holding on to it. He told me where to put pressure at certain places on her head, neck, and shoulders. I was told to cover Mom's eyes last. I held my hands over her eyes until the pain stopped and I no longer felt God's and my combined energy flowing in and out of Mom.

Besides the pain, I felt powerful chills and goosebumps. I also felt and heard snapping sounds in my hands and our energy fields. She was healed, and I never heard of her having another migraine. I had no idea how long it took; time never entered my mind. I was six years old, listening to God's guidance and allowing His Spirit to flow through me.

That summer, Dad and Grandpa built a one-room, twelve-foot-by-sixteen-foot cabin for us to live in. It was not big, but to me, it was like a castle. The fresh-cut cedar and pine boards smelled refreshing and clean. The cabin had a large, deep sink with running water and a large wood stove for cooking and to keep us warm during cold weather.

We were able to have running water by divining to find the right artesian spring and then developing it to be able to build up enough water to keep a five-hundred-gallon wooden holding tank full. I was really excited when Grandpa let me use the divining rod to find the underground spring. The divining rod was just a willow branch Grandpa cut to look like a wishbone. I held the two outer branches in each hand, but instead of breaking them apart, I just held it in front of me as I walked.

When the middle branch dipped toward the ground, I would get excited, thinking I had found the right spring, but the force of the dip wasn't yet strong enough to make it a good well. I was surprised and in awe as to how it worked. Then I came across a spot that pulled so strongly it frightened me. I thought I was going to be pulled down into the ground. I forgot I could just let go of the rod. Dad and Grandpa saved me and gave me praise for finding the spring.

Dad dug gently into the spring, enlarging and clearing the area around it. Then he enclosed it within a cement box and put a pipe through the wall so it could fill the huge wooden holding tank. Then he connected two more pipes to the tank. One went to the cabin and connected to the faucet in the kitchen sink. The second pipe went to a water trough for livestock that we would be getting. Gravity did the rest.

One of my daily chores was to check the Artesian well for any signs of it drying up. I was also to look for bugs, drowned mice, or other critters. I couldn't see how anything could get in, but eventually I started finding water skippers and spiders. One day, when I opened the lid, a mouse jumped out! I screeched a little, but I knew it wasn't after me; it just wanted to be free.

When the cabin was finally finished, we had two sets of bunk beds because Mom was expecting a baby in December. Mom and Dad's bed was in the middle of the two bunk beds. I had one set all to myself until the new baby arrived. We didn't have a lot of room to move around, so we actually had to have breakfast in bed or go outside and sit on the picnic table.

We had a fancy outhouse that we all pitched in to make. Anyone who didn't help wouldn't be allowed to use it. We were doing all this work because we planned to stay in the Sierras. Dad and Mom told us they bought the campground and surrounding land, a total of 147 acres. I was thrilled we were going to live there year-round. God kept His Word, and so did Mom.

In August, when Mom discovered the hospital was thirty miles away and the highway next to our home sometimes closed during the winter, she and Dad decided to go back to the city until after the baby was born. Consequently, we didn't register at the local school. I was disappointed, but I knew we were coming back. Dad even promised Mom a bigger house next year. We packed up what was necessary and left the rest in the cabin and our grandparents' trailer.

I actually looked forward to visiting Allie's Catholic school. I was interested in knowing more about God from the experts. I was filled with wonder and awe over the nuns and priests, especially their commitment to God and his teachings. I had notions of becoming a nun, of serving God and marrying Him or Jesus, whomever it was they married.

When Allie and I walked into the Catholic classroom, a nun welcomed us with a fake smile, showed us where to sit, and handed us each a book. She talked about a specific Bible verse. She read and talked so fast I wasn't able to understand what she was saying. Her energy distracted me; it was cool and felt stuck, not flowing. She encouraged us to read for ourselves and to meditate.

I couldn't find the verse, nor did I understand what "meditate" even meant. I quietly waited with the rest of the students until she spoke again.

"Are there any questions?" she asked, giving all of us a look that said, "Don't ask." Allie raised her hand while the rest of the students hung their heads and stared at the floor. Through clenched teeth, the nun asked, "What?"

"I don't understand any of it," Allie said quietly.

"Are you stupid?" the nun snapped.

I couldn't believe my ears. Allie had been born premature, and as a result of not having good medical care, she had needed to be kept warm by being wrapped up in a blanket in a shoebox and then put in my parents' oven. This might have caused some brain damage; she was a little slow in understanding things, especially if one spoke too fast.

"No, I'm not stupid!" Allie challenged.

"How dare you speak to me in that tone!" yelled the now crimson-faced nun as she walked quickly to her desk and grabbed a wooden ruler. She hit my sister across the back of her hands with that ruler and then quickly tucked it into a pocket in her dress. Then she hit Allie over both ears at once with her bare hands!

I couldn't believe what I was witnessing. Nuns were supposed to be kind, loving, patient wives of God, knowing all His ways and laws. They were commanded to share God's love with the world. I jumped up to defend Allie.

"Stop it! You can't hit her. I am going to call the police. You are evil. You're not like God!"

The nun's eyes bugged out as she turned even more crimson and came at me with the ruler raised, ready to strike. Catching wild animals had given me quick reflexes, so when she got close to me, I was able to grab the ruler out of her hand. There was a flash of fear in her eyes as I again yelled, "Stop it!" The students backed me up by chanting, "Stop it!" over and over.

A priest came charging in because of all the noise. "What is going on in here?" The nun, students, and I all spoke at once. The priest told everyone to calm down and sit. After hearing all sides of the story, he sent the nun to her personal living quarters and took Allie and me to the head priest's office. We sat there until Mom arrived.

We were ushered in to talk with the head priest about what had happened. I kept insisting someone should call the police because the nun had attacked Allie and me. We were put on suspension. I didn't know what that meant, either.

I told Mom that this place and the people were liars; they were not who they said they were. "This is an evil place; God is not here. Don't make us come back here, please!" I was so happy I was just visiting for the day. Poor Allie had been going there all along. No wonder she didn't look like she enjoyed going to school. We never went there again. I didn't bring it up to God, either. I knew He knew what was in the hearts of people and He would take care of this big lie.

Our mini-revolution at the Catholic school was beneficial to both sides. The Catholic school wouldn't have us disturbing their teachings, and we were happy to be in the public school. There were a lot more people in the new school. The energy was much different than the heavy, yucky one at the Catholic school. There weren't many happy or glowing spirits, but at least there were some, and laughter was heard every day.

Moving back to the city for the winter turned out to be a good decision. It ended up being a dangerous winter in the Sierra Mountains. Massive storms brought deep snow over the whole region, including our ranch. Roads were closed, houses were buried in snow, and food and water had to be flown in to the stranded.

Some homes were crushed by the weight of the snow. People had to dig the snow away from vents and chimneys so they wouldn't die from carbon monoxide poisoning. I didn't know what that was, either. I was told it was an invisible gas that kills people and animals because it doesn't have a smell. I wondered how anyone could ever be saved if they were breathing it.

I believe this was another lesson in how God takes care of us. When our plans are foiled, we get angry and disappointed, but in the end, we learn it was the best thing to happen.

Dad told us the cabin would have been our coffin for sure. I didn't understand that, but all the adults agreed. Our lives had been saved, including that of our unborn sibling, a fourth daughter who was born in early December. Mom and Dad named her Renée.

During this time, the evil man started coming back around. I guess he thought it was safe. He tried feeding Val food and talked like he wanted to be friends. Val wouldn't accept his bribes. The evil man again tried enticing us girls with candy, but we ran into the house and told Mom he was back. When she went out to confront him, he was gone. Val was barking and jumping at the fence in the direction he had fled.

After Christmas vacation, we heard that the evil man had been arrested for hurting children and been sent to prison. We were glad to hear he would no longer be bothering us or anyone else.

I dreamt of going home to the Sierras. I thanked God for making this all possible.

A New Life
& New Lessons

After the summer of 1952, we would never have to go to a big city school again. It was the beginning of a new life. In the city, we had had our own rooms, electricity, indoor plumbing, telephone, and television. We had none of those things now. We all had to sacrifice in the mountains. Mom had the hardest time adjusting. She gave up more than we knew.

In the city, she had played the piano every day. Mom had also taught and let us kids play, too. But the piano couldn't fit in the cabin or tent, so Mom was storing it at her sister's home in the city. Dad gave up money to live in the mountains. In the city, as a longshoreman, he had made lots of money, but in the Sierras, he worked in a lumber mill for only $200 a month.

We children, of course, knew nothing of those things. We were learning about farming, survival, hunting, and building. I loved the outdoors. Grandpa and Dad taught me how to plant a garden and how to measure and cut boards for building sheds, stairs, animal pens, and fencing. We cleared land for pasture. We cut wood for cooking, nightly campfires, and heating for the upcoming winter. It was a lot of work, but I enjoyed it.

When the livestock arrived, I looked forward to feeding them. The soothing smell of hay, grass, and chicken and rabbit feed made me feel at peace. Working outdoors, mostly by myself, was like being in heaven. I didn't care to help cook or do household chores, but I was forced to do them anyway. I formed a lot of blisters in the beginning, but eventually my hands toughened up with hardy calluses. When all my chores were done, Val and I would go hunting.

The entire family would spend evenings around the campfire and picnic table, reading, playing board games or charades, and singing by lantern light. Then we would jump into bed in our comfy one-room cabin, and my grandparents would retire to their one-room camper. Every other weekend, we went on fishing trips to a lake or river and camped out. It was a wonderful, God-blessed life!

Dad promised Mom he would build her a real house that same year. We were very excited to be getting a new, bigger home. We were told we would each have our own room again and so would Mom and Dad. Mom was thrilled she was going to have enough room to bring her piano up from the city. She began looking at plans and colors.

One day, I noticed Mom was no longer joyful in her spirit. It turned out Dad didn't have enough money to build the three-or four-bedroom house he had promised her. His parents took over and funded the project, which became a two-bedroom house, and they were going to live in it, too! Since we were all going to be packed into the new house, it wasn't going to be much different than being in the one-room cabin.

We three oldest kids would have one of the bedrooms. Our grandparents would get the other bedroom, and Mom and Dad would sleep on a pullout sofa bed in the front room. Baby sister Renée would be in her crib next to Mom and Dad. There wasn't going to be enough room for Mom's piano. It was the first time Dad had broken his promise about a new house.

In our new living arrangements, I became angry with the way Grandma treated Mom. She treated Mom and us kids like we were beneath her, not worthy of her son. She would tell us how she and Grandpa were of royal blood from Spain and that their relatives were advisors to the royal court of Spain. They had a coat of arms to prove it, and the king of Spain had deeded her father a large parcel of land in California. Yet Dad somehow had Yaqui, Apache, and Mayo bloodlines, too. He had actually spent summers on an Apache Reservation when he was young. I didn't know whether to believe her story or not, and I couldn't understand why my grandparents couldn't have continued living in the camper trailer. Grandma had always bragged about how wonderful it was to live there.

My favorite and only real uncle, Max, came to visit that summer. He had been living with us in the big city. He was now living in our old house all by himself, and for companionship, he wanted his dog back! I couldn't accept this news. Val had always been my dog, our family dog. All this time, he had actually belonged to our uncle. Why hadn't someone told us?

I felt a deep, terrible loss. I was angry, and my heart was broken. Uncle Max promised to take good care of Val, but a couple of years later, we got word that Val had been poisoned. They believed the evil man had done it. He had been released from prison and seen hanging around the old neighborhood. He was actually seen near our old house.

I learned I couldn't control other people's promises or choices, good or bad. I couldn't trust promises from people. God always kept His promises to me, but people didn't. On top of that, around the same time, I found out that Santa, the Easter Bunny, and the Boogeyman were not real. My parents and other adults had been lying to me all this time! I was so sad my heart hurt. I was told not to reveal these lies to Lily and our newest sister, Renée. I was eight years old, and I never again completely trusted anything anyone told me.

That fall, during deer hunting season, Dad let me carry a long stick that represented a rifle. I was to treat it as a real gun. I was told not to drag it in the dirt or point it at or near any person or vehicle. I learned to walk quietly and to be sure I knew which way the wind was blowing so as not to alert the deer. There was a lot to learn about hunting deer and other wild game. It wasn't a game of catch and release, like Val and I had played. Real hunting was serious and permanent. I hadn't experienced a hunting kill, but because, during the winter months and early spring, we could only afford to feed and care for breeding stock, I was forced to learn about the harvesting of our farm animals. We harvested chickens, rabbits, and goats. I learned how to kill animals humanely and how to age and butcher their meat.

It saddened me to feel their life force, or spirit, leave their bodies. Their spirits were still alive; the earth seemed to become one with them. I knew they were not really gone, because God was a part of them, too; He had created them. Physically, they were gone, yes. Spiritually, they were somewhere. I thanked God for revealing this to me.

We didn't have electricity. It would be coming when our "white house" was finished. We called the house our grandparents built our very own white house for two reasons. First, Grandma had it painted white inside and out because it was the cheapest color. Second, she was our dictator in residence; she bossed around all of us!

A kind neighbor stored most of our meat in their extra freezer. We kept some meat in ice-filled coolers. Later, when winter came, we packed the coolers in the snow. The cold temperatures kept them frozen until we could get a freezer of our own.

We worked hard to make sure we had plenty of wood for cooking and heating. After the harvesting of the animals, our grandparents moved back to the city…freedom at last! They left sooner than usual because Great-Grandma was doing poorly and Grandma was asked to help take care of her.

Mom and Dad were now able to sleep in the second bedroom until my grandparents came back in the spring. They did this every year until the second one-bedroom house was built. That was Dad's second broken promise to Mom because of his parents.

Meanwhile, Allie, Lily, and I were enrolled in the local elementary school. School was great. I actually liked my elementary school teachers. They were happy and enjoyed teaching. They encouraged us and helped us whenever we needed it, and they didn't mind being asked a lot of questions—especially my first and second-grade teacher. The school had two or three classes in one room because there were not many kids. I had to take the second grade over; I didn't know why.

My second-grade teacher was Mr. Roscoe. His spirit glowed brightly. I looked forward to each day and learning something new. People in the mountains were very different from people in the city. They had a glow of peacefulness about them that city people didn't.

Even though I enjoyed school, I loved getting home and doing my chores. Being outside in the fall and winter was invigorating, and I could feel the presence of God more than any other time. There is a silence you can only hear when there is snow everywhere. It's so quiet you can hear snowflakes falling and landing on the ground. God and I became so close that I rarely asked questions. We were one all the time. I just knew things without having to ask. His thoughts flowed through my mind as mine did to His.

For instance, once, when I looked into one classmate's eyes, it felt like my brain and eyes were being twisted to the point of passing out. It looked as if there were two sets of eyes in there, one behind the other. One set of eyes was filled with fear, and the other looked blank.

The word "possessed" passed through my mind. I didn't know what the word meant, nor had I ever heard it before, but at the same time, I felt a heavy, evil energy coming from the girl, too. I instantly knew she had been taken over by an evil entity. Her own spirit was still in there, just not in control all the time.

She would frequently fall to the ground, squirm, jerk, and foam at the mouth. A teacher would run over and hold her down until the jerking stopped. During one particular episode, I reached out to touch her, but the teacher pushed me away and told everyone to stay back and not worry. The teacher told us our classmate was having a seizure and it would soon pass.

This student often vacantly stared and would start wandering away from the school. One day, she said she wanted to go home, but then she headed for the local cemetery. Another time, she ate a whole large tomato in small bites while sitting next to me at a picnic table. When done, she suddenly threw up a whole, skinless tomato. She pushed it toward me, saying, "This is for you." She wickedly smiled while wiping slobber from her mouth.

From the time I first became aware of it, the evil spirit inside her would mess with me, especially during our high school years. She once suddenly sat on my lap and peed on me. Then she jumped up, pointed at me, and yelled, "Pam peed on herself!"

The evil spirit inside of her made her do sexual things, too. She would sneak out at night and pick up men driving home from local bars, but she pretended to be me during her sexual adventures. This caused me to get in trouble with my dad and helped fuel the lie that I was the local slut during my high school years. I wasn't allowed to go on dates or go steady with anyone during that time.

The evil spirit seemed to be challenging me, but I didn't know what it wanted. When not possessed, the girl would cling to me and call me her best friend. I asked God to help us both, but nothing ever changed. He never said anything specific other than, "Love your neighbor as yourself." Forgiveness became much harder as time went by.

Speaking of forgiveness, one summer, a family's car broke down on the main highway next to our home. Dad gave the man a ride to a repair shop to get a tow truck. The couple asked Dad and Mom if they and their kids could stay with us while they waited for their car to be repaired.

There was nowhere else for them to stay. It would only be for three days, and they didn't have any camping gear or supplies. My parents let them stay, mostly for the sake of their kids. I didn't like their energies, nor did I trust them, but Dad told us to treat them as guests. They were in need of our help. We took very good care of them. Consequently, they took every opportunity to stay longer. The father told us he really liked staying with us because he felt like a king and his wife felt like a queen since we waited on them hand and foot. Plus, we kept their kids busy and happy. He kept telling us the part for his car hadn't come in yet; it was back-ordered. He told Dad that he felt bad it was taking so long.

Dad found out the part had come in two days after the breakdown. If he hadn't checked at the repair shop himself, we would have waited for who knows how long. When Dad forced them to leave after three weeks, they didn't pay for anything or offer to replace our food. They didn't even thank us. I was confused. We are to help one another and be grateful when someone helps us, but those people took advantage and didn't show any gratitude. They seemed to think it was their right or privilege to use us and our supplies without thanks or compensation.

I had felt the prideful, selfish energies about them from the beginning. But I held my feelings in check as Dad told me to, even though I really wanted to tell the man off every time he said, "Hey, sweetie, get me a glass of water," when he could have gotten off his butt to get it himself. Mom explained that some white people think they are superior to people who are not white. This was my first experience of feeling I was different in another way, other than my gifts. "Forgive" was the word from God on this one, too.

More Death Rituals

That October, after Dad's parents left the Sierras, we received the message that Great-Grandma had died and we needed to attend her funeral. I wasn't eager to go back to the city and all the sad energies. I wondered if the screaming women in black were going to be there again.

We arrived at dinnertime. The house was full of people, and my parents seemed to know everyone. After eating, I became sleepy. I asked Mom where I could sleep. She told me to wait as she went to ask Grandma who was sitting with a group of women in black. They looked a lot like the women in black from earlier, except they were quiet now and didn't have veils covering their faces.

Mom spoke to Grandma. One of the women turned around to look at me. She had a crooked smile on her face, and her eyes twinkled with mischief. Turning to Mom, she said something. Mom gasped and looked like she was protesting. After a few moments, Mom came back to me, took my hand, and led me away.

To my surprise and delight, we walked down the hallway to Great-Grandma's bedroom. We walked right in, and Mom sat me down on the bed. I had always wanted to sit or lie down on this bed. There were pretty pink flowers on the soft, comfy bedspread. Great-Grandma had never let any of us children get anywhere near it, but there I was, sitting on it; I felt special.

Mom told me it was the only bed available. She seemed worried. I was delighted. I pulled the sheet, blanket, and bedspread around me, snuggling in for a good night's sleep.

I remembered the last time I had been near this room and how Great-Grandma had floated up and then come back down. I wondered if she had gone up and out through the roof or out the window or door. I decided to use one of my gifts God had given me to feel which way Great-Grandma had gone to see if I could catch up with her or feel what she was feeling.

I reached out energetically to find her energy or spirit trail and followed it. Up I floated to the ceiling, but that was as far as I could go. I thought, *How in the world did she get out of here? Where did she go?*

Suddenly a voice said, "We took her and the bed out the balcony."

"No way! Why? How could that happen?"

"We did and can show you if you want."

I was really curious and eager to know where and how Great-Grandma had left.

"Yes, show me."

"Go back to the bed and hold on tight," the voice eagerly demanded. Instantly the bed rose and floated over the steps and out the now open balcony doors. It floated over the balcony and onto the sidewalk!

Everything looked just like the desert had, like a dream. I was definitely in a different dimension. The air smelled of rain. The streets and sidewalks looked wet. I was once more one with everything. I smelled and tasted the damp air with my whole spirit body, not just my nose and mouth. I felt so alive and free.

The bed rattled down the sidewalk. I hadn't noticed the bed had wheels on it until, all of a sudden, it hit a deep crack, almost throwing me off the bed.

"I told you to hang on tight!" an amused voice exclaimed.

"Did you almost dump Great-Grandma, too?"

"No, we went onto the power lines."

"Will you take me to where she is?"

"Sure, if you want to go there." This time, the bed and I were raised to the top of the power lines. We were going so fast that everything was a blur.

"How much further are we going? It is taking a long time. I have to be back for tomorrow's funeral."

"If we take you to where your Great-Grandma is, you will not be coming back at all, foolish one. You should be careful about who and what you ask concerning spiritual things."

I demanded they take me back. I heard an evil laugh, and then the voice whispered, "Find your own way back. Fly if you can." The laughter faded away into silence.

I couldn't believe I hadn't asked God about this or asked the voice who they were, nor had I reached out to *feel* them before going with them. God hadn't even warned me.

In the stillness, I soon felt the heavy, awful feeling of evil coming my way and started floating back the way I had come, following the power lines. When I came to the place where the bed hit the crack in the sidewalk, I floated down to the sidewalk, but I couldn't find the bed. I walked toward Great-Grandma's house, frustrated at how I had so easily been fooled.

As I walked, the evil presence grew stronger. I looked behind me, to my left and right. I couldn't see anything or anyone. My fear was getting stronger, and I wasn't sure I was going the right way. I couldn't walk well or run. My legs felt extremely heavy.

The sarcastic words "fly if you can" came to mind. I asked God to help me fly back to the house because evil was coming. God said, "You can fly when you surrender all of yourself to me, just like when we become one. Let go, and you will float to where you want to go." I took a deep breath and focused on being one with God; I felt myself floating again. As I lifted off the ground, I thought, *Fly back to Great-Grandma's house.* To my relief, off I flew to her house. I still wasn't safe. Evil was at my back and ready to pounce. Quickly I landed on the balcony of Great-Grandma's bedroom.

I wondered what I was going to tell everyone about the missing bed. When I entered the room, everything went black. Evil had me in its grasp. It held me so tightly I couldn't wiggle free. I kicked and punched at it, calling out to God to save me. I could barely breathe. I felt like I was going to die right then in evil's grasp. "Help me!" I cried out to God for the third time. Evil's grip loosened. I was finally free—free from the sheet and bedspread. I had been wrapped up in them tightly, not in evil's grasp.

What a dream! Or was it? I was in the bed. It wasn't lost after all. The balcony windows were closed, not open, and it wasn't pitch black anymore. I was very tired and fell back to sleep. Mom came in sometime later to wake me for breakfast. When I went to eat, the woman who had told Mom where to let me sleep came over. She asked if I had slept well. She looked as if she knew what had happened, as if she wanted me to tell her. I thought that she was last night's voice.

God warned me not to let her know, so I told her I had been very tired and had fallen asleep right away. She looked surprised and then walked away to another woman. They talked in whispers, looking at me, confused. I knew for sure it wasn't a dream.

Being my first funeral, I didn't know what was going to happen or what was expected. The experience affected me so much that I didn't go to another for many years. Grandma told me to say goodbye to the body of Great-Grandma. It was in a big box in the front of the room. People were walking up to the box, touching or bending down over it, and crying. Everyone looked very sad. I wondered what they were doing. I hadn't been expecting to be told to go up there.

I knew Great-Grandma wasn't there. She was someplace far away. They should be happy she was back with God, but what if evil had gotten to her? Anyway, Mom told me I didn't have to go up. I was too short to get up on the box, and I definitely couldn't climb inside.

Grandma forced Allie to go up there, and she wouldn't accept my not going. She came over to me, angrily picked me up, and carried me to the box.

"Say goodbye to Great-Grandma. Give her a kiss goodbye!" she scolded.

"No!" I cried while kicking and squirming. She pushed me head first into the box. I found myself face to face with the dead body of Great-Grandma.

My lips and nose touched the skin. It tasted and smelled awful. It burnt my eyes and the inside of my nose. I could hardly breathe. It felt cold and stiff. There was definitely no life, energy, or spirit anywhere in the body. I couldn't understand why they didn't know Great-Grandma was not that thing in the box. It didn't even look like her. Thankfully, I didn't have to go to the burial, which I found out later meant putting the box, called a coffin, and body into the ground and then covering it up with dirt.

I couldn't understand why the grown-ups were acting so weird concerning the lifeless body used by Great-Grandma. They must have forgotten or didn't know about the life of their spirit and where it lives after it leaves a body. Needless to say, I was eager to leave this place and get back home to the Sierras and school.

ACT II

DODGING EVIL

SCHOOL DAZE

The years passed quickly. It was the beginning of the 1957–1958 school year for my sisters and me. I was entering the sixth grade. The fifth and sixth grades were combined. The teacher wasn't as bad as everyone said she was going to be. She was a strict, no-nonsense type of person. She expected the best out of each of us, and we were encouraged to expect the best out of ourselves. She taught me to enjoy reading and all my other classes. I didn't want to leave elementary school.

The next year, I was in middle school, which was in a different building thirty minutes away in another small town. I didn't like riding in a school bus. There were metal bars on the seats, no seatbelts, and thin padding. It wasn't comfortable or safe. What were the adults thinking? Again, another law. We were innocent before the seventh grade. We interacted with each other mostly as equals. When we left grammar school, things changed.

Social life in middle and high school was like being in the big city. Everyone was going to and fro, involved only in their own worlds, planning how they could become popular and accepted by the cool kids and adults at the school. I overheard some kids putting down others, including me, to make themselves look good, and they joked about how they fooled their parents by acting like good kids. This behavior started in the seventh grade and escalated as we got older. Perhaps it was all the hormones of puberty.

Girls who hadn't liked boys two years ago now dreamed about them all the time. This continued all through high school. They wanted boys to like them because they just *loved* boys. They would do anything to get one, even if the guy was going steady with someone else. Some of the girls in ninth grade started wearing makeup to show off their beauty and tight clothes to show off their new shapely bodies. The popular girls would make fun of other girls' and guys' looks, hairstyles, clothes, and even shoes. I didn't like their energy, their words, or even their facial expressions. They deeply hurt the girls and guys they embarrassed by mocking them. Their laughter felt like knives piercing our hearts.

The ninth-grade boys were suddenly studs, hinting about their sexual expertise and the size of their penises. All this happened in just one summer. They talked like they had been having sex for years and knew everything about it. Some of the girls talked the same way, not only about the size of penises but also the size of their bras. An A wasn't good for a bra size. One needed to have a B, C, or D.

I wasn't part of the shapely size-B-and-up crowd. I had muscles instead of boobs. I was strong and lean. I was five foot two, one hundred pounds, and had brown skin and eyes and long black hair. I wore loose-fitting clothes. Outside of gym class, most people didn't know I had big muscles. I didn't hear anyone gossiping about it.

Sadly, even in this small country town, the worldly ways were healthy and strong. Evil is in the minds and hearts of people everywhere in this world, and I discovered that it started between the eighth and ninth grades.

Odd social behaviors not seen or experienced before junior high were now daily occurrences, and they continued through high school. It became quite evident that those of us who used to hang out, for some reason, couldn't anymore. It wasn't acceptable if you weren't part of the new groups created by the school.

Some think this is a natural progression everyone goes through. I was forced to go where the school wanted me to go and take classes they chose for me. Could they have been indoctrinating me into their system? Was this truly a natural progression?

I got along with most everyone fairly well. I was chosen as a kind of mentor and confidante by some. They would come to me for advice or to have someone listen to them about personal relationship issues. As if I knew about such things.

Yet, strangely, I did. Answers would come to me via God's Spirit, and I would speak what I heard. It felt like I knew exactly what I was talking about, even though I had never been in a romantic relationship with anyone, nor had I ever had the inclination. I just knew the *whys* of what boys and girls said or did. Then, just as now, it all boiled down to fear—fear of not being accepted by others, especially those deemed the elite of our world.

Fear comes from listening to the negative thoughts given to us by evil. It uses not only our own minds, but also friends, siblings, parents, and even casual acquaintances. We are told by society and the world what is expected of us. One must fit in.

The message I got while in high school was that I wasn't smart or tough enough to accomplish my dreams. The teachers and counselors put the fear of failure and unworthiness in my mind and heart. They should have encouraged me like my grammar school teachers had.

Parents and religious leaders are supposed to teach people how to live well. Who gave schools the authority to tell us how we're supposed to act or live once we reach a certain age? It seemed like programming to me. We had all been getting along fine without their input or separation into social classes.

The school environment made me and others doubt our place and value because we didn't fit into the desired status quo of thinking. I still have a hard time understanding the "I'm better or more acceptable in society than you are" way of thinking. Except for those who are extremely evil, who torture and kill others without remorse, there is no reason to think anyone is better than another person, absolutely none. I was taught by my parents and God that we all should treat others the way we want to be treated. No one is to consider themselves above another.

I didn't and still don't have anyone I would call an idol. I have been moved by a movie star, musician, artist, or singer's performance, but I have never screamed and cried over them just because of who they were. That always seemed to me to be overexaggerated emotional drama.

The worst for me, though, was being forced to be naked and shower in front of everyone in gym class. It was humiliating for all. *Why*? We had never had to shower after playtime before. I was told it was because we were becoming women and men and our sweat glands would make us all stink after sports. We had to be considerate toward others in classes after gym. That school year went by quickly, just like my showers.

I wasn't allowed to date during high school, which was fine by me because I had no interest in boys. When I was a senior, I was allowed to go to the prom. I went with the only other non-white person in school. It was set up by our parents. We had a fun time, even though it was the only time we had spent together in three years.

I was a junior when I became aware that I had a sixth sense. One of my classmates, Maggie, was teased and bullied, except when I was with her. One look from me, along with a burst of energy from my mind and spirit thrown in the bully's direction, would put a stop to it. Putting up my hand and pointing it at them would have drawn too much attention and might have caused "They" to hear about it.

There was a classmate, Ralph, who would pester Maggie every chance he could get. I thought he had a secret crush on her. One particular afternoon, he was merciless toward her. I tried to get him to lighten up and leave her alone without using my gifts.

Instead, he got even uglier. It got to the point where she completely lost control and screamed, "I hate you. I wish you were dead!" She said it with so much hurt and anger energy I almost fell over.

It hit me like a tidal wave. Instantly I was swept into the future. It was summertime, and I was floating next to a huge pine tree near a river. I recognized where I was. I heard a speeding car coming toward me. I looked closely into the car and saw Ralph and his older brother in the front seat, laughing crazily. For a brief moment, I thought someone else was in the backseat, but my attention was drawn to the front, and I noticed they weren't wearing seatbelts.

The older brother lost control of the car and drove straight into the tree. It was a terrible, helpless feeling not to be able to stop such a horrible accident, let alone to have to watch it. The passenger door flew open, and Ralph fell forward and then partway to the side. His top half was hanging out of the door as it slammed shut, seemingly cutting him in half. I had just witnessed his death!

Gasping, I told Maggie what I had seen. I knew she didn't really mean it. She was so distressed from Ralph's torture that she couldn't stop sobbing as she explained how he would torment her after school, too. She just couldn't take it anymore. I encouraged her to forgive him. He was just a silly boy. The more she reacted to him, the more he would keep teasing her.

I went to Ralph's house after school to ask him to lay off Maggie and find out why he was pestering her so relentlessly. He said he liked doing it. He liked seeing her face turn red, but he didn't do it to hurt her. He was just kidding around with her.

While at his home, I noticed his whole family kidded with each other. They said embarrassing and mean things, teasing each other constantly. Obviously, it was their way of showing love for each other. My family did it, too, but not to such a hurtful degree.

I went to Maggie's house next and told her I had discovered Ralph really liked her. It was his way of flirting with her. She was not impressed.

Later on, she mentioned Ralph had been nicer to her and she had told him she didn't mean what she said that day.

I didn't witness any more incidents between them at school. Her outburst didn't cause the accident, but it took me to the future to see what would happen to cause his death. Later, during the summer, news came down the pike that Ralph, indeed, had been killed in a car crash, exactly as I had seen it months earlier.

During high school, I received a few invitations to go steady, but the boys wanted me to have sex with them first. They promised to let me wear their school jacket or sweater. They would even publicly admit we were a couple. What an honor! Yeah, right. NO!

After getting these requests, I had an entirely different view of the girls who were wearing guys' school jackets or sweaters. It did seem to be a contest between the girls about who got whose sweater. It was a status symbol of some kind. Because I wasn't allowed to go on dates or have a boyfriend, the boys took advantage of this.

They claimed to have "had me" and said I was some kind of sex expert. My reputation spanned the whole county and beyond!

I worked the concession stand during school games. Boys from visiting schools and their team members would gather around the concession stand and stare at me. They would usually poke at a boy next to them and tell him, "Go ahead. Ask her." Blushing, one of them would come up to the counter and ask me if I was Pam. I would say, "Yes, what?" He usually would blush and run away.

One time, a boy answered, "We have heard all about you. Are you as good as they say?"

"What are you talking about?" For a second, I thought he was referring to an incident at a different school when I had used my special healing touch in an emergency.

I was walking through the school's parking lot when three boys ran in front of me, racing to see who could get to their car first. The winner got to drive. One of the boys fell to the ground, screaming in pain. Tearfully, pulling himself onto the hood of a nearby car, he yelled at his friends to grab his leg and squeeze it. The other two boys tried to help him but didn't know what to do for such a strong cramp, or charley horse, as some call it. I ran over to him, grabbed his calf muscle, sent healing energy into it, and swept off the pain. It took only seconds to stop his agony. They all looked at me as if I were a ghost that had just jumped out in front of them.

The boy who had suffered the cramp blushed and thanked me. I told him he was welcome and asked them to please not tell anyone. As I hurried away, I overheard them asking each other, "How did she do that? Who is she? I don't know her, do you?"

Back at the concession stand, the blushing boy respectfully said, "Sex! Will you have it with me? I'll wait for you to go on break."

I couldn't believe my ears. I was speechless for a moment; then I yelled at all of them to get away from me. Now I knew why there were always groups of boys hanging out near the concession stand, looking at me. I was in shock.

How and why would they think such a thing of me? I hadn't had sex with anyone, so someone must have told people that I had. I tried to find out, but no one knew who had started this rumor. The whole school knew about it, but I didn't have a clue. I assumed it must have been one of the boys who had asked me to wear their jacket or sweater. Because I had turned them down, they had made up the lie to protect their pride and reputation.

This was around the same time I found out the possessed girl from second grade was roaming the highways at night, picking up men on their way home from bars, and having sex with them. She was telling them her name was Pam!

Dad found out and was extremely angry. He demanded I explain my behavior. I swore I didn't do such a thing. He investigated further and got a description of a large-breasted girl, which certainly wasn't me.

My high school counselors tried to help me decide what I should do for the rest of my life. They asked, "What *do* you want to do?" I wanted to live on our ranch forever and raise and train horses. I was told it would take a lot of money and a long time to accomplish.

I discovered barriers were all around to keep me from doing what I wanted to do. Instead, I was encouraged to stay on society's path: go to college, get a job, and settle down. Of course, much of this depended on one's IQ, grades, gender, and skin color.

I looked into getting college money through the government by way of my Indian heritage, but I found out my people, at that time, were not a recognized tribe. We had never signed a treaty with the U.S. government because we had never been at war with them. But the tribe was given land to call their own in 1964. On September 18, 1978, the tribe became historically recognized. (They had to go to war by blocking an interstate highway and then telling an Arizona official they were at war so they could sign a treaty. It is a great story.) Now they have their own casino to pay for the tribe's needs instead of taking handouts from the government.

In the meantime, during those same years, my spiritual life and home life were full of lessons.

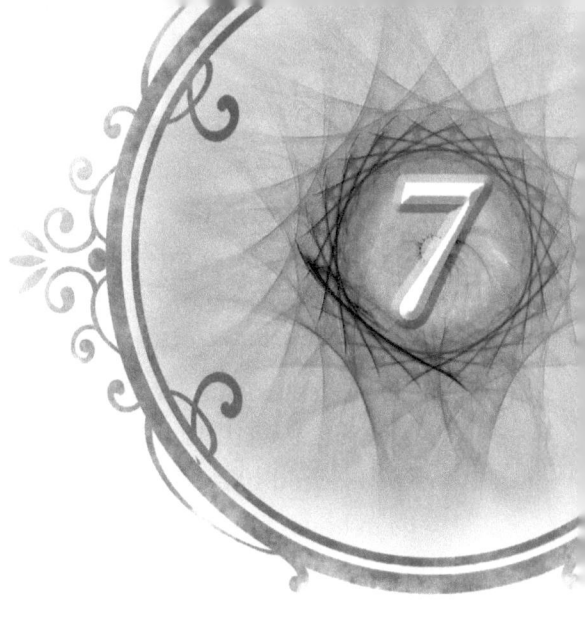

Church Dogma

I was taught to always tell the truth, but not hurt anyone's feelings, either. Isn't speaking partial truths the same as lying? And what about my secret? I was told not to tell anyone the truth about my gifts or "They" would come and take me away.

What if the truth would help a person more than the temporary hurt? Such were the moral dilemmas I thought about, along with other contradictions I learned from adults. They'd tell me that we are to behave well in society and obey or else suffer the consequences. But then they'd go and do the opposite of what they had told me to do. "When you are eighteen," I'd hear, "you can decide for yourself what you want to do or say. Until then, do as I say."

For example, in the same year I had to go to middle school, I was forced to go to the local Catholic summer school. It was called Catechism. Being able to receive my first Communion and, in a few years, be confirmed in the Catholic faith wasn't on my list of things to do that summer or any other.

There were three churches in the area: one Catholic, one Protestant, and one community church. They all claimed they were the only true church of God or Christ. Take, for instance, the community church, which claimed to be the 144,000 who, during the Tribulation, would be the only ones to be saved.

They invited my family to join their church, bragging they had over one million members worldwide. Dad was very good at telling truths beside his lies and fibs. He didn't sound rude, but he did cut to the quick. He always sounded humble, kind, and naive. He spoke to the pastor in a curious, child-like voice.

"I'm honored you have invited my family to join your church, but from what you have told me, there isn't room for us." The pastor was adamant that there was room for us. Dad continued: "I want to make sure I understand you correctly. You say you are the 144,000 chosen of God, the only ones to be saved during the Tribulation. So, we must join your church. Is that right?"

"Correct."

"You also say you have a million church members worldwide?"

"Yes, that is correct."

"Then, sir, I would like to know how your church chooses *who* will be among the 144,000?" The pastor's mouth was open, but nothing came out. Dad thanked him again for the invite, and we left. I will never forget that evening or the ones that followed regarding churches and their special teachings.

Evidently, since Dad and Mom had been raised Catholic, we had to be Catholic, too. I assumed it must be a law. Strange how, the older one gets, the more laws are needed. This was difficult for me to understand and accept, but off to Catechism, my sisters and I were sent.

My parents went to church twice a year, but they made my sisters and I go every Saturday or Sunday. Grandma, Dad's mother, was extremely Catholic and demanded her grandchildren become good Catholics. She had an altar in her bedroom with statues of Mary, baby

Jesus, Joseph, a couple of saints, the crucified Christ, and a picture of some Lady of Somewhere who looked a lot like Mary.

She put candles in red glasses in rows to light for prayers. She prayed a lot and crossed herself every time she walked past the altar. It didn't feel right, a bit dark and gloomy to me, and I didn't feel God's presence there.

Was being a Catholic different than being a Christian? I wondered if it was a religion, a church, or just a state of being. Grandma was mean to Mom and acted like she was better than us, but then she claimed to be religious and a good Catholic.

Because we were kicked out of the Catholic school in the city, I tried to have a better attitude at the new church. After all, the nuns and priest were different than those in the city. Maybe they would be nicer. I was surprised and happy when I found the nuns were quiet and gentle in actions and words and the priest was a spirit-filled man, always smiling and full of good cheer. He treated everyone alike. He made you feel just as important as the next person.

The first two weeks went smoothly. We learned special prayers and would get a gold star on a special card if we remembered them correctly. Those cards were beautiful, pastel-colored, with pictures of sheep with Mary and the baby Jesus. Another card had the whole holy family with golden halos around their heads and a lamb or donkey nearby.

They looked so loving, peaceful, and holy. I wanted to be holy, just like them. I treasured those cards and felt jealous and covetous when I didn't win the one, I wanted. I tried to trade cards for the ones I wanted. If I couldn't, I thought about stealing them! I couldn't believe what was happening to me. I was there to learn the ways of God. Instead, I learned the ways of the flesh and evil.

The rosaries were another temptation for me. The most beautiful ones were locked in a case in the church store and in the hands of the wealthy members. My family couldn't afford them, so we had the cheapest ones. I hadn't known we were poor before that summer. I was ashamed because I couldn't show my love for God by having expensive, beautiful things like everyone else.

White rosaries were the preferred color. White represented innocence and purity. Oddly, many of the adults had black ones, and we young had white ones. I wondered if it was because adults were no longer innocent or pure.

I never understood Mass; it was mostly in a strange language. I just followed the others; I even made the same scrunched-up face they did while praying really hard. There were, however, some who looked filled with the Spirit of God and had peaceful, glowing faces.

I was encouraged to sacrifice everything to please God, because, otherwise, He would be angry at me. If I didn't do as He, the nuns, and the priest told me, I was going to hell or, at the least, purgatory. No heaven for sinners. If I wanted to get to heaven, I had to pledge allegiance to the Church and God, go to confession, and give them the nickel or quarter my parents gave me to put in a basket that was passed around.

The priest would ask when I had my last confession, and then I was supposed to confess my sins. That was hard to do when you didn't sin. Sometimes I would just make up a sin, even if I didn't do it. Then he would tell me to pray a certain number of Our Fathers and Hail Marys, depending on the sin. Only then would I be forgiven and freed of sin. If you committed a really bad sin, the priest would throw in a couple of Apostles' Creeds to recite along with the other two prayers. The worse the crime, the more times you had to recite the prayers.

This was something you could do every week if necessary (it was actually kind of mandatory). The Catholic Church taught that God loved me but He was also angry at me. They made me afraid of getting Him angrier. I felt that if I messed up, I would go to hell forever.

This was completely opposite of the relationship between my God and me. I argued with the sisters about the true nature of God. They weren't happy with me. They wanted to know who had told me these things. I said, "God."

Looking at me as if I were some strange being, they asked, "Why would God talk to you? You must be talking to demons, not God. Stop listening to them and listen to us."

That made me angry. Demons—not God! I had to tell them the truth, even if "They" found out. I stomped my foot and strongly said, "God and I have been together since the beginning. He is love and is filled with kindness, compassion, and power all in one. He brings a great peace to my spirit and soul that no other person or thing can!"

They gasped and quickly took me to the priest for correction. After testifying against me, the nuns left. The room was quiet. The priest looked at me. He seemed to be in deep thought, rubbing his chin.

I was angry at the nuns but afraid of the priest. Was he one of the "They" who would take me away? Surely, I was going to be punished severely for speaking what was considered blasphemy to the nuns.

"So, Pam, you talk to God?"

"Yes, ever since I can remember, before I knew who He was or His name."

"Who told you His name?"

"My mom. She said His name is God, our Father. I just say Father most of the time. He is my Father more so than my dad. His presence is in me and all things. I even see him in you. You, too, are filled with His Spirit, aren't you?"

"Yes, I am, but not all who profess to believe have the Spirit or relationship we do. They do not understand the spiritual part of God as much as the laws, rules, and regulations they have learned from their teachers.

"I would like you to stop talking about your relationship with God and let the sisters teach their lessons. Learn the lessons and pass the tests so you can receive First Communion with your classmates. You and I know, and hopefully, someday they will, too. In the meantime, keep peace in class."

From then on, I just kept my mouth shut like in regular school. I no longer coveted the pretty cards. I just wanted to hurry and get this whole thing over with, receive Communion, receive the body of Christ in a wafer, and drink some wine.

It took me a while to understand Holy Communion. I first thought Catholics must be cannibals. I wasn't looking forward to eating someone's body parts. I finally understood the spiritual meaning after the priest explained it to me.

I didn't really get to know Christ very well, but baby Jesus was spoken of often in class. They hurried through the story of Christ. It didn't make sense to me, especially the part where He died for all our sins, yet there were still a hell, a purgatory, and a lot of people going to confession. I didn't really grasp the true meaning and importance of Christ until much later.

When I took my First Communion, I felt the loving, peaceful, uplifting presence of God in both the wafer and the wine as they went down my throat, into my stomach, and through my body. It was God's true Spirit. It was amazing. I felt all floaty. Strangely, I did not have the same experience with the wafer and wine until many years later.

My last religious ritual with the Catholic Church was Confirmation. I wore a white dress like I did for First Communion, but this time, I had to choose a new secret name. I was internally protesting the new ritual. I couldn't get myself to kneel willingly before a man called a bishop, whom I didn't know, and kiss his ring.

It felt wrong. What did this have to do with God, the Virgin Mary, or baby Jesus, let alone confirming my belief in the Father, the Son, the Holy Spirit, and the Church? Adults had some odd ideas when it came to rituals, religion, and churches. As I look back at those times, I can see how adults and others in authority took great advantage of a child's innocence.

I promised the priest I would go through the ritual of Confirmation for his sake. I would do it for him, even though he was being forced to go to a faraway church and we would never see him again. I liked him because he made it easier for me to endure the Church dogma.

I wanted to keep my word to the first person I met who knew the God I knew. Although we shared a personal relationship with God, I never told him about my gifts. Talking to God was one thing the priest understood. Seeing spirits and feeling emotions and others' pain was another story. After all, "They" were still out there somewhere.

While waiting for my turn, I watched all the others before me bow and kneel to a man dressed in a strange outfit. It reminded me of a picture I saw in a book when I went to the library with Allie. She told me it was about people who felt white people were superior to all other races. They were called the Ku Klux Klan.

The bishop's outfit looked like the picture I had seen, except the bishop wore a hat instead of a hood. Surprisingly, he did have the Spirit of God in him, just like my old priest. This confused me. He had a peaceful demeanor, and love shone out of his eyes. Still, it didn't feel right to my spirit. My heart beat fast. I was sweating, and I wanted to run away. The nun gave me a stern look. My parents and grandparents beamed with pride.

I remembered my priest's smiling face when I said I would do this Confirmation. I was angry because God hadn't answered me when I'd asked, "What do I do?" His Spirit was with me, just not talking. The person behind me gave me a rude shove and told me it was my turn.

I looked at the strange man closely as I walked up to him. Everyone was excited that he had come to our small town to take part in the ritual. They said he was famous. For what, I didn't know or care. I tried to see if there was any evil in him. He had none I could sense or see. I reached the spot where I was supposed to kneel. The nun gave me another stern look and pointed at the ground. Everyone was watching.

I just couldn't kneel before him, so I knelt to the right of him. He was going to ask questions about my faith, my new name, and the Church.

He would then bless and confirm me in the faith. I was to kiss his ring and thank him.

I was both excited and afraid of what was going to happen. He sensed my inner turmoil. Bending forward and toward me, he whispered, "What is wrong?"

"I don't feel it is right to kiss a ring or kneel before you or any man, only to God." I was very indignant.

"Do you believe in God, the Father, the Son, and the Holy Ghost?"

"Yes."

"That is really all that is necessary."

Surprised, I didn't know what to say or do. The nun was kissing her hand, practically yelling at me to do the same. I clumsily grabbed the bishop's hand and kissed my own hand, making it look as if I were kissing his ring. He blessed and confirmed me and then smiled.

I caught him watching me from a distance throughout the after-ritual brunch. He never approached or spoke to me again. I felt a peace about everything and knew God was pleased with my decision. I was delighted I didn't have to go back to Catechism ever again.

Going to church every Sunday, well, that was another thing. The sermons the new priest gave were full of fire and brimstone. He also hatefully condemned other churches. He told us that when we went to a different church for a wedding or funeral, we were shaking hands with those who were going to hell and that we were sinning for just going into other churches.

This made me increasingly angry, judgmental, and rebellious toward the Catholic Church. I am thankful God is the one who can see and knows the truth of everyone's heart and mind. God is the only one who has the right and authority to judge each of us, on Judgment Day or any other day.

Responsibility & Dependence

One November day after school, Grandfather was waiting for us at the bus stop. This was unusual; I knew something wasn't right. "What's wrong?"

"You'll find out when you get home."

When we got home, all of us kids ran into the house as fast as we could. We all asked at once, "What's going on?"

Mom, younger sister Renée, and Dad sat at the kitchen table. Two large suitcases were on the floor. The looks on their faces and their energy told me something was very wrong. Dad spoke in a firm, matter-of-fact tone.

"I'm sick. My thyroid is dangerously overactive. I've been told I only have twenty-four hours to live, so we must leave now. I need to get an experimental treatment of radioactive iodine. Your mother and I, along with Renée, have to go to the Mayo Clinic in Los Angeles for this special treatment. We don't know how long we'll be gone.

"Pam, I need you to take care of your sisters. Make sure there is plenty of food and wood for winter into spring. Do whatever you have to do to make sure there is enough food. (That was code for "It's okay to get meat out of season.") Your grandpa will help you get to and from the bus stop, and he will help haul wood and feed. You can drive the truck for short distances. (I had been driving short distances on the ranch since I was nine. I was eleven at this time.) Everyone will have to help each other."

We all cried softly as we hugged Renée, Dad, and Mom goodbye. I felt his sickness as I hugged him. I sent healing energy into him and asked God to please heal him. I had noticed he had been losing weight and didn't look like himself; his color had been off. I'd thought he was beginning to have another malaria attack.

He'd caught malaria during the war in the South Pacific. None of us kids were allowed near him during those times. He would be delirious from the fever and was dangerous to approach. Mother didn't think I should try to or could heal him. I asked God to heal him anyway and sent him healing energy. Dad seemed to have fewer attacks after that.

Allie was put in charge of the house, and I was put in charge of everything else. My heart and mind filled with pride. I felt very grown up, much more than when I had walked to Anna's years before. It was a week before we received word that Dad was still alive and getting the treatment he needed. Mom wrote to us to keep us updated on his progress. I was relieved and grateful, knowing God was taking care of him. I knew Dad was going to be okay. I just didn't know when he would be coming home.

The fall harvest was plentiful, but we needed more. I would take the .410 shotgun with me when I cut wood or cleared land. If any game popped up, I would take advantage. Deer season was starting soon. If I could bag a couple of deer, the freezer would be filled with enough meat to last through late spring.

One evening, Grandpa took me aside and told me it was time to get a deer. It was a week before hunting season opened, but I was worried about getting caught. We didn't have money to buy hunting licenses or tags, but we needed the meat to make it through the winter and spring. Grandpa reminded me that everyone would be sighting in their rifles all this week. It wouldn't be suspicious to hear gunshots, and there wouldn't be a lot of hunters roaming around.

I asked God for help. Once more, His wonderful words came to me: "Do not fear. I will provide for you as long as you need. Do not become prideful or greedy."

I was filled with relief, gratitude, and confidence. I could always depend on God for everything. Up to this point, He had protected me, answered my questions, and shared His knowledge, and now He would provide for my family and me.

The next evening, I went hunting. I was filled with excitement. On the way toward a well-used deer trail, my mind wandered. Would God really supply the deer? How? Where? When? Would it be far away or close? I hoped it would be close so I wouldn't have to carry it far.

To my surprise, in front of me, not twenty yards from the house, was a lone deer. It was a miracle happening before my eyes. The deer was eating a clump of grass on a hillside, the only clump in the whole area. I was completely caught off guard. I didn't know if I could get the rifle off my shoulder, aim, and fire before it saw or heard me.

I stood still and observed the scene before me. The wind was coming toward me, so it couldn't smell me. It would take a bite and then chew while looking straight ahead. It wasn't even moving its ears to listen. It was standing broadside to me, allowing a perfect lung or head shot. It had no idea I was there. I slowly took the rifle off my shoulder, pushed the safety off, aimed, and fired. I thanked God for keeping His word and felt grateful for the deer being a special part of the Yaqui people's life.

God had thought of everything: the distance, the hillside, the size, and no more weight than I could handle. I let the deer bleed out and field dressed it on the hillside. I then lay on my back to get the 150-plus-pound deer up on my shoulders to carry it to the hanging shed.

I didn't think I could shut out the feelings I had when harvesting our animals and transfer it to deer hunting, too. Knowing their spirits move on still didn't seem to make it okay to do. I felt a heaviness and an emptiness in my being, but I knew I had to do it.

I felt a sense of duty toward my family and Dad. I asked God to help me, and He did. It was as if an invisible shield dropped over my brain and heart, keeping me from feeling or thinking anything about killing a living thing. I was grateful to have a blankness come over me. It was as if I were experiencing an out-of-body moment. A part of me took a time-out.

Everyone was surprised. They had heard the shot but thought I was target practicing since it was so close to the house. After hanging and skinning the deer, we left it to age until it was a dark burgundy color and had a glaze over the meat. Then we butchered it and put it in our new, huge freezer.

Grandpa told me that we would need at least two more deer the same size or larger for us to make it through the winter and spring. In the next two weeks, God provided two bigger deer. They, too, were not far from home and on slopes, allowing me to lift and carry them back.

It was so easy and very satisfying to me. I was hooked. As the last two deer aged, we took down the two darkest halves to cut up, package, and put in the freezer. This left room for a fourth deer to be hung, if needed.

Everyone told me they were impressed with my work. I was confident in my abilities, and although I thanked God for providing all our needs, including the firewood, and for giving me the strength to do all I needed to do, I was getting full of myself. I discovered how easily evil can get into one's mind and heart.

Grandpa told me to go hunting for more venison. I was patting myself on the back for being able to track, find, and shoot my prey when a thought came to my mind. Just in case we had a long and hard winter, I should get four deer, maybe more. After all, there were five of us. Better safe than sorry, right?

Just like with the wood for heat, it's better to have more than not enough, right? After all, it was my responsibility to make sure my family was taken care of in those areas. Besides, God had promised to provide what we needed, right? With three rights, I was on a mission.

Determined, I went hunting. I walked a long way before even seeing a deer. The first one I saw was in tall brush, and I couldn't get a clear shot. It was now getting dark, so I gave up. The next morning, we finished cutting up and packaging a set of deer halves. Grandma commented that there was going to be a lot of meat from the three deer. I didn't process her comment. All I could think about was getting more.

I finished my chores early so I could get a head start. It was a long distance to where the deer had been the previous evening, and the thought of carrying a bloody carcass on my back in the dark was unnerving. Timberwolves, coyotes, mountain lions, and bears lived and hunted in the same area.

I sat for hours. Sunset was approaching, and I was disappointed that deer hadn't shown up. It was a well-used trail, so surely, something would have passed by before now. It was a good fifteen-minute walk back. I had to get the deer now or go home.

With closed eyes and a bowed head, I prayed, "Please, Father, you promised to provide us deer. I need one now." When I opened my eyes, I saw a deer coming out of the tree line from my left. It wasn't in a hurry.

I had to be patient and wait for it to get close enough for a clean shot. I could hear other hunters taking their shots before the half-hour-after-sunset rule. Finally, I was able to take my shot.

By the time I had field dressed the deer and gotten it up on my shoulders, it was dark. The deer was the same size as the first one, but it wasn't on a slope. It was extremely difficult lifting it onto my shoulders. I was worn out already and still had to carry it home. I knew the way by heart, but I couldn't see any of my landmarks.

I used energy waves or vibrations by extending my spirit energy out of my body to feel my surroundings. I also had all my other senses on high. I heard and felt many creatures running away from me. Some were deer; others were quieter, maybe rabbits. I was grateful to not feel or hear bears, coyotes, or any other apex predators anywhere near me on my twenty-minute walk home.

Everyone had been worried. They were angry that I had taken so long to get home. I was tired from the hunt and wanted to eat, take a hot bath, and go to bed. I couldn't remember whether I had thanked God for His provision, but He knew I was thankful for everything.

Grandpa teased me about the deer since it was smaller than the other two. My family joked that my hunting skills were failing. With my pride bruised, I was determined to find a bigger deer to bring home, even though we didn't need one.

There were only two days left to hunt. I told everyone not to worry, because I might be back after dark. I must have walked for miles and miles. I sat at lookouts for hours. I saw nothing, no fresh tracks anywhere. It was as if all the deer had left for winter early.

Finally, to my joy, a small herd of deer was making its way along a trail, which was covered on both sides by manzanita brush over five feet tall. It was dusk, and I couldn't see clearly. I could see a head pop out here and there as they walked up the trail that led to a ridge.

At the top of the ridge, each one stopped and looked back at me in silhouette, just long enough for a quick head shot. As each deer stopped, I could tell what size they were. The first four were small does. I knew two were bigger than the rest and one was a buck; I had seen his antlers earlier. I anxiously waited for him. He was a crafty one. When he got to the ridgetop, he kept his head down. I couldn't get a clear shot. I could only see his white rear end. The last deer was the bigger doe. I took my shot, asking God to make it a good one.

I could see a little by the light of the quarter moon, but it wasn't easy to locate the downed deer. As I followed the deer trail, something smelled rotten. This wasn't unusual in the wild. Animals killed by disease or cars, or otherwise wounded by mankind, would run off into the woods or brush to die. I ignored the smell, hoping I wouldn't run into a rotting corpse. I felt along the ground with my energy, hands, and feet until I bumped into the warm body. I got underneath her and lifted her onto my shoulders, dismissing the smells.

She was very heavy compared to the others because it was too dark and I didn't have time to field dress her. I hurried as fast as I could to get away from the area and closer to familiar territory. It was the hardest time I ever had getting a deer.

As I trudged along, I felt the chill of evil energy throughout my body, following and surrounding me. Was it evil or something else dangerous behind me? My hairs stood on end. I remembered fear was taken away when I called upon God for help. I asked for His help again. I felt His peace come upon me once more, and I was strengthened by it.

Despite my heavy load and the darkness, I was able to make good time. I was proud of myself for completing my mission. My family would be happy and wouldn't make fun of me anymore. Even though my mind was thinking those thoughts, my heart was saying something else. I was wondering if the doe was the rotten smell from earlier. She smelled awful.

I finally made it into the hanging shed. I was worn out, so I asked Grandpa to help me hang the deer. When we returned to the shed, he turned the lights on, allowing us to see what I had triumphantly brought home. It was the ugliest, sickest looking animal I'd ever seen. It smelled rotten, and there were ticks all over it. Grandpa told me it was the worst-looking swamp deer he'd ever seen. We both wondered why she was in the mountains.

She was old, and her hooves were full of thrush, adding to the smell. We opened her up. All her organs were diseased. Grandpa was disgusted. He complained, "Not even the dogs can eat that! Leave everything like it is until tomorrow when we'll be able to see to burn it.

You better get in the house and have your sisters look for ticks. Take a shower and wash your hair thoroughly. Hurry, get going."

I was ashamed of my pride and arrogance concerning God's promise. I had ignored His warnings. I had become prideful and greedy, and I had paid the consequence for my choices. I didn't dodge evil; I joined it. At least I had ended the deer's slow, agonizing death.

The next morning, we dug a deep pit, tossed in wood, and then poured gasoline on it. We tossed in the remains of the deer, more wood, and poured more gas. We let it all soak for a bit. Grandpa stood upwind from the pit and threw in a lit book of matches while quickly moving backward. There was a big poof of hot air that hit me in the face, forcing me to step back; the pit was instantly blazing.

We stoked the fire until there were no visible remains of the deer. We doused the fire with water and then filled in the pit. Walking past the spot would remind me of the consequence of not listening to God and my disregard of the sacred relationship between the deer and us Yaqui.

I was compelled to ask for forgiveness and determined to dodge evil. I began to pay more attention to the kind of thoughts coming into my mind. Evil doesn't stop. I knew I had to be more discerning. I wanted to depend on God's wisdom and provision, not mine. I was completely dependent on Him for everything. Life was much smoother when I listened to God.

Dreams, Visions & Nightmares

Something new started happening to me after deer season closed. I wasn't sure if it was because I was so tired from all the work and school stress, but I started dreaming. The dreams seemed so real that I wasn't sure if they were dreams or real life. Were they warnings, visions, nightmares, or malfunctions of my brain, or maybe a combination of them all?

The first dream was about Mom and Dad coming home. I wouldn't have so many responsibilities anymore. It made me happy and a little sad. I wasn't sure why or from where the sadness was coming. A wonderful dream, but not real. It had been four months since they had left, but no one had told us of any homecoming news.

Some dreams were old ones from when I was younger. The newer ones were full of detail and had an alien theme throughout. I was fascinated.

When I was five, I asked the question, "How did all this get started?" I knew God made everything—He had told me—but I always wanted to know how and why. I wanted more information. To my surprise, God didn't answer me in His usual way.

Instead, He gave me a dream. In the dream, two bald giants with large brains were in charge of an experiment in an enormous lab. They talked like God and I did, using their minds. I was able to hear them discussing whether or not to keep an experiment going.

They floated across the floor to a line of vats running against a wall in their lab. There seemed to be no end to them. One said, "I wonder how long we should keep doing this experiment. We have given them everything they need to accomplish the purpose for which they were created. Many choose the opposite path. We must keep looking for the ones who choose and keep the knowledge of walking and living the path of love and peace." They both sighed heavily.

Floating in the middle of the first vat was a type of island planet. They found a man who was living "the way" and put him into a second vat. I wondered if all the vats had land in them. They finally found a female living with the knowledge. They plucked her out of the old vat and put her into the new. Would this new couple make the experiment a success, or would it also be a failure?

"This is good," said one of them. "The man will no longer be alone." He made it sound like it had been a long time. I had no idea how long this experiment had been going on or if it was still happening. I figured that some really smart beings somewhere in the universe were helping God with His creations, or experiments.

Perhaps God was one of them? It made sense to me back then. I can now relate it all to Adam and Eve in the Garden of Eden. This gave me awesome energy bursts throughout my whole being. Is God, perhaps, an alien?

Another dream was about aliens and a past life. I was sleeping when explosions woke me. Planes were flying very fast, then stopping quickly, and then taking off again without landing on the ground or crashing. I jumped out of bed. The floor was rock-hard and cold under my bare feet. I felt different. I was taller. I looked down at my body and noticed I had big, strong muscles all over. I was in a stone building, like a castle. From my balcony, I could see a volcano nearby and a city below being fired upon by those flying machines.

They were darting to and fro, destroying everything in sight. I knew who they were. They came from the heavens, and their flying machines, called ships, were able to fly in and out of our world. We had a treaty and were trading with them. I was also a friend. I couldn't believe what they were doing.

A ship came up to my balcony and hovered. "Why are you doing this?" I asked.

"I am sorry, dear friend. Your leaders have plotted against us. When our leader learned of the betrayal, we received orders to destroy all signs of our presence and to kill all who know of our existence. You know we will see each other again, for you have learned our teachings well and have been living them. Until next time, be at peace."

The same green and red laser beams destroying my city and volcano were now coming straight at me. There was a flash, an explosion, and then darkness. I woke up in my bed on the ranch, gasping for air, wondering whether it was real, a vision of a past life, or just a nightmare.

I could still smell the smoke and feel the cold floor on my feet. I now thought for sure that spaceships and spacemen were real. Even so, this information didn't cause me to doubt God or our relationship. If he had created this world and us, why couldn't He have created other worlds and other beings?

At this time, I was also having flying dreams and experiences. They felt real. I wasn't sure whether I was actually dreaming or awake. These experiences happened both during the day and night. During the day,

I would be hot and tired from work. A cool breeze would come and lift my spirit into the air. I would fly up and down the currents of air.

I had to practice landing, but after a few crashes, I learned how to land back into my body. Learning to balance my spirit body on the air currents was a bit tricky at first, but when I trusted they would hold me, they did. I was convinced, through the dreams, that I was indeed both a spirit being and a physical being and able to switch between the two whenever I wanted.

It was now spring. Mom and Dad had not come home yet nor written about when they were coming. I woke up earlier than usual to do my chores. I planned on spending the entire day in the forest being quiet. I wanted to talk to and hear from God.

While in the forest, I heard a vehicle turn into our driveway. I wondered who it could be. My grandparents' dog was barking, so I thought it was a stranger. I heard voices filled with excitement and even some crying.

I was glad I was far from the house. I wasn't in the mood for company. To my dismay, the alarm bell rang, meaning I had to get home as soon as possible. I grumbled all the way back, walking as slowly as possible.

When I got close to the white house, I could hear talking and laughter through the open windows and doors. I didn't recognize the car, but I did recognize the voices. Mom, Dad, and little sister Renée were home! The radioactive medicine had worked, but Dad had to take thyroid medication for the rest of his life.

Both Mom and Dad looked tired and pale. They had been through a very stressful time, and it showed. Renée was a toddler and was getting into everything. She spoke in long sentences I couldn't understand, but her "yes" and "no" were very clear.

One day, the local news, which was really just gossip, notified us that two classmates had committed suicide and another had been killed in an auto accident. This triggered a bunch of dreams about death, my death. I wanted to know what would happen when my body died. I didn't want to make the mistake of following just anyone, like I had done with Great-Grandma.

I made myself dream of all the different ways one could die. Every time I died, I would find myself floating in the air above my body, just like Great-Grandma. It would be silent like in the desert years ago, and there would be the same golden glow surrounding me like when I was in Mother's womb and when I cut my foot.

In every dream, a voice behind me would joyfully say, "Welcome home!" I would turn toward the voice. A man in a gold-braided white tunic would be floating behind me. He would smile while taking hold of my hand, and then he would fly us toward a bright light shining on the horizon.

I was extremely happy to be going home, but we would never make it to the light. I would wake up. I was convinced more than before that humans are really spirit beings who don't die. Our bodies do, but the real us goes home, back to where we came from, just like I knew when I was three. Fear of a physical death left my mind and heart.

During the same time, I had a recurring nightmare about two men in trench coats who were out to kill me and weren't going to be stopped by anything. The nightmare started after the television and Channel 8 became part of our family. Mom and Allie had become addicted to soap operas. When their shows were on, nothing else mattered. If anyone asked for anything, they would wave their hands at you to go away or tell you to wait for a commercial.

Evidently, this affected me more than I had thought, because my dream was all about abandonment. My mommy didn't love me anymore. She wouldn't leave the TV to help me. The TV and Channel 8 changed our lives forever. We didn't play games, sing, talk, or read stories as a family anymore. We started to drift apart. I did what I liked to do: be one with God, work on the ranch, and dream dreams.

The year I turned sixteen, I had a dream come true. I finally got a horse. Not my dream horse, but she turned out to be exactly what I needed. She was a prelude to my life when it came to men. She had been treated terribly by them, but in the end, she overcame her distrust of them. Later in the same year, a big change happened in my relationship with God.

Temper Tantrums & Lies

I was happy my parents were home. It meant I could relax a little. The doctors told Dad he might die of leukemia because of the radioactive iodine treatment. But it was either dying now or in twenty years; he chose the twenty.

Although I was glad to have my parents and sister back, a part of me was angry about the changes in my daily routine. My parents didn't want me to stay in the wild for long periods of time. I was to stick close to home. They never told me why; they just said I could not wander far.

I felt trapped, even like I was in a cage. I wanted out. I felt unappreciated, too. I started getting mad over things I couldn't do anymore and being made to do what others wanted. They had given me all the responsibility while they were away, and now they were treating me like a kid.

My anger would turn into rage at times. I would throw and slam things, punch pillows, and scream loudly in frustration. One of the perks of living in the wild with a national forest all around was that no one but my family and the wildlife could hear me act out. Mom gave me pillows to hit and permission to scream out my frustrations. She wanted me to release my stress so I wouldn't hurt myself or others. She had a temper, too, as did her mother. It might have been a Yaqui trait. Or was it the Italian and my dad's side? Perhaps all.

The main problem for me was that whenever I had a tantrum and threw, kicked, or smashed something, it would ricochet back and hit me.

One time, while splitting wood in a fit of anger, I hit a wet stump so hard that the double-edged ax bounced back and hit me on my face, cutting a hole over my left eye. The blood flowed so thick I couldn't see or stop the bleeding on my own. I thought I had killed myself. I definitely had gone on a warpath against myself.

Slowly I learned to not give in to my anger. I learned to not react to it by screaming but instead to surrender it by breathing out and sighing. In other words, I learned to give it to God and let Him show me how He would work it all out.

I must confess, to this day, I still have episodes of anger from frustrations. This may be my thorn in the side to keep me humble. I embarrass myself whenever I give in to it, and I worry about how it may affect others to see me in such a state. God is not weak. I am.

Summer was going by quickly. With Dad and Mom home, the chores didn't take as long to do. Because of all the wood we had gathered the last few years, that fall chore was done early, leaving me time to do other things like fishing in a nearby creek.

The creek was about a half-mile away in a canyon. It was filled with a trout called brookies. I always took our dogs, King, a full-sized collie, and Prince, a border collie.

I liked going there to catch fish by hand and splash in the cool water. I learned how to catch fish this way by watching my dad throw large lake trout onto the shore when it was too risky to pull them ashore while they were still hooked and on the fishing line. Sometimes he would scoop the fish up with both hands, and sometimes he would shove a finger into the gills and then toss it onto the shore. Mom would hold the fishing pole for him.

I used to take a fishing rod to the canyon creek, but thick brush and willows made the pole useless. I remembered how Dad had scooped the fish onto land and then we kids would pounce on them, keeping them from flopping back into the water. I figured it would work for me, too, as the creek was not very deep or wide and the fish were always in pools or under logs and the bank. I just had to block them from escaping.

I would look for the fish and see them scurry into a pond under the bank or a log. I would slowly and patiently creep up on them, making sure they didn't have an escape route, and then scoop them onto the bank. It was great fun and very rewarding. They were good eating.

One morning, after chores, I decided to go fishing in the canyon creek. Both dogs happily came along. We were in good spirits. I was giving thanks to God for just plain being alive and able to experience this wonderful life. As I reached out in spirit to God, a breeze came along and lifted me up and out of my body. Since I had been dreaming about flying and having live experiences, I wasn't afraid. I was enjoying the freedom it gave me.

I heard Mother calling, and I flew over to where she was standing on the porch, just to see if she could feel or see me. She kept calling my name. I flew right up to her and asked, "What?"

She suddenly turned pale and looked scared. She was looking all around and even reached out to feel the air around her. She called me again frantically, using all three of my names. That meant I was in deep trouble and better answer her in person.

I flew back to my body, which looked frozen in step. Both dogs were sitting next to it. I walked to the house, where Mother was still standing on the porch. I asked her again, "What?"

"Pam, what did you do?"

"Nothing. I was on my way to go fishing."

"Something strange is going on." She looked around in fear. "I felt something next to me just a minute ago. It reminded me of the strange things that happened when my mother was alive. Anyway, I don't want you to go to the creek. It is too far away. I will be going grocery shopping later, and I want you nearby."

"Aw, Mom, I don't need to go with you. I'm old enough to be left alone. While you were gone, I did fine on my own. Please, let me go fishing."

"No, and that is final."

I was frustrated but kept my composure. "Can I go to the big meadow instead to play and hunt? If you need me or are ready to go shopping, just call for me or ring the bell."

"Well, okay, just for a couple of hours."

I was again happy, but I was also angry. Why did grown-ups always get to tell you what you could and couldn't do? People in authority always take your freedom away. I was determined to take mine back.

I thought I was so clever because I had tricked Mom into letting me cross the street to go into the bigger meadow. From there, I could sneak back across the street from the lower end of the meadow and go to the creek without being seen. And it was a faster way to get there. (Guess who gave me that sneaky thought?) I *again* fell for the temptation to think only of myself.

I ran as fast as I could with both dogs at my heels. We snuck back across the highway to the creek. The dogs and I were hot by the time we reached our destination. Splashing in the cold water cooled us down. I caught three fish but had to release them. If I took them home, Mom would know where I had been.

We had so much fun I forgot all about the time. When I noticed it was getting darker, I knew I was in trouble. If Mom had been calling or ringing the bell, I couldn't have heard her. I jumped up and headed back. The quickest way to get across the highway without being seen was over a deep ravine. A tree had fallen across the ravine, making a perfect natural bridge.

The barkless tree was about ten inches in diameter and around eight feet above the rock and sand below. I had crossed over it many times with dry tennis shoes, but my shoes were wet that day. In my haste, with the dogs close at my feet, I slipped off the tree and fell to the ground. My ankle felt like it was broken. The dogs panicked and ran back and forth on the tree, trying to find a way down. The sides of the ravine were too high for them to jump down or for me to climb up.

I was in big trouble. Boy, it all seemed familiar. Again I had made the wrong choice. I had listened to the wrong thoughts. All of a sudden, the dogs took off. They had never before left my side. What was going to happen to me now?

Thoughts of mountain lions, bears, wolves, and coyotes flowed into my mind. They all were going to eat me; no one would ever find me because I wasn't where I was supposed to be. I would be a bleached-out skeleton by the time someone found my body. How foolish could I have been? Why had I disobeyed?

Well, at least I would be going back to my spiritual home, back to God. "B-but I don't want to leave yet!" I cried like a baby and begged God to help me. He didn't answer. I felt abandoned by God and my dogs.

I prepared myself for the end of this earthly life. I buried my head in my hands and sobbed. Then I heard a voice above me. "Little girl, why are you crying?" I glanced up. A man was standing on the fallen tree. He wore a white tunic with gold braiding. *Is he my guardian angel?* I wondered. I had been told that everyone had one, but God had never told me I did. I had always assumed He was my guardian.

I blurted out what I had done, confessing everything. He didn't say anything. I looked up to see what he was doing. I was surprised to see him looking up into the sky, his hands lifted and a look on his face that seemed to ask, "You sent me here for this?"

The man looked down and told me, "Just follow the dogs back

home." I cried again, explaining that the dogs had run off, leaving me all alone. When I looked up again, the man-angel was gone.

While waiting for my doom, I heard noises coming from the upper part of the ravine. I couldn't see anything, but I could hear branches being broken. Something big was coming toward me. I imagined it had to be a bear. I cuddled up inside a small cave in the wall of the ravine. I threw dirt over and around myself, hoping I would be hidden.

It got closer and closer. I closed my eyes and held my breath. The next thing I felt was the hot, stinky breath of an animal, a cold nose, and then the comforting warm licks of two dog tongues. They had found a way to me. What the man-angel had said was true!

I grabbed them both by their necks, and they helped me get out of the ravine. It wasn't easy, but the dogs took me to the spot where they had been able to get into the ravine. From there, I was able to climb out slowly.

To my surprise and relief, in front of me, at the top of the ravine, lay a walking stick. It was on smooth, sandy ground, and there wasn't another sliver of wood in sight. I knew it had been put there by God. What were the odds that a walking stick made of driftwood and in the shape of a crutch for someone my size would be lying within my reach? (A miracle!)

God was faithful, even though I had not been faithful to Him or my mother. I thanked Him for saving me and giving me the crutch to get home. Using it to lean on, I hopped as fast as I could, with my faithful dogs running by my side.

When I reached the lower meadow, I heard the bell ringing and the urgent calls of Mom and my sisters. I wondered how long they had been calling. When I knew they could see me, I slowed down and took it easy. I called back, "I'm coming!"

"Where have you been? Why haven't you answered us? What happened to your foot?" they all asked at once.

I answered somewhat truthfully, "I was in the lower meadow. I didn't hear you calling until a few minutes ago. I sprained my ankle when I slipped off a log."

Mom was glad I was home and took care of my injured ankle. I had told the truth, just not the whole truth. I didn't want to get into trouble and be forbidden to go back to the creek.

I was able to stay home and ice my ankle while everyone else went shopping. I thanked God for helping me stay safe despite my bad choice. I accepted the injury as punishment and as a reminder to obey my parents.

☙ ♦ ❧

God and I had a falling out in my sixteenth year. It was very traumatic. During that time, I was all about me—my wants, my feelings, and my gifts. Looking back, it must have been a mix of hormonal and emotional surges keeping me from staying in the Spirit, throwing me into a fleshly state of mind. I call it teenager-ism. It was my biggest temper tantrum ever…well, until menopause.

The fallout with God came to a head because of a combination of hormones, the Catholic Church, and Grandmother telling me that it was God's will things were not going my way. She said I must have been sinning. I didn't think I was sinning. I wasn't doing anything the Church or my God had told me was a sin.

I questioned God's protection and sovereignty. Why hadn't He helped those who had committed suicide? Why hadn't He protected my classmates who had been injured terribly or had died in car crashes? Why were my pets being hurt or killed because of human error on my family's part or from being attacked by predators?

Why hadn't He talked with me about these things happening at home and at school? Why hadn't He protected me and mine like He had promised? Maybe I was spoiled. After all, He had given me His word, and nothing had happened that had caused me to doubt Him in all the years up to that point. But now I felt my God wasn't who He said He was because He had broken His word.

I didn't think my sinning was the cause of these events. The only things that might have been sins were my temper tantrums, when I lied to Mom about going to the creek, and when I ate a crushed bag of peanuts I found on the floor of the cash-and-carry store.

I didn't think it was wrong when I picked them up and ate them, but when Mom smelled the peanuts on my breath, she asked me where I had gotten the money to buy them. I told her the truth: I found them on the floor. I thought that since they were crushed, no one would want them. Rather than let them go to waste, I decided to eat them.

Mom told me it was the same as stealing from the nice woman who owned the store. I was shocked. I never thought they belonged to her. I thought someone had bought them and dropped them. After Mom told me it was stealing either way, I was sad and ashamed. How would I know to whom they belonged? Mom gave me a nickel and told me to go back into the store, apologize to the owner, and pay for the peanuts.

I confessed to the owner what had happened and promised I would never do it again. The owner was surprised and grateful. She hired me to help do inventory every year until I left for college. She told me it was because she knew she could trust me. I was paid five dollars an hour!

(I now could buy all the peanuts I wanted.) I also went to confession, so I should have been cleansed of any sin.

All the while, the nuns and new priest were teaching the opposite of what I knew about God. I was confused and angry. God wasn't talking to me. Where was He?

I thought the Church and Grandmother must have been right after all. Their mean God was the real God, and I had believed a demon. I stood outside and yelled at the sky, "They say it is God's will, Your will, that everything is going wrong in my life. You're not protecting me like You said You would. You're not who You told me You are.

"I hate You. I don't want anything to do with You. Stay out of my mind!" I screamed at the heavens, feeling let down, angry, and abandoned. I left my God's side because I was led to believe that He had left mine first. I wanted nothing to do with the Catholic God, either.

Lucifer had gotten a hold of my mind, and I didn't even realize it. I began walking, living, and thinking in my own wisdom, my own power, without any God. My gifts were changing. I was now in control of them. I was confident that I could expand my powers by myself. I didn't trust anyone else's word. *Everyone lies,* I told myself, *even my God!*

☙ ◆ ❧

Mom told me I had to go to a doctor for a Pap smear—my first. This was something all women had to do after they started menstruating. She told me a doctor would examine me to make sure I was healthy and everything was normal, whatever that meant. Mom trusted in doctors for everything, and my grandmother was a hypochondriac; she considered it a badge of honor to go to a doctor more than anyone else.

Mom told me the doctor would put his fingers in my vagina and then insert a cold metal thing to keep it open so he could take a swab of my insides. Whatever was on the swab was what they would use for the test. I didn't want to take this test, but again, it seemed to be a law.

A nurse made me take off my clothes and put on a gown. It was open in the back. She told me to lie on a small bed she called a table. It had what looked like stirrups on it.

"What are those for?" I asked.

"Those are for your feet, or actually, the heels of your feet. When the doctor comes in to examine you, he will ask you to put your heels in them and scoot down closer toward him. I will be here to help you."

"Okay," I said hesitantly, wondering, *Who came up with this idea?* A balding, chubby, male doctor wearing glasses came in full of smiles. He introduced himself and shook my hand with his pale, limp, sweaty one. "Hello, Pam. I will be examining you today and taking the Pap test. I understand this is your first time."

"Hi. Yes, it is my first time."

"Well, I will be very gentle and move slowly. But if you have any discomfort, let me know right away."

"Okay, I will."

Both he and the nurse told me everything would be alright. They showed me the tool he was going to use. It looked like someone had put two deformed shoehorns together. He then showed me how they came apart like a car jack to hold my vagina open. I was afraid it would break me or get stuck.

I stiffened when he put his fingers inside me, and I unconsciously squeezed down.

"Don't worry. Just relax," he encouraged me. "It will be a little bit cold as I slide this in. You will feel some pressure. Really try to relax for me." The nurse left the room.

He pulled out the jack. I really did try to relax, but it was hard to do. He was moving his fingers in and out and around my vagina. He also pushed down on my stomach in the area of my ovaries. He then told me he was going to take the swab now and it could be uncomfortable but would only last a few seconds.

It felt like he was poking me with something sharp, and I yelled, "Stop! That hurts!"

"Okay, that part is done. Don't worry. I only have a few more things to check out. Just relax."

He touched and poked me all around, inside and outside. He started making weird noises and kept asking me if it felt good and if I was enjoying what was happening. I told him, "It isn't hurting me, but it feels weird."

I was tense because I sensed something was not right, and I was afraid he might hurt me again. There was a sheet hiding my view of what he was doing. Being my first time, I thought it was the way they did Pap smears. I had no idea I was being molested.

After three months of going back for Pap smear checkups, I finally asked Mom if she enjoyed her Pap tests and if they felt good to her. Mom said no and asked why I wanted to know. I told her because the doctor kept asking me if it felt good and if I was enjoying what was happening. I asked her, "How often do I have to take them?"

Mother told me that was not right. She was so sorry the doctor had molested me. She was especially angry after I told her he did it every time I went in for a checkup. He had scheduled my checkups every two weeks, for my health, of course. I no longer went back to that doctor.

Mom gave me the following advice: "Getting raped or molested will not kill you, but fighting it will. Let them have their way. Let it go, especially if they are white. No one will believe you over them. I'm so sorry this happened to you. Let it go. Forget about it. You will be fine." Since it hadn't felt good and Mom's advice seemed logical, I didn't make a big deal out of it. I put it out of my mind.

I wondered if Mom or someone she knew had been raped or molested. Had her mother spoken the same words of wisdom to her? Being Indian and treated less than human in Arizona might have been the reason she had been given such advice. I never asked her. Instead, I followed her advice and forgot it ever happened.

My first exposure to sex was through breeding animals on the ranch. I thought of it as an act for reproducing, not for recreation. At one of our annual barbeques, the adults were talking about expecting new babies.

Earlier in the week, Dad had told me to pick out doe rabbits in heat and put them into the buck's cage to breed. After the doe flipped the buck off three times, I could take her out and put in another doe, repeating this process until all the does were bred.

I noticed all male animals bred from behind and on top, often biting the female on the neck or back. I wondered if humans did that, too. At the barbeque, Dad made a joke about not having any more rugrats in the house, and curiosity got the better of me. I loudly asked, "Dad, does Mom flip you off three times when you are breeding like the rabbits?"

Everyone burst into laughter. Some even spit out their food. Their faces were red, and tears fell down their cheeks.

"No, honey, she doesn't."

"Oh, okay." I went on with my dinner, not giving it another thought.

That was the extent of my sexual experiences before going to college. Mom's advice soon became my mantra: forget about it, and you will be fine. But I wasn't fine. It kept stewing deep inside.

A Long Walk on the Dark Side

After leaving God behind, I was free, prideful, and arrogant toward any authority over me. I couldn't wait until I turned eighteen. I would then be free from all who seemed set on oppressing me from being who I was and how I wanted to live my life. Even so, I didn't really know what all that freedom would entail.

When I was a senior in high school, I was convinced to follow my counselors' and parents' suggestion to become an accountant. My parents decided the best school was in a city in southern California. They told me the city was nicer and smaller than the last city in which we had lived. I wouldn't know for sure until I actually felt and experienced the energies. The school was near friends of my parents, and they offered to let me live with them. My parents were excited, knowing I would be in good hands.

After graduation, I spent the summer enjoying my family and all the farm animals. I had hoped I'd have a car to drive at college, but there wasn't any parking where I was going. I would have to carpool with my guardian to his work and then take the bus from there to the college.

Then, after school, I'd take the bus back to the workplace. It worked out perfectly because we both had the same hours.

Mother drove me to her friend's house in the city and helped me get settled a week before school started. She wanted to make sure I felt comfortable with everyone and the bus routes. I was a good match with her friends. Mom was satisfied with everything and returned home. She reminded me to call every week to let everyone back home know how I was doing.

It was the mid-sixties when I started college. I was seventeen and pretty naive about life in the city. Everyone seemed to be having sex and expected sex all the time. I saw men as dogs, trying to hump everything in sight. They spoke about sex like it was their right. Just like in high school, the boys bragged about the length of their penises and how good they were in bed. I guess they thought that girls would be turned on by that. The men looked at women as just another notch for their belts. They talked like it was a contest to see how many women they could sleep with before they died.

Many women I met were just as bad. I was shocked by their boldness as they threw themselves at both men and women. Then they'd tell everyone how enjoyable, horrible, or funny the experience was for them. They were proud to be in charge of each encounter. They used the men and women whenever and however they wanted, just like men did with women. To them, there was nothing wrong with their thinking. After all, they saw it as just sharing love with their neighbor and anyone else they wanted. It was the *peace* (piece) and love generation.

Sex just wasn't a big deal to them. It wasn't anything special, just an awesome sensation you should experience as often as you could. They told me that God, after all, had created us to experience those awesome sensations as a reward for reproducing the human race.

Interestingly, none of the people acting this way seemed to believe in a god of any kind. And I have to admit I wondered how sex would feel.

"Awesome sensations" piqued my curiosity, but I didn't have the urge to try it out with anyone…yet.

What the doctor had done to me didn't sound at all like anything they described. I pretty much stayed away from it all. I went to college, studied, and declined any offers for dates or parties for a couple of semesters.

Peggy, a friend from high school, decided to attend the same college. She rented an apartment near the college, and I would stay over on weekends. My guardian didn't allow me to go out during the week. But when I stayed with Peggy, I could go out and do things without having to be home at a certain time.

I faced my fear of roller coasters at the boardwalk; they had a giant one. Peggy talked me into riding it, and four rides later, I was finally able to let go of the safety bar. I hadn't felt so much fear since learning about "They," the Boogeyman, the evil man, and the bear that was going to eat me in the ravine. I didn't have God in or with me anymore, so fear was more intense. Without acknowledging God in my life, I now had a fear of death, but I did end up enjoying the roller coaster. It felt good to let go of the fear, and now I was ready for Disneyland!

We would take a bus to Disneyland and spend the entire day until closing. We would also go to other tourist spots like a wax museum, Knott's Berry Farm, and the zoo. We would go down to a boardwalk and sunbathe on the nearby beach. We had lots of fun and met men, too. One night, Peggy and I were invited to a party by a couple of guys we had met, and we decided to go check it out. We definitely felt awkward entering the house. There were biker people in leather, people in Levi's, and some were scantily clothed. We were in casual hippie attire.

They welcomed us with smiles and laughter and offered us drinks and drugs of our choice. We knew nothing of the drugs offered, except for pot, which I had tried at a friend's party the summer before I left the Sierras. I faked inhaling it but still got high because I get contact highs even off of high or drunk people. I had also tried wine and beer but didn't like either one.

A large biker offered me a whiskey of some sort. I thought I was going to choke to death. Everyone laughed and told me I should take another swig to make it feel better. The warm feeling down my throat and into my stomach actually felt comforting and called for more, but the burning sensation at the top of my throat and the taste in my mouth wasn't enjoyable.

They promised one smaller swallow would help. Since they were the experts, I took a smaller swallow. It was almost the same burning, choking reaction for a few seconds, but then, quickly, everything felt smooth. All I felt was a warm, cozy feeling in my throat and stomach. It still didn't taste good. Someone slapped me on the back to congratulate me for finishing the challenge and then handed me a joint.

I watched people smoking pot and noticed they would sometimes cough and choke on it, too. To not be made fun of again, I took a tiny hit off the joint, just like I did the first time I tried to smoke a cigarette. After a bit, I was feeling everything. My gifts were triggered. I misjudged the effects of all the high people, whiskey, and pot. I was floating out of my body again, but I wasn't in full control.

Although it was fun, it was a learning experience, too. Pretty soon, I was quite confident and fearless. A fuzzy warmth flowed through my body. Evil was seducing me into its world. I closed off God from my mind and heart. I no longer listened or walked in His Spirit. I was now fully in the flesh. From that night forward, I thought it was good to use my gifts for myself. I fell for the lie. I didn't have a clue I was doing evil things. I was doing what came naturally to humans.

During that time, both men and women offered to have sex with me, sometimes both at the same time! I couldn't see or understand how two girls or two men could even have sex, let alone engage in a coveted threesome. Gosh, at that time in my life, I wasn't sure how a man and a woman would go about it, either—until the one night when I was manipulated by a handsome man I met during a trip to Disneyland. He worked there and knew of a special place he wanted to show me. He was selfish and arrogant. He thought he could do whatever he wanted, and he did.

He boldly took my virginity and a piece of my soul. He laughed and even bragged that he had taken my "cherry." As far as I'm concerned, he was evil in its purest form. He turned off a switch deep in my spirit, heart, and mind, thus beginning my hatred toward men.

Besides him, there seemed to be men everywhere, whistling, gawking, sneering, undressing me with their eyes, and saying very risqué things. I became wary and disgusted with men. Still, I hoped someday I would find a special someone and achieve the elusive orgasm.

I didn't know how addicting evil could be. I was disgusted by it in others, yet I was deceived and didn't acknowledge it in myself. The longer I stayed in the city and the more I dated, the more I became coldhearted, selfish… evil.

It all started while I was going to college and trying to fit into society in the city. I would go on dates and accept drinks from men, even though I was underage. I would accept drugs that were offered because they told me they were good; I never considered that they might be dangerous.

I would be told we were going out to dinner and a movie and end up at a house or apartment because they had supposedly forgotten something or had to go to the bathroom. They'd say that I might as well wait inside instead of out in the car. This excuse would also be used after dinner and a movie.

I was so trusting in the beginning, but it eventually became the usual course of dating. I was told by some that they didn't pay for everything on the date to get nothing in return. I didn't think I was *evil*-evil, just a bit naughty. I didn't love others as I used to. "Compassion" was no longer in my vocabulary or heart. I had a deep disdain for all men, period. I couldn't figure out why they were so attracted to me. I had small boobs and was tiny, like a kid, a whole five feet two inches tall and 110 pounds of muscle, not beautiful like the women they already had in their clutches.

The point came when I had finally had enough and decided to play the game men played. I wanted to have the orgasm about which they all talked. I decided I wasn't going to be used or a victim anymore, so I started to use and manipulate them. I attacked first. I became the man, a brazen woman, like the ones I had been shocked by when I'd first moved to the city. I chose with whom, how, and when I had sex. I again chose to join and not dodge evil. I was in control, or so I thought.

A LIFE FOR A LIFE

During the thirteen years I walked on the dark side, I was drugged and date-raped more than I would like to admit. Even though I thought I was in charge, they managed to control me to their satisfaction, never mine. They were useless to me after they had their orgasm, and I told them to their face they weren't any good at sex as far as I was concerned.

I became tired of this way of living. Even school no longer interested me after one of my professors tried to take me somewhere other than the bus stop when he offered me a ride. I quit college and moved back to the mountains, away from men and sex—or so I thought.

On the Greyhound bus home, I fell asleep in my window seat. After a while, I woke up to my breasts and private parts being fondled. I thought I was dreaming, but when I opened my eyes, a strange man was leaning on me from the once-empty seat next to me!

I tried to jump up, but he pressed hard against me and told me to stay put and be quiet. I looked around to see if anyone would or could help me. Most were asleep. I didn't know when this guy had even boarded the bus. His demeanor and energy told me to be quiet or else.

I sat there, letting him do what he wanted, feeling helpless and embarrassed. The bus driver was watching.

A woman across the aisle was also watching, but she was giving us disgusted glances. She would look away and then turn and watch some more. No one ever asked if I was okay with this stranger fondling me. I made eye contact with the driver to help, but no one wanted to get involved. This went on for some time until the bus stopped.

I thought, *Finally, the bus driver is going to help me.* He hollered the name of a town, and the guy on top of me jumped up and said, "Thanks!" as he headed to the open doors. I looked to see what town we had stopped in, but it was pitch black, with no lights or signs anywhere. The bus driver said something to the guy about "next time" and then slammed the doors shut.

I curled up in my coat and tried to fall asleep, this time sitting in the outside seat so no one could trap me again. I often wondered whether they would have done something to help me sooner if I were a white woman.

I was thankful to finally get home. I needed to take a break and wash off the experiences of city life and the bus ride. I needed to get back to nature and spirit. I spent a lot of time in nature, riding horses, and fishing. I also read up on the occult, witchcraft, and other assorted spiritual teachings of religions and philosophy. I was trying to find what I had lost, the "oneness" of God and the love I had felt for and from Him.

I was intrigued by the "I-ness" and selfness of other teachings. I practiced many, along with the occult, becoming proficient in the tarot, Ouija, divining, spells, and reading people. None of these made me whole or feel like I did when I was young and one with God. Instead, I had pride, selfness, and arrogance in the knowledge I achieved. I didn't need any god. I had my higher self.

I became one of the people I used to dislike. I was now the one who thought and felt I was above all others. I looked at others as inferior, lost beings, easy marks to take advantage of and manipulate to do my bidding, to fill my needs and desires. I was being fooled by evil into thinking that I, in the end, was helping others, showing a type of love and compassion.

All the while, I was looking to be whole, or one not only in spirit but also in the flesh. I was seeking the elusive orgasm. I was told it would make me feel complete, even if only for a short time. Evil was always dangling some kind of carrot for me to reach for in the flesh, distracting me from what I really needed: a personal, spiritual relationship with God. I was about to feel the consequence of my choices.

※ ◆ ※

One morning, I woke up sick. I had heartburn so bad it choked me. I felt weird, like I had a heavy ball in my abdomen, but I wasn't swollen. Mom made me go to a doctor. The doctor ran a multitude of blood and urine tests and gave me a pelvic exam and an x-ray.

While I was sitting in the exam room, waiting for the results, the doctor came in and asked me how long ago my last period had occurred.

"I'm not sure, around two years ago, maybe longer. I've never been regular. I was told it was because I did manual labor. Why?"

He didn't say anything. He just turned and walked to the window. He stood there, looking out for a long time with his arms behind his back, rocking back and forth.

"What's going on?" I asked, thinking something was happening outside.

"I'm looking for the three wise men to arrive," he said in a mocking voice.

"What?"

"You are at least five months pregnant. You must have had a period."

"Well, I haven't. I did have sex, but I have not had a period for a long time."

I tried to remember who I had been with five or six months ago in the city. I had put all that behind me. I didn't want to remember any of it. I knew the consequence of my choices, once again, were going to touch many lives, not just mine.

This news started an entirely new set of humiliating experiences. I was the talk of the medical professionals. I was sent to many specialists and had many tests. I was afraid they were going to hurt the baby or me. Technicians would say, "Oh, it's you, the miracle pregnant girl. Stop lying. You had to have had a period." The medical people were always whispering behind my back. All along, I had been worried people might have thought I was a party girl but not a liar.

Hey, it was the sixties. Random sex was acceptable behavior for much of society at that time, but not for my dad. He was hurt and ashamed of me. He forbade me to keep the baby. If I chose to keep it, I couldn't ever come home; he would banish me. Mom tried to talk him out of it but to no avail. I was kept a secret from everyone.

Mom and I moved to another state so I wouldn't be seen by anyone locally. I felt so ashamed and alone. After a while, we couldn't afford the medical bills or rent. Mom talked me into going to the local welfare office. They agreed to pay my medical bills and help me, but *only* if I promised to give the baby up for adoption.

They informed me I wouldn't be able to see or hold the baby once it came. They told me it was the best way. A priest and a few women who had given up their babies came to share their stories. They wanted to help me, a seventeen-year-old, decide what was best for the baby and for me. They posed questions: "You will soon turn eighteen. How will you find a job and raise the baby? Who will take care of it if and when you are working? You won't have family to help. You will be all alone." They painted a bleak picture of single motherhood. I knew deep inside I wanted to keep the baby, but they convinced me to think I wouldn't be capable.

When it came time to deliver, they took matters into their own hands and induced labor. Mom was going to be with me all day, but par for the course, nothing happened except that my water broke. The doctor was in meetings all day. When they tried to reach him to deliver, he couldn't come. They gave me drugs to slow down the birth. When the drugs wore off, they called the doctor again. This went on for the rest of the day. I was afraid and felt abandoned by both the Catholic God and the God of my youth. Even more bizarre, I also felt abandoned by the doctor, and even by evil.

Mom had to go back home because my sister Lily was graduating that night. No one knew about my condition except for Mom and Dad. I was all alone. After Mom left, I was once more given drugs to induce labor. This time, the pain was horrific. No one had prepared me for that!

They gave me more drugs to put me out. Then they gave me drugs to wake me up during the delivery. I woke up to excruciating pain. My belly, pelvic area, and spine felt like they were being torn apart. I screamed with pain and then passed out. When I woke up again, someone was telling me to push, and someone else was squeezing my neck and shoulders. I didn't know what was happening or how long it had been happening. During my drug-filled delivery, I was in and out of consciousness. I woke up with sore everything.

It turned out that my doctor never came, so an intern took over. Mine was his first delivery. He didn't cut me far enough, so when the baby came out, I was torn clear to my anus. He did his best to suture me. I didn't know what it all meant, but I could feel it. The next few days were a blur. I was kept mostly drugged up, per doctor's orders. I faintly remember the social worker coming in to get me to sign papers, but I couldn't hold the pen and didn't know what she wanted me to sign. She tried it two days in a row, but physically, I just couldn't do it.

Finally, I was able to stay awake long enough to ask a nurse what I had. I was told I had a big, beautiful boy. My heart broke, yet I was glad he would have a home very soon. I asked the nurse if she could bring him to me so I could hold him. She told me it was against the rules when an adoption was being done, but if I were to go for a walk down the hall, I could take a peek.

I did try to sneak a peek, but I was caught and escorted back to my room. I saw babies, but I didn't know which was mine. I was kicked out the next day. Hopelessness settled into my soul. I was to meet with the social worker in three weeks, on a Monday, to sign the final papers. I would finally be eighteen, the legal age to sign away my baby.

On that tragic Monday, Mom drove me, but she wasn't allowed inside the room. She waited outside. I was told earlier it was going to be very private. Only the social worker, a witness, and I were supposed to be in the room.

When the social worker and I walked into the room, however, five people were already sitting around a large oval table. I was embarrassed to have so many people watch me sign away my baby. It was supposed to be a private meeting. The social worker told me this was normal; witnesses were needed.

I felt the energy of the people in the room. The couple sitting across from me was probably the adoptive parents. They looked at me differently than the others and were holding hands under the table. They felt and looked like they had empathy toward me for what I was about to do, but they were very excited, too. I read the form the social worker handed me. At the bottom was a question I didn't understand. It was next to where I was supposed to sign my name.

"What does 'under duress' mean?" I innocently asked. Everyone at the table gasped. The couple suddenly looked afraid.

"Oh, that has nothing to do with you, dear. Just go ahead and sign," the social worker urged.

"What does 'duress' mean?" I pressed.

"It means you are being forced to sign or do something against your will. It has nothing to do with your case. Just sign it."

"Oh, okay," I said while deliberately checking the box saying I *was* signing under duress.

Everyone had a fit. "No!" they all said at once. The social worker grabbed the pen out of my hand and blotted out my checkmark.

I started crying and exclaimed, "I am under duress. My dad will banish me from the family if I keep the baby. You told me you wouldn't help me unless I put the baby up for adoption. How is that not under duress?"

"I-it isn't… I-it's just your situation, n-not duress," the social worker stammered.

Everyone was holding their breath. I sighed and then signed. I felt completely helpless and alone. A piece of me died that day. I buried the hurt and agonizing sorrow, along with all the other experiences I had been through, as deep as I could and went back to the ranch to heal.

I was full of hate. I hated my dad for making me give away my baby, the men who had had sex with me, the doctors who didn't believe me or take good care of me, even myself for the choices I had made. I was disappointed in myself and Mom for not standing up to Dad and the social worker, who, it turns out, suddenly got a promotion.

I had lost all faith in men, and now I lost all faith and trust in humanity and the God of my youth. I buried the memory and emotions of giving up my son deep down in my soul. The pain was too great to bear. I gave the life of my son into the hands of strangers to give him a better life. Now I had a new life, too, but to what end?

This world sucked. I was bitter and vowed to be in complete control of all aspects of my life from then on. Evil was winning, despite the sweet inner me trying to come out all the time. She was still pouting in temper-tantrum mode, not strong or grown-up enough to accomplish any real change.

When I finally left the ranch, I ended up in Reno, Nevada, "The Biggest Little City in the World." Just my size. Even though I hadn't officially finished college, I could still work as a bookkeeper. I had earned excellent grades and had only one final to take to get my degree. The college told me I could take it anytime I wanted. I just never wanted.

After many phone calls and checking job listings, I was excited to be asked to go immediately to a business looking for someone just out of school. I hurried down to their office. It was only five minutes away. This was almost too good to be true. I walked into the building with a big, happy smile, expecting to be working right away.

When I walked in, to my surprise, everyone stopped what they were doing and looked at me as if I were a great threat to their lives. The energy coming from them was fear and disgust. I looked behind me, but there was only a well-dressed woman escorting another woman to the exit. She was apologizing for any inconvenience concerning an interview, explaining that the position was filled. I thought it had to be me. After sending the other person away, the woman turned to me and asked, "Can I help you?"

"I'm here at the request of Carol. She hired me by phone about five minutes ago, and I'm here to fill out the paperwork."

The woman turned pale, her eyes opened wide, and she stammered, "Oh, m-my. Th-there has been a m-mistake. I just filled the p-position ten minutes ago myself." She backed away from me, not taking my outstretched hand, as if I were a leper or something.

"Is there another position available?"

She answered me in a very condescending manner, talking to me as if suddenly I couldn't speak or understand English at all. "Are...you...sure...you under-stand...the skills...needed... for this work? You should...try...going...to...your...people...on the... Res-er-va-tion." I couldn't believe my ears. She didn't even wait for me to answer. She turned quickly and walked away.

I responded angrily, "Of course I have the skills to do the job well, and I do know I don't want to work for the likes of you!" I stormed out of the business and cursed it for being evil. I wished bad luck upon it, feeling very strongly it would fail.

I forgot that words spoken in anger could make a curse come true. I vented all my anger, frustration, shock, and hurt feelings into those thoughts and spoke the words, "So be it!"

That was the beginning of using my gifts for spells and curses, and good deeds, too. Anger brought out my immediate reaction to fight back. No forgiveness or overlooking a person's condition of spiritual anemia. This was the first of many racist comments from white people in my life. I wasn't surprised when, within a few months, that business closed forever.

I was too young to work in a casino, and no one wanted a mixed-blood Indian to work with their finances. So, I worked in a fast-food restaurant. I learned how to be a fry cook, waitress, and cashier. I was able to use my already-honed skills from home as a floor sweeper and mopper.

I liked working there. Everyone was nice and fun to be around. Three of my coworkers and I became roommates. The night shift crew talked me into going with them to a pool parlor after work. They taught me how to play pool and billiards, and I really took to it. It was a fun place to go for people under twenty-one. They also introduced me to cruising and dragging on the strip.

I was still living in the flesh and still seeking the ever-elusive orgasm. Virginia Street in downtown Reno was where young people went to hook up with others for partying, making out, or one-night flings. We cruised every Friday and Saturday night. We would go to parties together or hook up with guys on our own. We never brought them to our place.

I met many different types of men in the next year and a half. One almost strangled me to death on a double date. I was saved by one of my roommates. I should have paid more attention to those red flags I would get when meeting someone new, no matter how cute they were or how good the sex was. I learned the hard way, so I didn't date anyone for a long time after that.

I focused instead on researching mystical arts. I tried stretching my abilities to the limit, like willing cue balls into the pool table pockets, turning signal lights to the color I wanted when I wanted, and guessing what color the next card in the deck was.

I practiced astral projection, which is when my spirit leaves my physical body to travel wherever I want to go. I interpreted dreams, cards, and omens and tried to see people's auras. I stretched out to feel by energy or spirit only, more often and further than before. I concentrated on an object or person only in my mind to see and touch them energetically or spiritually. I was surprised how easy it was to do, even at long distances. Though I didn't have the same relationship with God that I had before, I was "educated," I knew spirit was real, and I was a spirit person in a physical body. I had control of my spirit more so than my flesh. I wanted to return to the spirit dimension when I finished this physical life. During this time in my life, I wasn't walking with God.

Instead of using my gifts for the good of all, I was using them all for my good. I wanted to become powerful in my own right, to do whatever I wanted, when I wanted, to whomever I wanted. No one was going to mess with me and get away with it ever again. The battle between good and evil raged on, and evil had the upper hand.

I had heard about a new fad called past life regression. At first, I thought it was silly, just another way for people to make money. People are always looking for answers in the dark arts more than in God's arts. But I was curious. I'd had so many dreams of the past that, perhaps if I went back, I could find out more about the alien people. Curiosity got the best of me when people I knew had discovered they had been an animal in their first life memory.

I made an appointment with one named Davos. He asked if I would be okay with other people observing our session. I didn't mind. I was just anxious to see what I was going to experience. Before arriving, I was to concentrate on going back in time. "Ask spirit to come forth and take you back to your first life," Davos had told me. I had also been told to repeat the request. There was no rush. "Take as long as it takes," he had directed. I spoke those words over and over in my mind and out loud. It was kind of like hypnotizing myself.

When I arrived at Davos's home, I greeted the observers, but I felt like I was drunk. I kept repeating, "Spirit, come!" I forgot to say the other part about my spirit going back in time.

Soon a strong wind hit the building. Everyone in the room was startled. I opened my eyes to see what had happened. Behind Davos was an open closet. I saw three spirit beings standing in it.

They looked like smoke men. Two were light-colored and one was dark and wearing a hooded cape. The light smoke spirit men's faces weren't covered, and they looked familiar; however, I didn't know them. They definitely were sending bad energy toward me. They were angry and seemed intent on killing me. *Wait a minute*, I thought, *those are the two trench coat men from my old recurring nightmare!*

I didn't say anything. I wanted to see if Davos knew what was going on in his own house. He was sitting across the table from me. His eyes were closed.

He said, "Don't be afraid. I will ask them what they want. I won't let them hurt you. You must have said something wrong." It felt safe to relax and wait to see what was going to happen.

As soon as I relaxed, the two light-smoke spirit men slowly came toward me. They floated through the table and stood behind my shoulders, one to my left and the other to my right. Suddenly, in unison, they attacked me, pulling my head back over the back of my chair. They were trying to break my neck! I struggled against them, holding my neck very stiff and pushing myself forward. I couldn't believe they had become solid and were now trying to kill me.

Their eyes were filled with hatred. I wondered what I had done to them. When Davos saw what was happening, he spoke in a strange language and drew symbols on the table. I didn't recognize or understand either, but the two smoke spirits released me and returned to the closet.

The black spirit paced back and forth in the closet, sending me angry, evil energy. Davos apologized for what had happened. He hadn't thought the spirits were going to be violent. He told me to wait while he let the other spirit into him so they could talk.

A few minutes passed. Davos turned toward me and said, "Look into my eyes, and you will see the spirit. It wants to speak to you."

I looked into Davos's eyes. His whole countenance changed into the dark spirit inside him. There, before me, was the most beautiful, handsome face of a man I had ever seen, but the energy coming from him was both fearful and enticing.

I felt pure love for and from him; I was drawn in like a moth to the flame. When I reached out to touch the mesmerizing face, his true nature came forth. Suddenly I saw the vile, evil being named Lucifer. "I finally have you in my grasp!" he said with a sneer.

All the love I had felt for and from him instantly turned to hatred. His eyes turned black and bottomless. An evil laugh came from deep within him. It felt like he wanted to kill me, too. I started to call out for help, but he was in the one person I needed to help me. I thought I was doomed again. Davos started to chant and again drew symbols on the table. Another strong wind came from a different direction, and then all three spirits disappeared.

"What just happened?" I asked. I was in shock, along with the rest of the people there.

"Don't worry. They're gone and won't come back. You know the one, but the other two are from your future. They will hold you back from being all you can be. They want to kill you both spiritually and emotionally. Let's continue your past life regression session."

"Are you sure? Will I be safe? I worry they will come back when I'm on my journey in the spirit realm."

"Oh, yes, they're gone. Just be sure to say the right words this time." He laughed.

This time, I concentrated on my spirit going back in time. It was interesting how it took form in my mind. I started remembering everything I had done earlier in the day, then back to yesterday, then the day before until the days and hours were flashing by in my mind's eye. It reminded me of the TV show *The Wild, Wild West*. It would show flashing pictures of all the actors in past scenes.

I found myself in Mom's womb and then in a long dark tunnel that resembled a tornado. I flew through it extremely fast, heading toward an opening. I didn't know if I was at the top or bottom. There was a blinding burst of light, and then I found myself lying on the ground.

Half asleep, I brushed flies away from my ears and eyes with my hands, which were now paws. My tail twitched up and down, and I could smell the earth, grass, and nearby brush. I knew I was a large cat. I was lying partially shaded from the sun.

I heard a horrendous sound coming from my left. The noise hurt my sensitive ears, putting my nerves on high alert. I ran from the noise as fast as I could, with my powerful legs pulling and pushing me forward. A pungent scent flowed into my nostrils. It smelled of the dangerous two-legged ones. I had a strong hatred of them. I pictured them all in a long line with noisemakers roaring loudly. I couldn't get their smell out of my nose. I ran faster. Not watching or paying attention to what was ahead of me, I ran past a large bush and straight into a two-leg with a spear. He thrust the spear into my chest. The shaft broke off when we both fell. I smelled his scent and fear, but I was wounded and needed to run and hide. The others were too close.

I found a large patch of brush and hid in it until dark. I knew I was dying, but I felt a deep need to get revenge on the two-leg before I left that life. Limping out from under the brush, I searched for my killer's scent trail. I picked it up where I had been attacked. I followed the scent until I came to the two-legged's camp. It was dark, but the whole camp was lit up by fires. I walked around the encampment, searching for his scent. No one else mattered. I finally found him. He was standing guard.

I snuck close to him. Every muscle in my body was tense, and my tail twitched rapidly as I prepared for battle. When he turned around to check the fire, I leaped onto his back and sank my teeth into his neck and my claws into whatever part of his body they could grip. My teeth sliced through his flesh, crushing his bones. I tasted his warm blood as it flowed into my mouth, and I felt his life force leave his body.

I felt proud and pleased I had finished my hunt and gotten my revenge. When the rest of his kind noticed I had killed him, they all attacked, stabbing me with their spears until my body was dead. I heard them yelling as I tasted and smelled blood, both his and mine. I didn't feel pain or emotion as I floated back into the darkness of the tornado.

Another bright light appeared, and I headed toward it quickly. When I stopped, I was in a massive building with a large staircase on which many people were walking down in a line to greet me and others. It was right out of a movie scene.

Men and women were dressed in white wigs and wore fancy clothes. The men wore suits with ruffles instead of ties, and the women wore corsets and big hoop skirts. One by one, they bowed in respect and kissed a huge, ugly ring on my hand. But their fake smiles and laughter told me they all feared and hated me.

The other people in line with me wore military uniforms or fancy suits. They had smug looks on their faces and looked down on everyone. I politely smiled. I was perplexed, however, as to who or what I was exactly and wondered why everyone hated me. I also wondered why I didn't experience a death. The scene just faded away before my eyes. I again drifted into darkness.

ಞ ♦ ೞ

A faraway light beckoned. When I came into the light, it was actually dusk. The sun was setting behind the majestic mountain range looming before me. The moon and the Milky Way lit up the night sky. I sat on a horse and gazed at the beautiful sight while rolling a cigarette.

I glanced over a large herd of cattle, looking for any sign of trouble or breaking of ranks. A cowboy was to my right. We were far apart, yet I felt as though we were one as we watched over the herd. It was the best feeling I'd experienced so far: peaceful and calm.

There were no feelings of anger, hate, or fear or thoughts of revenge in my mind or heart. I felt completely whole and at peace with everything, even God. How did I know or think of God? No other memories filled my mind. I was rejoicing in this life, period. I didn't want to leave that past life, but I had no control.

Once more, my spirit flew into the dark tunnel. I passed by a long line of flashing lives. I didn't get the chance to see what they were about because I didn't stop at any of them. Finally, I came to a stop. I was standing, looking at a lunar eclipse. In fact, I saw three lunar eclipses at this one stop. I wasn't alone, but I couldn't see the people with me. I didn't see the tunnel anymore and figured I wasn't going any further. I was disappointed I didn't see aliens, alien ships, giants, or other planets.

Then I heard the voice of Davos. He was calling me back to the present. It took a few minutes. When I opened my eyes, I was back in the room where I had started. Those who had come to observe had questions. Davos told them to wait a little bit so I could get over the "jet lag" and settle into the present. Once I was settled, I shared what had happened. Everyone sat in silence as I went through the lives I had experienced.

To this day, I'm not sure what to believe. I know what I experienced, but it was my first and last past life regression session. It's not clear whether they were real past life memories and not suggested ideas from

Davos, who told me that the three lunar eclipses were in my future and had something to do with the two gray-smoke spirit men.

Sadly, I really didn't learn much from any of them. I considered the lives I had experienced during the regression session, the emotions I had experienced, and the consequence of my actions as a cat. My best past life turned out to be a cowboy, who was one with God and His creation, just like I was in the beginning of this life.

I wouldn't do it again or recommend it to anyone. Although negative past events in this life should be acknowledged and forgiven, they make us who we are today. They shouldn't be used as an excuse to stay that way, especially if you are unhappy. I knew I had to surrender my past and forgive myself. I couldn't change the past and figured it would be best to concentrate on this life, the present, and look to the future.

By age nineteen, the partying and doing whatever I wanted to whom I wanted was no longer a challenge. It was easy, boring, and dangerous. I needed to move on. But what was there to do for the rest of my life?

Love? and Marriage

Life wasn't challenging, fulfilling, or even fun. David, a guy I was dating off and on, wanted to marry me, but I didn't love him. There were red flags, too. David would smooth-talk his way out of trouble whenever he was caught doing something wrong, whether it was a speeding ticket or getting caught flirting with another girl. He always portrayed himself as a type of savior for me. He promised to protect me, provide for me, and love me better than anyone else.

He was quite proud of the fact that he could talk people into doing things he wanted. He called himself a silver-tongued devil. His smooth-talking and his steady job convinced me I was better off with him than with anyone else, so I finally agreed to marry him. Since he wasn't Catholic, we couldn't have a Catholic wedding, which didn't break my heart at all. We found a non-denominational church that agreed to wed us.

Before the wedding, I went in for a doctor's appointment. They found some cysts on my ovaries that needed to be removed and said I might need a hysterectomy. They would determine whether that would be necessary during the surgery. I was ready to accept that I would never have another child, a fit consequence for my past transgressions. David disliked hospitals and would do anything to avoid going in one, but he did drop me off.

In the recovery room, I felt the strong presence of a man. It felt like we had known each other forever, like we were meant to be together. *Those dang drugs!* I thought.

"Don't leave me," I begged. "Please stay with me."

I heard a man's voice answer, "Don't worry. I won't leave you."

I sighed with relief. A few minutes later, I felt his hand leaving mine. I immediately reached out. "I told you that you can't leave me. I need you here by my side. I think we belong with each other. I don't want to lose your presence. It makes me feel safe." I was unable to open my eyes. I soon slipped away into a deep sleep while tightly holding his hand.

A nurse woke me up for breakfast. I remembered that I had been operated on when I felt the sutures. I had faint memories of an energy I had felt a strong connection with and needed to have near me. As I ate breakfast and thought about the upcoming wedding, a good-looking male nurse came in, sat on one of the visitor chairs, and said, "Good morning, Pam. I'm Michael." He had a big smile on his handsome face and a twinkle in his beautiful green eyes.

"Good morning," I said hesitantly.

"You don't remember me, do you?"

"No, I don't remember seeing you before, but your energy is familiar. Oh my gosh! You're the guy. The guy I wouldn't let leave me." I was so embarrassed. I didn't know what to say or do.

I was wearing a gown with my backside exposed. My legs were unshaven, my hair was a mess, and I didn't have on any makeup. He was so darn cute. I wondered why I was acting like a teenager with a crush. *Hey, you're engaged. Get a grip on yourself*, I thought while I fussed with my hair and tried to cover my legs anyway. "I'm such a mess," I stammered.

He had the best laugh I had ever heard. "You look just fine. Don't worry about a thing. "Anyway, I'm an intern and was in the operating room with you. I have already seen all of you, every inch."

I blushed. My heart raced, my stomach did flip-flops, and chills ran through me from head to toe as he smiled and gave me a long look of approval. He changed the topic by asking how sore I was feeling. He told me he had rounds to make but he would be back later, maybe to have dinner with me.

I was in a huge turmoil. The feelings I had for Michael were as strong now as they had been in my drug-induced fog. I wondered if he was the one for me. As I sat there in my little fantasy dream world, someone else came into the room. It was the last person I was expecting: my fiancé, David, with flowers in hand.

He had refused to come in with me before the surgery, saying he would give me a day or two to feel better before coming by to visit. He was uncomfortable being there; his eyes showed his fear and readiness to leave as soon as possible.

I was blushing again, this time with guilt. *Hmm... I guess he really does love me*, I mused. Still, I went back and forth over my feelings for Michael and the lack of the same kind of feelings for David. I was confused. Was evil tempting me to break my word to David? I wondered why I suddenly had a conscience. I rarely listened to it anymore. I was in control of me. What was going on?

Around dinnertime, I was breathless as I waited for Michael. As soon as he entered the room, everything else disappeared. We talked about each other's plans, hopes, and dreams. The electricity between us was intense. My guilty conscience made me tell him I was engaged.

He was surprised, but he also admitted to having strong feelings. He suggested fate was involved. "Maybe you're not supposed to marry David.

"Think about it, Pam," he insisted, blowing me a kiss as he left the room.

I wondered what it would be like to kiss him. I had never kissed anyone with a mustache. Was it prickly or soft? His eyes were warm and inviting. I could have gotten lost in them for days. A part of me was saying, "This is what you have been searching for." Another part of me was saying, "This is so wrong. You have pledged yourself to David. Don't be tempted by lust." I told myself to sleep on it and wait to see how things worked out.

The next morning, I was full of expectations when my surgeon stopped by to examine my sutures. He told me they didn't need to do a hysterectomy, but he also said I was so scarred from the cysts that, sadly, I couldn't have any more children. He then said, "Well, you can go home today. Everything is looking fine. Just take it easy for the next two weeks, and I will see you then at my office. I already booked the appointment for you."

I mustered up a smile and a thank you. The nurse, seeing my disappointment, said, "Don't worry. I'll tell Michael you were released early and were unable to say goodbye. We all know about your situation and are hoping everything works out for you both." She giggled and smiled reassuringly.

Everyone knew about my situation! A shot of fear went through me. What if David knew? He *was* acting different lately. Maybe he had spies or special powers. I went home, rested up, and took the pain pills as directed, which, in turn, gave me hallucinations. I was advised to stop taking the medication. I then picked up from where I had left off: making wedding plans.

Three weeks later, I was headed for my car to go grocery shopping when a motorcycle pulled up next to me. Suddenly my stomach was full of butterflies. The rider removed his helmet and shook his dark hair. Then my eyes met those green eyes and that smile: Michael!

"Hey, beautiful, can we talk?" It was incredible to hear his voice. I felt faint and couldn't believe he was standing before me. "I've tried to forget all about you, but I just can't. Have you had enough time to decide what you want to do about us?"

DODGING EVIL

I melted at his gaze. I wanted to run into his arms and kiss him. I had been dreaming of (and dreading) this moment.

"I quit my job at the hospital and bought a conversion van," he continued. "I want to head east. I want to see where I'm drawn to stay, and I want you to come with me. This, whatever we have, is strong, compelling, and undeniable. I want to see it through to the end. Don't you?"

A part of me yearned to say, "Yes!" Another part of me, the practical me, said, "No, you can't. You gave your word you would marry. Everything is all set. You have always kept your word. You can't stop now." I couldn't decide between the two men. Which feeling was right?

David promised security, but Michael promised passion. With David, I knew I would be taken care of, but with Michael, I had a profound spiritual and physical attraction I didn't feel with David.

What was the right choice? I was truly torn, but because sex was not a priority for me (even though I still hadn't had an orgasm), I didn't trust that the strong attraction would bring me ecstasy or completeness. I had been fooled before.

Sadly, I told Michael I couldn't go back on my word. I told him that if we had met earlier and I hadn't been committed to someone else, I would have loved to go on an adventure with him. Both of us had tears in our eyes as I reached out to touch his hand one last time.

He leaned down to kiss my hand, lightly brushing it with not only his lips, but his mustache, too. It felt amazingly soft. He looked into my eyes and asked for a goodbye kiss. I told myself it was the least I could do, knowing I had really wanted to feel a kiss from him since the first time we had met. Temptation is so mean and makes it tough to make choices!

Our lips met, and time seemed to stop all around us. It was hard to pull away. *Darn, I shouldn't have done that*, I thought. I was afraid David would find out and hurt us both. I pushed away from Michael, blushing. "Goodbye. Have a safe trip, and I hope you find what you're looking for."

He smiled. Ooh, that smile! "Thanks, but I think I already have." As he rode away, David drove up! I wondered if he had spies everywhere. He seemed to show up at the strangest times. He leaned out the car window and, with his usual smirky smile and left eyebrow raised, asked, "What are you up to?"

"I'm just going shopping. You're off work early. Want to come with?"

He had other things to do.

Months later, while visiting a friend in the hospital, the nurse who had taken care of me stopped me in the hall and told me a chilling story. Michael had indeed left the hospital. He told them he had someone in mind to go with him.

She thought it might have been me, but he came back to ask if anyone else wanted to go with him. Another nurse who had a crush on him wanted to go. He reluctantly agreed. Less than a month later, the nurses got word that Michael and the other nurse obviously hadn't gotten along. Apparently, she whined and complained a lot, and in a fit of anger and frustration, he had killed her and dumped her body somewhere along the highway. He was now in prison.

All the what-ifs went through my mind. It was an example of how someone or something can feel and look beautiful and seem wonderful and right but then turn out to be the complete opposite.

My parents gave David and me the perfect church wedding and reception. David was, indeed, a self-proclaimed silver-tongued devil. He had everyone fooled. After the reception, my new "loving" husband informed me I was now his property and was to obey him in all things.

A few weeks later, he told me he didn't want kids because he didn't want any of his kids to be called half-breeds. He knew I couldn't have children and was just being mean. Thus began the mental abuse. We were married for seven years. They were not all bad or all good years. It was a growing time for both of us. I learned I couldn't always get what I wanted, but I did get what I needed.

Most of our emotional and spiritual growth comes through trials and tribulations. It seemed all the difficulties I faced started with a choice I made. Some jobs I had during those seven years turned out to be learning opportunities, too.

I worked as a telephone operator, a telemarketer, a salesgirl for Macy's, and a massage therapist. I also worked one day at the local welfare department. I found out immediately that I couldn't work for such an evil place that traps people into poverty, punishing them for getting on their feet. For them, it was easier not to work and just keep having kids.

All those jobs taught me to think seriously about what I was doing. They seemed to be legit businesses. Each had a good and bad side. I had to choose to either continue deceiving people or quit. In each one of those jobs, people looked down on me because of my race.

I fell back into working as a waitress. It was honest work; I enjoyed the people and places where I worked. Race didn't seem to matter in this line of work. I made great tips throughout the seven years I was married to David.

We lived at my dad's ranch because neither of us had jobs in the city anymore. Dad told us on our wedding day that if we ever needed a place to live or help finding work, we were welcome to stay on the ranch. David really wanted to take advantage of the offer. We were living in the old cabin Dad and Grandpa had built long ago. At least it was our very own space, and we didn't have to share it with anyone. I worked at a local restaurant as a waitress, and David worked as a logger. Things went well until he received an inheritance from his grandmother and had an affair with an old friend and ex-neighbor of ours in the city.

I had been delving into the black arts with my gifts and knew he was having an affair. When I confronted him, he admitted he was cheating. I told him to leave. Good riddance, I told myself, but I was devastated and angry. I wanted to beat them both to a pulp, but I knew they were not worth it. Instead, I settled for witchcraft attacks from afar. I didn't want to kill them, just make them hurt like they had made me hurt.

They had ripped out my heart and guts. I sent that pain to them both whenever I felt them together. I didn't know for sure whether it was working, but I felt better after doing it. At the same time, I prayed that God would bring him back to me. What a goofball I was! But it felt wrong for us to break up. Our oath to each other had been for better or for worse, for richer or poorer, until death do us part. Again I was conflicted.

One voice said, "To hell with him!" The other said, "You made an oath, so forgive him, even though he broke his." I cried a lot, not knowing what to do.

I started reading the Bible and even made a deal with God. If He brought David back, I would do anything He asked of me, especially in the biblical last days, if I were still alive.

Two weeks later, David came driving up to the ranch. I met him at the front door of the white house but kept the screen door closed.

"What are you doing here?"

"I want to return your dad's rifle. I forgot it was in my truck, and I want to talk to you."

He handed me the rifle, and I put it in my family's gun closet. Mom left the room so we could talk in private.

"What do you want to talk about?"

"How have you been?" he politely asked, using his charm.

"I've been good," I lied. "Why do you care all of a sudden? It didn't seem to matter before."

"I'm sorry about what happened, and I would like to come back home if you'll let me."

"Why should I trust you? How do I know you won't do it again? More important, how do you know you won't do it again?"

"Honestly, I can't promise it will never happen again, but I will try not to. I do love you, and I have missed you. Please give me another chance."

"I don't know. I'll have to think and pray about it. What changed your mind, exactly?"

He shuffled his feet and looked down at his hands. "I think she's after my money. I want you back, and I think you have been using witchcraft against us."

"What?"

"And just in case you have been," he nervously whispered as he started to pull a small, knitted pink talisman out of his wallet. I was only a few feet from him when the talisman suddenly flew out of his wallet and hit me on my chest. He explained he'd had a good witch make him a protection talisman against me.

When the pouch hit me, my breath was taken away for a few seconds. The pouch fell to the floor. As I snatched it up off the floor, I felt the witch's energy. I grabbed all her magic power meant to harm me and threw it back at her tenfold. I felt her and the fear I caused. I felt powerful and in control in that moment. I sneered at him, telling him she wasn't powerful enough to stop me from doing whatever I wanted to anyone I wanted.

The witch's fear was so great that I suddenly had compassion toward her and David. I swept most of my anger away from her, leaving just enough so she wouldn't try again. I then asked David why he thought I had used witchcraft.

"Well, every time we got together after you found out about us, we would have terrible gut aches, headaches, and chest pains, like we were having food poisoning, heart attacks, or someone was ripping our insides apart.

"I knew you had been dabbling in the occult and thought you were practicing on us. After all, I really don't blame you. We did do you wrong, but she came after me, and I gave in. You know how weak men are, especially when it comes to women who are ready and willing. Please, forgive me. Let me come home."

I could tell he meant what he was saying. A part of me still wanted him to suffer, if he was really suffering.

"You came here asking to come home, but you brought something that could have hurt me. I don't know what to think. I'll need some time to decide what I want to do. Call me next Friday night. I'll know by then."

I wondered if God had anything to do with David's sudden change of heart. If so, I must honor His answer to my prayer. At that moment, I had a headache.

Part of me was prideful. I now knew my witchcraft worked. I could do anything now. That power trip didn't last long, though. I soon gave in and forgave David, and we decided to start over. We left the ranch and moved to Oregon, then to Lake Tahoe, trying to find a place we could call home. We stayed in Tahoe for a year before moving back to the ranch. We built an addition onto the old cabin and made it a home of our own, even though we didn't have indoor plumbing.

We did well for a while. Life was simple and good. Around six months later, I thought David was trying to make me think I was going crazy. He would play mind games on me. He would tell me things and then later contradict what he had told me. When I corrected him, he would get a worried look on his face and then gently touch my forehead. "Oh, honey, are you feeling alright? I never told you that. Are you sure you're alright?"

This went on and on. I didn't know if I was coming or going. I even dreamt he was trying to kill me. I would wake up to see him standing next to my side of the bed, arms raised above his head with an ax in his hands, but he was also lying next to me in bed.

He caused me to doubt myself and my memory. I foolishly thought he wouldn't lie to me about anything. One day, I was so distracted by thinking how I had misunderstood what he had told me that I didn't even notice I was actually holding a spoon I had been feverishly looking for to stir my food! He kept saying that something was wrong with me. That it was all in my head; he had nothing to do with any of it.

I was too gullible, I believed him when he said he wouldn't lie to me. I should have known better, especially when he smiled his smirky smile and raised his left eyebrow.

One night, I was awakened by the presence of someone next to my bed. It said, "Pam, wake up!"

I opened my eyes. I couldn't see anyone, but I definitely felt a presence. It actually pulled on my arm strong enough to lift me out of bed. "Follow me," the being urged.

I was hesitant but didn't feel evil intent. Besides, it was holding me tightly and pulling me in a hurry. I didn't get a chance to put on any clothing. As usual, David was sound asleep. The being led me outside to a clearing and then gently lifted my chin up to the night sky. Before me was a bright star or the moon fluctuating like a strobe light. One beam fell onto my forehead and landed between my eyes, the spot most people call the third eye.

I was amazed at the feeling it gave me, both physically and spiritually. I felt like I was plugged into a wonderful power source that made every cell of my being come alive more than any other time I could remember. It also felt familiar, like I had experienced it before. I heard a deep, powerful voice say, "Come!" The word vibrated throughout my whole being. The power in that voice was compelling and incredibly strong.

I was both excited and fearful. I reached out in spirit up into the beam of light to feel who or what was calling me. I was enveloped in the most wonderful warmth, peace, and endless love that could only come from God.

"COME!" the voice said more insistently. Again the voice vibrated throughout my whole being. I opened myself up, surrendering my heart, mind, and spirit. I became one with the beam of light and with whatever or whoever was on the other side.

I floated peacefully up into the magnificent, bright light. Suddenly a different voice called out, "Stop! Don't go. It's Lucifer. He is tricking you into going up high just to drop you!" I stopped immediately.

I knew that if I was only in the spirit, he couldn't hurt me, but if my spirit was in my body, he could drop me. I looked down to see if my body was on the ground. If it was, I had nothing to worry about. To my surprise, my body wasn't on the ground. Frightened, I lost connection with the awesome light. I fell hard to the ground, on my bare bottom.

"See, I told you so!" the voice bragged.

I pondered that event for days afterward. I wondered why I hadn't recognized God's or Lucifer's voice. I'd heard both before. Was it some other entity's voice? I researched in my Bible concordance to find references to the voice of God. I found a verse where Jesus said, "Those who know Me know my voice." Did that mean Jesus was the other voice, the one that had warned me? Or the one that called me? I needed to know more about Jesus. I asked God to send me someone who could help me listen to the right voice.

The next day, for the very first time ever, Jehovah's Witnesses came knocking on my door. They were eager to share their knowledge. When they asked about my life, I told them about my delving into the occult world but that I now wanted to know Christ and his voice. All of a sudden, they became fearful.

I didn't understand their fear. They were adamant that Jehovah was all-powerful, their protector, and provider, yet they acted as though they doubted he would protect them. They came three more times. Each time, they crept into my home as if they were going to be attacked by some monster demon. I reminded them that my occultic behavior was in my past, but they still were concerned.

They mostly talked about the Old Testament, the law, and the end of days and not so much about Christ. Their teachings reminded me of the

Catholic teachings: condemnation, judgment, and fear. I finally asked them to stop coming.

I kept praying for help in learning what I needed to learn about Christ. I also needed to know how to deal with David's mental abuse. He was killing me emotionally and spiritually. He did resemble one of the men in my trench coat nightmare and the smoke spirits from the past-life-regression mix-up. Could he actually be one of them?

I didn't want to use witchcraft or my gifts to mess with his sanity. I was trying to become a Christian. Besides, we had been married in a church. I needed to keep our vows. So, things got worse until, one day, I woke up DEAD.

ACT III

SURRENDERING

Awakening

I felt void, empty of all emotions; I felt absolutely nothing. I wasn't even afraid. I thought I must be dead, but I could move my body and felt the pinch I gave myself. My spirit was still in my body. *What is going on?* I mused. A voice came to my mind, reminding me about my wedding vows and how they were valid "until death do us part." It continued, "You are dead in spirit and dead emotionally. You are set free. You can leave David. Remember all you have learned so far and start anew. Try again to live well."

I felt strange yet calm. The same voice told me I must leave the ranch and David. It spoke without emotion. David wasn't home, so I was able to take everything I needed and pack it into my car. He had bought the car for me from one of his friends. He didn't like being bothered to drive me where I needed to go and then come pick me up.

I walked over to the white house and told my parents I was leaving. I was taking Koda, my female German shepherd. I wasn't sure where I was going. I would let them know, but they had to promise not to tell David. I would file for a divorce as soon as possible. I needed to find a job and a place to live first. Dad gave me a hundred dollars and told me not to worry about anything except myself.

David, as usual, showed up just in time. He drove up while I was walking back to the cabin and my car. By the time I reached the cabin, he was reclining in his La-Z-Boy with his favorite music playing and lighting up a big joint. He hadn't noticed the car was full of my things and Koda was waiting to go for a ride.

I knew he wouldn't leave of his own accord. He had put a lot of money into our house. Nevertheless, I had to make a change. Our relationship was dead; besides, the spirit had told me it was time to go. Dad told me he would let David stay a month or two until he was convinced I wasn't going to return.

I boldly told David I had woken up to the realization we weren't good for each other. I was done. I was leaving. I told him how I was empty inside and my emotions were gone. I would file for a divorce when I got enough money saved, unless he wanted to pay. Of course, he declined to pay. David told me he would drive the truck off a cliff if I tried to take it; he also told me I better not try to get any of his inheritance money.

"I don't want your money or truck. I just need to get away from you."

Once more, David told me I couldn't survive without him. He told me I would be back, crying for forgiveness, within a month. He snidely laughed, raised his left eyebrow, and, one last time, said, "You can't make it in this world without me." I turned my back to him and walked out.

I drove away from the one place I could call home, where I used to feel safe and loved. David was there now, so I had to leave. It was no longer my home. It had been ruined. I was ruined. The one good thing was that I felt nothing. I was empty inside. I wasn't angry, fearful, or sad.

Koda would give me a kiss for reassurance every few minutes as we drove to…where? I hadn't thought about where I was going. I just drove until I reached Reno and had to put gas in the car, but I didn't want to live or work in Reno. I headed south toward Carson City, but then I turned west, up a steep mountain and back to Lake Tahoe. It was a beautiful drive up the mountain and down into the lake's basin. It suddenly felt like home. This was where I was going, to Lake Tahoe, the place where people go to be healed in spirit. It is a holy place to many Native tribes.

Many years ago, I was told by a medicine man that one comes to Tahoe to be healed and renewed but must leave afterward or they will go insane.

"Look around you," he said. "The white man is crazy because of living here too long. They have become drunkards, drug users, fornicators, and unhappy, lost spirits. You will become the same if you stay too long."

My older sister, Allie, had been living in Tahoe for a long time. She worked in a casino's hotel laundry room. My younger sisters and I would spend time with her during our summer vacations, after graduating from high school, and when I got back from college.

I became friends with her friends and their children. Jay, the son of one of Allie's coworkers, and I became close friends. I trusted him because we had known each other a long time. I ran into Jay while driving around the south side of the lake, looking for places to rent.

He offered to let me stay with him until I could find a job and a place of my own. We were a bit cramped in his small apartment. I called from Jay's phone to let my parents know I was safe and where I was staying.

The next morning, I went to one of the casinos, boldly walked up to the slot manager, and asked him when he was going to hire me. I took him by surprise. He smiled and said, "You can start tomorrow if you can get a sheriff's card."

That caught me off guard. I quickly drove to the sheriff's office and applied for the card. Anyone who works in a casino must have a sheriff's card. It proves you have a clean record. It must be carried on your person when working in a casino. The officer told me it could be a couple of days to a week before I would get it. I suddenly panicked. "I was told to start work tomorrow," I whined. *Why are you whining?* I thought. I was even pouting. Was I getting feelings back?

"Don't worry," the officer said, jerking me out of my head. "I'll give you a temporary one until the background check comes through. Then you will get a permanent one. The casinos are always hiring people and wanting them to start right away," he complained. I was so happy. I was off to a good start. All I needed to do was find my own place to live.

I returned to the casino and presented my brand-new temporary sheriff's card to the slot manager. "Wow! I didn't think you would get one so fast. You must know somebody. I guess I better keep my word. You can come in tomorrow at 10 a.m. Your shift will be from then until 6 p.m., but since you are here now, you can fill out all the paperwork and meet the day shift head cashier."

I really liked everyone I met that afternoon. The only downside was I wouldn't be paid for a whole month! Their policy was to hold two weeks' pay, and if you cleared the background check and were a good employee, they would catch you up on the next two-week pay period.

At least I knew for sure I would get paid every two weeks. Now all I needed to do was find my own place, which turned out to be harder than I thought. Many landlords had been burned by casino employees who gambled away their paychecks, and they didn't want to rent to me without a big down payment and security deposit.

I drove around, looking for an affordable place to rent. I saw a rental sign advertising a rental for seventy-five dollars a month. It was in a cute complex with five cabins facing a communal courtyard with what looked like a motel. I hoped utilities were included and pets were allowed.

Pulling into the courtyard, I saw a woman with three young children helping her water plants. I asked her about the rental. The woman and her husband turned out to be the owners of the complex. She was a gentle soul, and her children were well behaved. I could see and feel the Spirit of God in her, too.

Unfortunately, she had just rented the seventy-five-dollar cabin, but she had larger rooms and cabins available. They were $150, $175, or $250 per month. I asked to see the room for $150. I was surprised at the size of the unit. It was a large, fully furnished studio apartment. It had a separate fully furnished kitchen and a full bath with towels. Utilities were included, and I could have a dog. It was perfect!

I felt this was where I should be, but I had a small problem. I only had eighty-five dollars. I explained my circumstances and told her I could pay half now and, in four weeks, I could pay the remaining half plus half for the next month and then pay seventy-five dollars every two weeks. I also volunteered to pick up after my dog, rake the courtyard, and do any other chores that needed to be done. That would leave me with ten dollars to last the month. It would take a miracle.

She told me she needed to speak to her husband and asked me to call or come back later that evening. I went back to Jay's place and told him about the room. He wanted me to stay with him longer so I could save money, but the unit could be gone by then. Anyway, his place was too small. That evening I called, and to my surprise and joy, he had agreed to my offer, but I had to go over right away. He wanted to meet Koda and me first. I packed up all our stuff and headed to our new home. I thanked Jay for his hospitality and asked him to keep in touch.

The husband was a stern-looking man whose demeanor demanded respect, yet I could see he had a soft heart inside. We all got along well, and they had me sign a lease with the terms I had requested. Best of all, no deposit was required. They gave me the keys, and Koda and I moved in that night.

The next morning, I headed off to work in my uniform, a white blouse and black skirt. I made sure Koda had plenty of fresh water and a full food dish. She was housebroken and experienced in being left in a house alone for long periods of time. My first day was quite the day for me. I learned everything about being a change girl. During each shift, I could purchase any special of the day at lunchtime for only $1.05! That perk came in handy during the long month of no pay. When I ran out of money, I didn't know what I would do.

While roaming the casino, looking for customers, something wonderful happened. There in front of me was a dollar bill just lying on the floor. No one was around. The casino's policy was finders keepers when money was on the floor, unless it had a casino wrapper on it, was in a jackpot bag, or was a casino chip. Those had to be turned in to the head cashier.

Any change left in slot machine trays was supposed to be put back into the same machine or turned in to the cashier, but most everyone pocketed it. I was taught by a long-time employee how to palm the left-behind coins.

I never noticed so much change being left behind or money on the floor before or after that time of need. Don't get me wrong; it wasn't a lot. It was just enough to get necessities like a pack of cigarettes, lunch, or a can of dog food. I always took home a doggie bag for Koda, too.

On my days off, Koda ate part of her canned food, and we shared the popcorn and soda crackers I got for free from the casino coffee shop. I drank lots of water; it made me feel full. During that time, my landlord invited me for dinner twice, sending me home with leftovers.

I learned to ration everything and to give thanks for what was being provided. They were the best landlords I have ever had the privilege of renting from. They prayed before dinner and talked about God, too. They belonged to a local Christian church.

She gave me a King James Bible to read. Since I didn't have a TV or radio, I spent many hours reading the Bible, but it was very difficult. The style of English was hard to understand. I usually just skipped over all the hard words, including all the "begots." I couldn't make heads or tails out of it at first.

The month finally ended, and I received my paycheck; I paid rent as promised. I actually earned enough to pay next month's rent, too.

Time went by quickly. I was happy and content. That dark emptiness no longer overwhelmed me. I went dancing almost every night, played pool for small amounts of money or drinks, and played slots off and on. I always won.

On one of my days off, Jay came to visit, and he offered me a new drug that was in town. He told me it wouldn't make me sick and contained no man-made chemicals. The high should last around four hours or so. He told me it was an awesome, natural high and the drug was holy to Native Americans. It was meant for spiritual awakening and enlightenment. I was very interested in taking the Mescaline. It sounded exactly what I was looking for at that time in my life.

I took it, but I felt nothing for about an hour. I decided to go down to the lake to sit and wait for it to take effect. It was a subtle high. I didn't even realize I was tripping. I was extremely relaxed; everything was glowing and alive, just like when I had first come into this world. God was in and of everything. I was soft and fluffy, like everything around me. I *was* everything around me.

I couldn't get the smile off my face. Everything I saw or touched was vividly alive. Emanating from the center of the universe was an energy or life force that had all things breathing in the same rhythm, making us all one. All my senses were on full capacity. I was one with God again.

I felt a strong urge to get into the water, to feel it against my skin, through my body and spirit, to become one with it. I held water in the palm of my hand, letting it flow through my fingers. It shimmered like diamonds in the sunlight, making beautiful bubbles as it landed back into the lake, becoming one body once more. It reminded me how all creation is truly one.

We all—animals, humans, water, and sand—are different in shape and form, but spiritually or energetically, we have come from the same source. I came to the realization that the water I picked up out of the lake was still the same lake, but just a smaller part. My separating it from its origin and changing its form for a short time is similar to my being born into the Earth realm.

In my mind, the lake represented God, the origin of all creation.

When I poured the water from my hand back into the lake, it became whole once more. This is the same as when I left the spirit realm and why, when I and others leave our bodies for good, we will return to God, becoming whole once more.

I sat down to play with the sand and pebbles on the bottom of the lake near the shore. The water was exceptionally smooth and cool. The pebbles and sand felt wonderfully alive. Their textures were amazing to feel. It made me extremely aware that these things were made by design, not by accident.

I felt the presence or energy of someone coming toward me. I looked up. Jay was standing next to me. He said quietly, "How are you doing?"

"I am great; this is wonderful!" I was beaming with joy.

"I've been watching you for a while. I thought I better let you know you can't keep playing in the water; it will draw attention. The cops look for people who aren't acting normal. If you were a kid, they wouldn't think twice about you playing in the water. As an adult, it's pretty weird. They'll think you must be high to enjoy such a trivial thing."

"Hey, have you felt a tree yet?" he asked. "I know where we can hug some trees and not get in trouble." He grabbed my hand, leading me to a nearby forest.

It is hard to describe the feeling the trees gave me. Each tree had different bark and leaves, yet they felt the same. Each had a life force or spirit of its own, yet they were also one with me as with the universe and God.

We were all breathing in the same rhythm. My heart slowed to match the universal heartbeat. I wanted to feel this alive and in touch with all things every day, just like when I was young. I was in complete peace, whole. I loved everything and everyone because we all are one.

I seemed to be getting higher rather than going down. Jay told me everyone could have a different experience and a different length of time before it wore off.

"How long can it last?" I asked.

"I've heard some have lasted up to twelve hours."

"Twelve hours! You assured me I would be down by now! How can I ever trust you again?"

"Don't worry. You have complete control of how you react to anything that happens. Never panic. Tell yourself you are in control, and you will be. Drink lots of water and eat lots of food; it will help." His words settled me down. I made a mental note. I would take this mescaline again, but on my first day off, not the second, just in case it lasted longer.

During my mescaline high, I listened to music. I really listened, hearing and feeling it truly for the very first time. It was wonderful, and so was the refrigerator. I had never known how soft and cool it was before that night, either. I binged out on dinner. I felt hungover the next day, but I was hooked on that kind of high. I was lucky it wasn't easy to get. It was an entire month before it was back on the streets. The next time, I was prepared.

I asked Jay to buy me as many hits as he could. I wanted to have a stash for when I wanted to take it and not have to wait for it to come back to town. I planned on cutting them in half or quarters for more frequent but shorter highs. All Jay could get was four hits, and one was his. I was disappointed and angry.

"It was all he had left by the time I found him," Jay explained. "It takes time to make, and it sells fast. It is the real deal."

I had to use it sparingly. When the next month came, I still had some left, but I was eager to replenish my stash. This time, though, Jay brought me some weird-looking capsules.

"What is this?"

"It's the same mescaline, just made differently. It is ground up to a fine powder and put into a vegetable-based capsule. You can't see any of the fibers like in the old pills, plus they are smaller and easier to swallow."

I thought it was a great idea. We took it at the same time and waited.

In about ten minutes, we could feel it starting. This trip was extremely different than the previous ones. I didn't like what was happening at all. It felt dreadful to my body, mind, and spirit. It didn't bring harmony; it brought chaos! It made my gums very tight and dry, making me gnash my teeth. Every fiber in my body was clenching, too. My spirit went into hiding.

I could feel bubbles forming and popping like tiny explosions in my brain. My heart was having trouble beating. I started to panic. "Jay, what is going on?"

"Wow! They must have cut this with strychnine like they do acid. That's messed up!" He was extremely angry and apologized for not checking. "Don't panic. Like I told you before, make your mind be in control. Make your body calm down and just wait it out. Listen to your favorite music, sit outside, and hang out with your dog. She will help you feel safe."

Jay had to leave. I did as he advised, making it through the terrible six hours of pain and agony. I felt what an animal must feel when they are poisoned by strychnine. What a terrible way to die. It felt at times that my heart was being suffocated.

My brain cells felt as if they were blowing up and reforming over and over. I was able to see through my skin. I watched my blood flow through my veins and muscles, and sparks of energy shot from nerves to muscle and tendons as my brain told them to move.

It was beautiful to see; the colors were soft and soothing. I was in awe at the design and function of the human body, but the gnashing of my teeth and tightening of my body weren't worth it.

It was nothing like the pure, smooth, life-giving, uplifting, enlightening mescaline, which was a natural high. This man-made poison tried to make God's work "better," yet it only caused terrible side effects, even death. I never bought it again.

I made my little stash last as long as I could. It was the first time since I was a young girl that I felt one with God. When the mescaline was gone, so were those sweet times with God in spirit. I slowly returned to the fleshly way of being.

I was twenty-six and filled with marital and spiritual despair when I experienced an unusual encounter that led me back to God. I was playing nickel slots on my day off. I had used my gifts often to find slot machines ready to hit. Because of my super "luck" with the slots, casino security always watched me closely; they thought I was using some kind of cheating device. I had already won thirty jackpots, adding up to around $250.

As I pulled the slot lever, I unexpectedly felt a presence coming toward me. It came from the highway next to the casino. I felt it pass the casino and then turn into the parking lot and stop. It came into the casino and went down into the coffee shop. It stayed there for about a half-hour, and then it moved back up into the casino toward me.

It came close and stood next to me. I didn't look up. I didn't want it to know that I knew "it" was there. Was it a human or a spirit being? It moved away from me. I took a quick peek. "It" was a black man. He walked around the casino once more and again stopped next to me. He stood there for a few seconds and walked away.

In the meantime, I kept hitting jackpot after jackpot, enjoying myself immensely. I still felt his presence in the casino. He came and stood next to me for the third time.

"Yep, you are the one. The one I was sent to save. The devil has his claws deep in you. God wants to set you free. Do you know the name of God?"

I fought the urge to laugh. "Are you serious?" I asked. "Of course, I know a name of God. It is Jehovah."

"Oh, you do know His name. Well, do you know Jesus?"

"I know of the name. He is the Son of God and was crucified and then risen, but I do not know Him," I replied smugly.

He warned me that while he would be sharing with me knowledge about Jesus, people would come by and try to interrupt our conversation. He also said that the slot machine I was playing would dry up so I would have no choice but to give my full attention to what he was going to tell me. I laughed at that statement.

The machine was under my power. It wouldn't dry up unless it ran out of money. The coin tray was overflowing. As he talked on and on about Jesus, the payouts started to slow to a trickle, and indeed, strange people kept coming by and literally pushing him away from the machine he was leaning on or standing next to, definitely interrupting him. They looked like they were hypnotized or following some behind-the-scenes directions.

Finally, I had nothing to stop me from listening. The machine did dry up, and his Jesus talk eventually made the weird strangers go away. He asked if I would go to his car to listen to a tape God wanted me to hear.

I laughed, thinking, *Now I know what his play is all about.* I figured he just wanted to get me in his car for who knows what and had probably paid those people to harass him, too. What a con!

"I tell you what," I said. "I'm willing to go out to your car, but only if my friend Jack goes, too. I will then know for sure you are sent by God. He will be off duty in a few minutes."

I knew my coworker Jack would never agree to it. He had been beaten badly by a group of eighteen-year-old black men while others had stood by and just watched, so he disliked black people. Only God could make Jack agree to go to a car with a black man.

While waiting for Jack, I cashed out, keeping two dollars to play a nickel slot while the man told me his story. He was an ex-Catholic priest who had been living and studying at the Vatican for many years. The more he learned, the more he realized that the Church wasn't the one God had begun.

Of course, it proclaimed to be, but its actions were far from it. He didn't know what to do. He had given his whole life to serving God and the Church, but he really just wanted to serve God. He knew he couldn't continue to be a Catholic priest, so he asked God to show him what to do. God answered his prayers.

God told him to denounce his position, travel to America, and then go to Lake Tahoe, to a casino where God would show him to look for a woman. God would point her out to him three times. He was to ask her, "Do you know the name of God?" and then tell her that the devil has his claws deep into her and God had sent him to help save her. He finished with, "I am to have you listen to a tape before I leave here and go to my next destination."

Why me? I wondered. I had been there and done that. Could I really have a relationship with God like I had once enjoyed?

As Jack walked up, I looked into his eyes to see if I could detect disdain or anger at seeing a black man with me. I didn't see either. In fact, he smiled and held out his hand. "Hi, I'm Jack," he said. "Who are you?"

"He's an ex-priest who came all the way from the Vatican to save me," I explained. "He has a tape in his car that God wants me to hear. Will you come with me?"

"Sure, let's go."

My chin hit the floor. I couldn't believe my ears. Did he not see the man was black? Or was I seeing a white man as a black man? Only God and the man knew for sure. Jack and I never spoke about the color of the man's skin.

The tape was about some secret items the Vatican had hidden. Some of the items would be given to the Antichrist in the last days to reveal who the Antichrist would be. We were asked to not say too much about what was on the tape until it was time.

Jack told me he thought the guy was from God and the message was indeed meant for me. I then began my quest for Jesus. A lot of roadblocks began to appear, too.

Roadblock number one happened a week later on a Friday night. I was working in the casino coffee shop and was taking a pot of hot coffee to one of my tables. My customers were smiling and reaching for their cups when my right foot landed on a knife that a busboy had dropped on the linoleum floor.

It caused me to lose my balance. My foot slipped out from under me, and I fell backward, throwing the coffee pot behind me. I fell to the floor with a thud and felt a shooting pain in my back. I couldn't get up or move my legs.

The coffee was spilled all over, broken glass was scattered, and customers were worried. Someone sent for security, and they called an ambulance after they saw I couldn't move. I was rolled out on a gurney and taken to the hospital.

I was injured so severely that I had to stay three days for observation. I couldn't walk without help. Luckily, workman's compensation paid for everything, but that next Monday, I received word that I was fired for not showing up on Saturday.

Because of the right-to-work law, it was the casino's policy to fire anyone who didn't show up to work on a weekend, no matter the reason. I was in too much pain to worry about work. Workman's comp and a state aid program paid all my medical and housing expenses during that time.

I healed and was able to get back to work in three months. Jay and my sister Allie helped me during that difficult time. Jay and I kept in touch for a while after that until he fell in love, got married, and moved to Vegas.

One evening, when I got home, I was shocked to find David sitting in his truck outside my apartment. I had sent him the divorce papers to sign, but he was supposed to mail them back to me, not *bring* them to me. A shiver ran through me as I approached my door. I pretended

I didn't see him. He rolled down his window and yelled, "Hey! Can I come in? I need to talk with you."

I made sure my landlady saw him when I let him inside, leaving the door open. Koda was glad to see him, but she lay down next to me. David wanted me to show him all my music records. He was sure I had taken some of his.

I knew I hadn't, but I let him look anyway. While looking, he asked me where I had been since I wasn't home right after work. I was curious how he knew what time I got off work. Like before, he always showed up at just the right moment and seemed to know things he shouldn't know. He was probably the "witch" in our relationship.

I told him I had just joined a tae kwon do class. He became serious. "I didn't think you meant it when you left," he continued. "I just knew you would be back in a month, but you never came back. Your dad told me to leave because you weren't coming back. Then I got the divorce papers. I want my car back. You can have the bike to ride if you want. Then I'll sign the papers."

The bike was a 350 Honda Enduro, a street-legal dirt bike we used to ride together, but it needed work. He didn't want to fix it himself. He was being "generous" by offering it to me. It would be the only thing I would have from our marriage, besides freedom. I agreed to the exchange; after all, the car was in his name.

I needed to wait for payday until I could find a motorcycle shop to fix the bike before winter. Once the bike was fixed and stored for the winter, I would have to walk or take a cab until spring because I couldn't afford to buy a car. David agreed to wait.

Two weeks later, I drove to Reno to hopefully find a repair shop that would be able to fix the bike. Besides a tune-up, I wanted to turn her into a mini chopper, to make her a lowrider by taking off the springs that cushioned the ride and gave it height—or, in other words, hardtail the bike.

I wanted lots of chrome, including glass packs. The front end was already extended, as it was a half-dirt, half-street bike. I also wanted a purple, chopper-style gas tank and a sissy bar.

Everyone laughed at my idea, even the repair guy. After I went through all the details with him, he liked the challenge and thought it just might work. As far as we knew, it was definitely a first. We made arrangements, and I left him with a deposit to seal the deal.

He took all the money I brought with me that day. I knew I could get the rest of the money by using my gifts playing shill slots. A shill in a casino is a plant (either human or machine) who generates a lot of money for the casino. They purposely win a lot to get others excited to win, too.

All I had left to do was get the title, register it, and somehow get it to the repair shop. I gave the car back to David. He signed the divorce papers and gave me the title for the bike. Then a friend hauled it to the bike shop for me. My mini-chopper was finished, paid for, and back to Tahoe before the next big snowstorm.

I parked it inside my apartment for the winter. I was proud to be able to make the bike my own. Fixing up the bike my way represented my new freedom and independence from David. I was finally my own person, not someone's plaything. I was taking something broken from the marriage, like me, and making it new.

Although I was dabbling in Christianity, I still dabbled in the black arts, mostly regarding slot machines and a few people I was messing with for fun. I felt great about myself and my life.

I was beginning to see how God had been working behind the scenes. I wanted to get back to where I used to be spiritually, but it was a time of ups and downs in my spiritual growth. Evil still invaded my thoughts. I tried to ignore them when they came, but the flesh was strong.

I met a couple who opened a palm, tarot card, and fortune reading shop. They also held séances. I hung out there on some of my days and evenings off. I found it all intriguing and discovered a lot of readings were done based on their ability to read people.

They asked key questions to determine what the person wanted to know or experience. The only reading I thought was legit was the tarot. The draw of the cards was amazingly accurate. I learned the cards never lie, but they also are not definite. You can change an outcome by choosing another path. I wondered why people came to the couple for answers instead of going to God.

I reminisced about how it had been between God and me when I was younger. I had read the Bible and prayed enough to know that if I asked and waited for the answer or actually read the book, I would find answers to my questions, like when David had cheated on me and "killed" me.

Around that time, while reading the Bible, I was reminded of those wonderful days of my youth. Even though I wasn't close to God at that time, I still knew He is God. Even though I wanted to know Jesus, I wasn't convinced I needed him or God to be involved in my everyday life. I was taking care of myself and my gifts in the way I wanted, yet I yearned for the relationship I used to have with God because I wasn't empty inside with Him.

Once in a while, I would call upon God for help and then remember that I could handle it myself. After all, I reasoned, He hadn't been there when I had needed Him in the past. That voice in my head would remind me, "He wasn't who He said He was." I was doing my own thing, enjoying myself and all the world had to offer me.

One evening, I remembered what it had been like to be one with God. I felt peaceful, joyful, and my spirit and flesh were whole. I didn't need or want anything. I wished I could be like that all the time for the rest of my life. But the feeling came and went as quickly as a thought or a breath. I hoped *someday* I'd get that oneness back.

As time went on, a group of us at the casino found a four-bedroom beach house for rent on the lake. We decided to move in together. The rent was cheaper for all of us: two couples and two singles. It had a large fenced yard for Koda.

Although I was sad to leave my wonderful landlords and apartment, allowing Koda the freedom to roam in a yard instead of being locked indoors all day or night was the deciding factor. Koda and I would occasionally visit them.

One night, after moving into our new beach house, I had an out-of-body experience, I found myself on what I can only describe as a lighted grid. The brightly lit lines went to and fro as far as my eyes could see. Spirit beings were gliding upon them. Some were gliding slowly, while others went very fast.

I wondered what they were doing and why. A man glided right up to me. I stepped back, thinking I was in his way. He wasn't angry or in a big hurry. A beautiful white and golden glow around him made his shoulder-length gray hair, mustache, and beard glow as if a holy halo was in and all around him. His kind smile put me at ease.

"Excuse me," I said. "I didn't mean to get in your way. What are you all doing? Where are you going?"

"We are sent to help or save others who are crossing over before their time. You will also, but not right now. In the future."

At that moment, he showed me the future. I saw three spaceships shooting red and green laser beams along the fault lines and volcanoes in Washington, Oregon, and California. The whole West Coast was falling into the ocean from Washington State to San Diego, California!

I watched myself flying on the grid to San Francisco, where I jumped into the ocean among crumbling buildings to pull out a drowning man, who, when I looked closer, turned out to be a dear friend and roommate at the time. I gave him the choice to stay on Earth or to come with me to the spirit side. Before he could answer me, I was suddenly back in front of the man on the grid. "Who are you?" I asked.

"I am Alan Watts. Please, remember my name." He glided out of sight, heading southeast.

The next morning, while having breakfast with my roommates, I shared what had happened the previous night. The roommate I had seen in the future stopped eating. His eyes wide with wonder, he asked me, "What was his name?"

"Alan Watts."

He jumped out of his chair and ran to his room, returning with a book. "You're really freaking me out," he said with a quiver in his voice. "That is the name of the man who wrote this book. He was a famous preacher, philosopher, and healer. Before he died, he told his family and followers he would send a sign or word if the spirit world did indeed exist. You just proved him right. You have to get a hold of them and let them know!"

I got chills throughout my body once more, thinking my out-of-body experience was real and not in my imagination. "They will just think I'm crazy and will laugh at me. No, thanks." I jokingly added, "Well, you better stay away from San Francisco in the future. You know I don't know how to swim and won't be able to save you, let alone dive down deep to grab you!" We all laughed.

Years later, while writing this memoir, I did contact the Watts family and inform them of my encounter with Alan Watts. He was polite but dismissive. He mentioned something about a dancing white mountain goat. My roommate asked me about a possible meaning the white dancing goat might have had to Mr. Watts. While I have not read the book, it describes how, every morning, while Alan Watts sat, he observed a white mountain goat dancing across from him on a high ledge. The daily observations went on for some time, but then, one day, the goat didn't return.

In answering my roommate's question as to a meaning, I explained that goats always express their joy of life by jumping and prancing around, especially in the morning. Mountain goats are nimble-footed, so doing it on a cliff ledge would not be odd, and they are white. Spiritually, it could mean God was showing the joy we all should have for just being alive, but it all could end suddenly, without warning.

It had been two years since I had divorced David, and I was having fun working in the casino and playing slot machines. I convinced myself I was making the machines pay out for me. I would concentrate on the energy coming out of the slots because they had a special energy about them when they were ready to hit a jackpot. I would be drawn to touch a machine. By the jolt of energy coming from it, I could tell almost exactly how much money it would take to hit a jackpot.

I found a partner who would play the slot machines for me when I couldn't. I would tell her which ones to play, and then we would split the take later. The slot bosses and security would still watch us when we played to see if we were cheating. We were just lucky. She had a sixth sense about the machines, too. Sometimes we would feel them from a distance, as if they were calling us.

One day, Dad approached me about borrowing some money to save the ranch. He had borrowed money from some lending company and used the ranch as collateral. A balloon payment was due, but he didn't have the funds, and no one in the family could help. He knew of my luck with the slots and asked me to get money for the loan and property taxes.

I couldn't believe he had put our home in jeopardy. He needed $10,000, but I didn't have enough money saved to help him. Dad called an emergency family meeting to discuss the situation.

I came up with what I thought was a brilliant idea. I suggested we find a lawyer who could help us stop the ranch from being lost by having Dad declared financially incompetent. Then he wouldn't have the authority to sell off or borrow money on the ranch and possibly lose our inheritance.

Boy, that didn't go over well. Everyone jumped on me like a pack of wolves. "Our dad isn't crazy or mentally ill!" my sisters screamed at me. I hadn't said that, but they wouldn't let me explain what I had meant by being financially incompetent. They kept yelling at me, so I returned to Tahoe.

When I got home, I suffered from a horrible headache. I couldn't eat, sleep, sit, or even lie down. Aspirin didn't work. I didn't know what to do, especially since I couldn't relieve it myself. The wind off the lake was blowing strong and was exceptionally cold that day. I thought that if I went down to the lake, the cold wind might help. I stood out there for twenty minutes. I was freezing, but the pain didn't stop. I decided to go back in and lie down to get warm. Maybe then the headache would stop.

Back in the house, I climbed into bed. I was shivering. I took two deep life breaths and relaxed the best I could. I made myself stop thinking about losing the ranch and how hurt and angry I was at my family. I wanted to raise horses. I wanted to live my life there. I panicked. I was going to lose my home! It was all about me again.

I continued to breathe deeply; the way God had taught me to release pain. When I stopped fretting, a quiet calm finally came over me. That once-familiar voice spoke to me again, "Who does the land really belong to?"

I thought about it. "God created it for us to enjoy and take care of while we are here," I said with revelation and sadness.

"He gives, and He takes away. If you desire anything more than a relationship with Him, you will lose both. He will give you your heart's desire. Trust in Him. He is with you always. Remember, you are never alone," the voice reminded me.

Suddenly my headache was gone. I had received clarity over the situation. I thanked God for helping me to get over it. The world wouldn't end if the ranch were lost. Something else would take its place, and it would probably be better for me in the long run.

Evil gets what it wants by lying, stealing, manipulating, and even killing to accomplish its goals. The wicked seem to have all they could ever want, but they are usually quite lonely and fearful that someone will do to them what they did to get their money and power. Backstabbers and swindlers are always looking behind their backs, wary of others who may be lurking to harm them. Dictators and some politicians are good examples of this.

I learned that God will give me my heart's desires, but if those desires are selfish, immoral, or harmful, there will be consequences. Even if I get what I want here in this world, I can lose what could have been mine in the spiritual realm. Then, when I die on this side, I'll lose all that had been acquired here, too.

It boils down to what in my heart is truly important. I learned to accept what happens and trust that good will come. It may come a few years or months down the road, or even when I return to the other side, but it will come. Nevertheless, I asked God, if it was His will, to please help me get the money to pay off the loan. I was instantly spent and quickly fell asleep.

That night, I dreamt I was in the casino, working as a cashier. It was an extremely slow Monday. I was bored and asked my shift manager if I could take a short shift to play the slots. He agreed. I discovered I had only one dollar to spend.

My instincts or Spirit told me to change the dollar into four quarters and play a double-quarter machine. I walked among them slowly and was drawn to a double-quarter machine near the main bar. The energy was very strong. I put in two quarters and pulled the handle. Nothing. I tried again. The handle was tingling, as was my stomach. The wheels went around and around. I held my breath as I saw one, two, three, four bars hit on the center line. Then the fifth and sixth slid past. I won thirty-five dollars! That one jackpot led to my winning enough money to pay off the loan. The ranch was saved!

I woke up and wondered if the dream was a premonition. *Could I really do that?* It was an exceptionally slow Monday; I was working my usual ten-to-six shift. I looked in my wallet. All I had was a dollar for lunch. According to my dream, that was all I needed. I mumbled to myself, "Dreams can come true." I was bored at work, and the dream kept coming to my mind. I questioned whether it was from God or evil and whether it was my imagination or my gifts at work.

I went back and forth thinking about it. *Should I go for it?* I wondered. Not far from me was the double-quarter machine from my dream. Two hours passed, and it was time for a break. The shift boss, who was also the slot manager, came over and jokingly asked if I was still awake. We both laughed. I took the chance to tell him about my dream, asking if I could have a short shift to win a bunch of money. He laughed. "Sure, I would like to see you win. I don't believe it will or even can happen. Nobody is ever that lucky. That's why they are called "dreams."

I got four quarters for my dollar and walked to the double-quarter machine. The rest is history. Even though I won the money to pay off the debt and the taxes, Dad refused to take it. He told me he had it covered already. I felt it was because of the financially incompetent scheme I had suggested.

Years later, I discovered that my sister Lily had taken out a loan to pay off Dad's loan. With my winnings, I paid off all of Dad's other personal debts that I knew of, but I never told him, and I asked the people not to tell him.

My so-called lucky streak lasted until I became a full-fledged Christian. My slot partner told me I had changed sides and that was why I wasn't winning anymore. Well, it seems to have been a correct statement. I haven't had the same sensitivity toward slots ever since.

Once more, I was bored with daily life. My spirit was yearning for a fuller life, like when I was young and had been one with God in Spirit, as we Yaqui believe is possible without the help of drugs.

ON THE FENCE

I needed to make changes in my life, have goals, find my purpose, and set priorities. I stopped trying to find the legendary, evasive orgasm and someone to love as a life partner. Everyone I met just wanted to use me for sex, lodging, or money. I started staying home more often and began reading the Bible in earnest. I had been on the dark side for too long, and it was hard to concentrate on the Word of God. Spirits (demons) distracted me by making the letters turn into big black spiders that crawled all over the pages, blurred my vision, gave me headaches, and even locked me in my own house!

I couldn't open the curtains, windows, or doors. While sitting or walking around the house, I would feel a hot breath on my hands and arms, like something panting heavily. I would see many tiny spirits partying on my bed, laughing, drinking, and dancing. Some even bounced up and down on the bed like kids. Once in a while, they would give me a dirty look as if they were mad at me about something.

The first time I saw a tiny spirit was at the casino. One of the cashiers I worked with was known to be a bit off in the head. I was warned to watch out for her outbursts. But she didn't seem off around me; she was kind, soft-spoken, and mostly quiet.

One afternoon, while waiting for her to count out the booth, a strange thing happened. She was trying to count the money, but she was being bothered by something flying at her face. She said quite loudly, "STOP IT! Get away from me," while swatting at the air around her head. I thought a fly or maybe a bee had flown inside the building, but when I looked more closely, I saw just the head of a tiny spirit flying at her. Its face and eyes were filled with hatred toward her. I was shocked to see it, but not as shocked as it was when it realized that I could see it. The tiny face immediately disappeared from my view, but it kept attacking her.

I told her what I had seen. She was relieved and said, "No one has believed me. They attack me all the time, here, at my church, and even in my house. I am so tired of them. I can't get the sleep I need. I pray all the time, but they will not leave me alone. I hate them!"

"I'm so sorry you have been going through this. Have you rebuked them in the name of Jesus? Have you used anointing oil on yourself and all entrances of your house, including the windows, to stop them from getting in? Have you claimed the blood of Christ on yourself and your house? Why hasn't your priest come to your aid?"

"No one believes me. You are the first person who can see them and believes me. I think I need an exorcism."

"I do think you need help. I hope you find someone to help you." I didn't know what else to do. I thought one had to be a Catholic priest or some holy man to exorcise demons. From the movies I had seen, they didn't have much luck. I felt so bad for her.

The Spirit led me to give her one of Koda's puppies to be a companion to her and protect her. She was very happy and seemed to have fewer interactions with the demons. When she retired, I never saw her again, but I continued to see "them."

I saw many little demons at the casinos and in bars. Then, eventually,

I saw them in my own home. I watched them sit on people's shoulders and whisper in their ears, and then a fight would break out. The tiny spirits would laugh and celebrate. They would climb over the slot machines and jump on the shoulder of a person playing, and after they whispered in their ear, the person would get angry at the slot machine. The person would also violently push people away from the machine if someone got too close or tried to take it from them.

The demons caused chaos and laughed with glee when they got someone to lose control. I noticed they were all over my bedroom. I told them they could stay as long as they didn't mess with me or anyone I brought into the house. We peacefully coexisted for a long time—that is, until I began to change sides.

Despite all the spiritual warfare, I kept reading the Bible. I gleaned promises and enlightenment from God's Word. The Bible helped me to overcome the attacks from my old spiritual colleagues of the dark side. I was encouraged by words such as, "Only the Spirit of God can teach you the ways of God and give understanding, not man," and, "The spirit of man returns to God, but the body returns to the earth. Dust to dust, ashes to ashes, but the spirit and body of animals return to the earth."

All of these verses confirmed the things my God had told me, including what Mom had told me of the Yaqui belief, and all I had experienced early in life. They encouraged me and confirmed I was on the right path, especially when the tarot cards told me I had found the key to all wisdom. The cards never lie.

During my journey back to God, I engaged in a battle between God's Spirit and my flesh, which was really serving and listening to Lucifer, the liar. I would speak to my friends about the benefits of each side. I couldn't make up my mind, and my friends asked me to please choose one. They said they would follow me whichever way I chose. That didn't help me.

I couldn't make up my mind, and I didn't want to be responsible for their spiritual choices. I needed to choose one way or the other for myself, but how? Both ways were pulling on me, and each seemed right to me at that time.

I read in the Bible, "Each person shall make their own peace with God." So, I punted. An acquaintance of mine who belonged to a coven had been after me to join them for some time. I asked him to inquire whether the other members would let me join.

In all my wisdom, I thought that if they accepted me, perhaps I belonged on that side after all. If not, then I must choose the other side. This was my way of not directly choosing. I could blame them for my choice, just like Adam blamed Eve and God for his choice. I didn't want to be held accountable, either, especially if I chose wrong, like I had done many times before.

It took some time, but eventually my acquaintance contacted me. He told me yes, but they were going to test me before I could join. I was told to be prepared for the coming weekend. It was late, after midnight, when two pink clouds approached me. I heard the words, "Follow us," in my mind. I left my body and floated up to the ceiling, between the two pink clouds. Instantly we were flying extremely fast and heading for Southern California.

We flew above the rugged rocky shores, on which ocean waves crashed and roared. We slowed down to go through a narrow opening in a rock cliff. I was curious why we didn't just go through the rocks like we had the roof of my apartment, or just fly high until we reached where we were going and then drop down.

The pathway zigzagged until we came to a large open circle in the center of a giant maze. In the center of this opening was a huge, flat rock on which a naked girl was lying. A group of people in robes with hoods covering their faces were swaying and chanting.

A man holding a knife was standing in the center over her. The chanting was getting louder; the rhythm was hypnotizing. I found myself swaying and humming with them, but I didn't enter the circle. I stood at the entrance.

The man in the center looked into my eyes and said to me in my mind, "Come, enter into me, and we will sacrifice her together. Then we can be one forever!" I was pulled toward him. It was an amazing feeling being in him, being *one* with him.

He shared with me the sense of love and belonging I hadn't felt since I had been one with God during the cowboy past life episode and on the mescaline trip. But this feeling wasn't peaceful or fulfilling. Instead, it was a powerful, gut-wrenching feeling of evil, lust, and selfness. The flesh (ego) was undeniably in control.

We held the power to take life from this girl, whom I didn't even know. There wasn't regret, just a lust for more power. I was all caught up in the scene before me. It took me a minute to notice that I was seeing out of his eyes. I felt his emotions and the knife in my own hand. I was really one with him!

The overwhelming emotions rising up in me were frightening and yet irresistible. When it actually came time to thrust the knife into her, I wouldn't do it. "No! I will not kill!" Instantly I was back at the entrance of the circle and then quickly dragged back to Tahoe by the pink clouds. My acquaintance came to my house the next day and sadly told me I had not passed the test.

I wasn't going to join. I found my true path. I broke the news to my friends. I chose to seek knowledge of Christ, God, and the Holy Spirit. It created a division among us. Some wanted to follow. Others didn't want to give up their fleshly desires or change their way of life.

We had many conversations about the pros and cons of my big decision. I told them they were free to choose their own spiritual paths. I didn't have the right to tell them what to do, but I had found the one way that appealed directly to me and my spirit. This was, and should be, a deeply personal decision.

I had read and learned about philosophy and different religions, but

I liked the concept of surrendering myself and allowing the Spirit of God to fill me, to reignite that little spark inside me. I wanted God to teach, guide, and empower me to overcome the flesh and its destructive desires. Then I could become one with Him, filling that empty spot deep within my soul that nothing else could permanently fill. This also aligned with the Yaqui belief of being one with the creator and all creation.

One friend of mine, Demetri, was livid. "You will be all alone out there where you are going," he challenged me. "No one will follow you. No one believes there is a God or a devil. You choose to be good or evil; it doesn't matter, because there is no heaven or hell. Love has no power. It is just an emotion we have been told is more important than others.

"The real power is in anger and hate. With these, we can kill and rid ourselves of people and things we don't want around us. You will see. You will be begging to come back to this side."

He had confided in me once before that he had never felt love from anyone before me. Sex was love to him, and he wasn't sure what he felt between us because we had not had sex. I gave him a big hug and told him I would still love him no matter what. I asked him to let me show him the power of love.

"How can you do that?"

"I have been sharing God's love with everyone I know. That is what we have between us. Please come over tomorrow afternoon, and I will show you how the love of God feels; it isn't just an emotion."

I invited some friends who had chosen to follow God and Christ to come over and prepare for the meeting with Demetri. We prayed and asked God to reveal His love to Demetri and to us.

The next afternoon, when Demetri came over, I sat him in the middle of our circle. He was nervous. I explained to him what we were going to do. "You will sit here in the middle. Just sit still. See if you can feel or sense anything at all. You can open your eyes or close them.

"We will sit in a circle around you, holding each other's hands. Then we will ask God to let His love fall upon us all. We will become one in the energy and power of love. We won't touch you. God will touch you, revealing Himself to you."

It took less than a minute. I could feel the presence of the Spirit of God fill the room. I asked God to reach out and touch all of us, especially the one in the middle of the circle.

I told the others to envision and ask God to touch and fill Demetri with love. Doing this would let him feel for himself the power of God's peace and love all around and in him. The entire circle was in a state of bliss, but then Demetri panicked.

"What are you doing? Who's touching me?" He opened his eyes, but no one was touching him or even near him. He asked us to stop. He couldn't take it anymore. The feeling frightened him. It wasn't comforting to him like it was to the rest of us. He asked again what we were doing to him.

"We aren't *doing* anything to you. We are sharing God's love with you spiritually. We prayed and asked God to reach out to you in love."

He admitted it was indeed a fantastic feeling, but it was so strong he couldn't handle it. He felt he was going to die. Fear of death kept him from surrendering to love.

I didn't understand. We stopped. I worried we might have scared him away from God and true love. After all, we were new to this kind of stuff. He left quickly.

A few days later, he came back to talk. He told me he had been really frightened, yet he wanted more, just not so strong. He had never experienced such a powerful high before. Deep inside, he was craving more but was afraid.

I told him he could tap into God's love anytime he wanted. All he had to do was remember what it felt like and then let himself go back into that state of being by taking deep breaths and letting them out slowly.

He could control it somewhat, but he should just surrender. It would change him completely for the better because he would never be alone or feel unloved again. We practiced together until he was comfortable with God's love.

As I pursued my journey toward God, Christ, and the Holy Spirit, I lost contact with Demetri. I heard he moved away, but I didn't know where. I often wonder what happened to him and whether he ever found peace with true love, both spiritually and with someone. I hope he did. We gave him a very real point of reference.

During that time of spiritual growth, I would play pool or go dancing and gambling on the weekends after work. I had heard of a guy who was a really good pool player. He was winning so much money that no one would play with him.

I played for money, too. A few people who had lost to me told me to go play with the guy at the biker bar. There were four bars on the strip. Two were across the street from each other, and one was considered a biker bar.

While I typically preferred the quieter bars on the west side of town, I liked a challenge. I was told to look for a guy named Tyler. I found him at the biker bar, playing a game for twenty dollars. When he won, the opponent angrily threw a crumpled twenty at him and left. He asked if anyone else wanted to play. No one wanted to take him on for twenty, so he offered a ten-dollar game, then a five-dollar game plus a drink. There were no takers.

I watched him as he laughed and then offered a one-dollar game or a drink. He was so cute with his pouty face, and he genuinely looked hurt that no one wanted to play with him. His hazel eyes looked blue, then green, and sometimes a light brown, depending on his mood.

He was slender yet muscular. He dressed like a biker, with an unbuttoned sleeveless shirt and leather vest that showed just enough of his hairy chest and six pack. He wore a bandana on his head and was extremely tanned.

I was attracted to him in many ways, but I could see he was a mess spiritually and emotionally. He didn't like rules or someone telling him what to do, which was evident from the puppy he had snuck in that was quietly sleeping under the pool table. I was impressed. It was only three months old and well trained.

Part of me wanted to run away, and part of me wanted to stay and fix him. I decided to play pool to get to know him. He was surprised that I offered to play for ten dollars, but he just wanted to play for a dollar and a drink. I agreed. I won the game. No surprise.

I could tell he hadn't played his best game, and I hadn't either. That's part of being a hustler in pool. He was very likable, friendly, and had a great sense of humor. He also had a deep sadness in him, too. We hung out off and on that summer, riding our motorcycles, fishing, and playing pool. Nothing serious.

Around that time, I had to give up the beach house. One of the couples got married and moved to Europe. The other couple got married and wanted their own place. This left us two singles to find new roommates or go our separate ways.

We couldn't find anyone we both wanted to live with, so my roommate decided to follow a girl he had met back East. I was on my own again. I found a studio apartment with a kitchenette near the beach and downtown for seventy-five a month, including utilities.

When winter came, I found out Tyler was homeless. His roommates had left without telling him, leaving him to deal with the landlord. It turned out Tyler had given his roommates money for rent, but they hadn't paid it. One of them had even stolen his tools for work.

He and his puppy were sleeping in his broken-down car. I took them in, and things grew from there. We fell in love and decided to stay together for life. He was also raised as a Catholic; no wonder his spiritual condition was so messed up.

It was definitely crowded when Ty and the puppy moved in, so we moved to a one-bedroom cabin with a fenced yard for our dogs.

Although I was studying the Bible to find out more about Jesus and doing whatever I could to restore my relationship with God, I still worked at the casino, smoked pot, and went drinking, dancing, and gambling with Ty.

We went on fishing trips on our days off and in the evenings after work. He supported my search for Jesus but didn't participate. He had already been baptized by the Catholic Church and had been an altar boy. Life was good, and we were happy together.

The more I read and understood, the more I wanted to do as the Bible directed. I didn't know any church people except for my ex-landlady. I didn't have anyone to talk to about the things I was reading, the things my heart wanted to know. I hadn't completely surrendered myself to the point of having personal talks with God, like in the beginning.

My flesh was still in control. Each day, I fought to stay in the spirit, ignore the flesh, and dodge evil influences. I was at the crossroads of my life. Should I commit to follow the spirit path or stay on the fleshly, worldly path?

I was sitting on a fence, looking down, leaning way over toward Christ, back to God. I just couldn't let go and jump. Every time I was ready to jump, a voice would say to me, "What if it is all a lie? What if you jump and find out it was all for nothing? You know that if you do jump, you will die!"

FINDING BRIAN

The urgency of that voice caused me to listen and freeze, to choose not to jump. I now understood why Demetri had let fear stop him. I would pray, asking God to give me the strength to use His knowledge, power, and guidance. "What should I do? Whose voice should I listen to?"

I flashed back to the night I fell from the sky because I didn't know which voice to believe. Almost every word I read in the Old Testament was condemning me to hell. There was no escaping the penalty of sin, which was death—not only of the flesh, but also the spiritual connection to God—and the torment of that sinful decision for one's spirit life forever.

I wailed and rejoiced with King David in the Bible's Psalms and was given hope when God forgave him every time he failed in the flesh. Even though he sinned, he was forgiven by God, but he did suffer the consequences of his actions, just like I had.

King David was forgiven because he had faith, the same faith that Abraham, Job, and others had in the books of the Old and New Testaments. They had faith in God's promises. Most importantly, none of them were perfect. They all had their weaknesses, too. The best part I read was that a Savior was coming and all things would be made new.

The stories of the nature of mankind were enlightening, especially the history of the chosen tribes of Israel. It was encouraging to know that God wants to have a relationship with us, despite our nature to stray from His love, provision, and protection. We want to do it our way, to live our own way with no consequences.

We want to do things without help from anyone, even the one who created us, He who knows us better than we know ourselves. In the Old Testament, a prophet said God knew us before we were in our mother's womb (Jeremiah 1:5).

I can testify that this is true because I knew God before I came here. Yet this world and its ways, Lucifer, with his lies and half-truths, convinced me I was wrong. I was convinced that everything I had experienced must have been just the imaginings of a child's mind.

I wondered at the people who lived during the time of Christ. They had witnessed so many miracles, and yet they had still been convinced that Christ was evil and must be crucified. I wasn't much better than they. I had lived an exceptionally real relationship with God, my Father. He had protected me, provided for me, and guided me through many trials. Still, I had left his side, just as He had said I would many years before it happened.

I yearned to have that relationship again. I was given hope. I knew by accepting Christ as my Lord and Savior that I would be reunited with God once more. We would become one again, just as I knew was possible from my childhood and the Yaqui teachings, but this time, it would last forever!

The more I learned about Christ Jesus, the more I knew how important He was for my spiritual life with God and all creation. No sinner can reach the Father except through Christ. When I was still, I could hear a voice repeating the words of God and Christ that I had read in the Bible: "Deny self and let me fill you. When you accept me (Christ), all things are new. You are a new creation, with a new and right mind; you will be reborn through me. The old is dead and every sin is tied to a millstone, thrown into the deepest part of the sea, never to be brought up again. You will be a child of God, a co-inheritor of the things of God, with Christ, your brother, Lord, and King. We all will be one, as Christ and the Father are one, in Spirit."

As I looked back over the past thirteen years, I saw the protection and provision God had done for me behind the scenes, just like He had said He would. I had paid the consequences of my choices, just like everyone else.

I now knew which voice I was to listen to and obey. Words would come to me when I had a problem or situation in which I needed God's wisdom and power. I was very excited. I was again communicating with my Father and I could feel His presence more each day.

It wasn't as it had been in the beginning. I felt guilt and shame for doing what I swore I would never do. I couldn't forgive myself for being fooled by evil and surrendering to the flesh. I hadn't dodged evil at all. I had joined it.

Now I knew I was finally making the right choice. I was jumping off the fence and into the arms of Christ. I was going to die to the flesh and be reborn in the Spirit. I accepted Christ as my redeemer. I faintly remembered reading about or hearing that getting baptized was essential. It was an important part of being saved by Christ. It became a persistent thought in the back of my mind. I needed to get baptized ASAP.

It wasn't easy getting baptized. I called every church in the phone book, and I went to some churches and found the doors were locked. A few of them had answering machines, and I left messages that I wanted to get baptized as soon as possible.

Those who answered my call said I would need to be a member of their church for at least six months before they could baptize me.

(Interesting how that was the same residency time required to get a divorce in California.) No one seemed interested in baptizing me. I was shocked. The Bible says nothing about belonging to a particular church or a waiting period before getting baptized.

The Bible says every believer is a saint, a part of the true, real church. I was confused about this new development concerning my path back to God. I read the Word as it appeared to me literally and how it made me feel in my spirit heart.

I must be baptized, I thought, *or I won't be saved*. I was in a panic. To make things worse, I then had a premonition that I was going to die in an earthquake. I was at work, walking toward the restroom, worrying about how and when I could get baptized.

Since I had been raised in California, I knew what an earthquake felt like. That day, the tremors were light at first. I was surprised but then I remembered that Tahoe was still an active volcano. As the tremors strengthened, it seemed they were coming straight to me personally. The tremors grew stronger and stronger. Suddenly I felt a deep rumble, and the building started rocking and groaning.

I tried to keep my footing to get to the restroom and under the sink. I heard a noise above me. I looked up in time to see the ceiling cracking and falling on top of me, along with the hotel's upper floors. I fell to the floor and looked up, stunned as I realized that I was still alive.

A coworker saw me fall and came running to help me up, asking if I was alright. I was confused at first when she told me she hadn't felt the earthquake. I then knew I had just experienced a vision, a premonition that I was going to die in an earthquake. But when? I didn't want to die unsaved. After work, I went straight to my former landlady to ask her what I should do about it all. She was surprised no one wanted to baptize me. She said she would speak to her church elders and get back to me.

Two days later, two young men came to my house. We had a lengthy conversation in which we quoted Bible Scripture to each other. They felt one must belong to a church to be baptized. I reminded them how Christ and all the apostles had been baptized without belonging to a church. I reminded them about the story of Philip, who, while in Samaria, was directed by an angel of the Lord to go down into the wilderness area of Gaza. There he saw an Ethiopian in a chariot, reading Scripture. He shared the gospel with him, and when they came upon a body of water, the Ethiopian asked to be baptized. Afterward, the apostle was instantly taken away by Spirit, finding himself in Azotus (Acts 8:26–40).

I also reminded them it was written that we should meet together with like-minded people to encourage one another, especially when we see the last days' prophecies being fulfilled. Scripture didn't mention a specific church or denomination.

The disciples and apostles of Christ went around sharing the good news and baptizing, healing, casting out demons, and performing other miracles everywhere they traveled. No specific churches were mentioned to which the people belonged.

The two young men were surprised at my knowledge of the Word. They invited me to meet with their elders. They felt there shouldn't be a reason for me not to be baptized in Christ's name. After all, no one was ever baptized in the name of a church, right? I was so relieved to hear those words. Time was running out for the earthquake to hit.

At the time I received the premonition, I became connected to the earthquake's energy. I could feel it surge and then fall and then again build up pressure. I was told by Spirit it was coming fourteen days from the Monday on which I had received the vision. It was getting closer and stronger. I tried not to panic and trusted that God would do something. I had faith in Him and His Word. Humans were causing the mistrust.

When I finally met with the head of their local church, he said he was sorry but there were rules and regulations he had to follow. He wanted to help me. He made an appointment for his superior to meet with me on the following Friday, just three days before the earthquake and my physical death.

At least they believed that I had experienced the vision of the earthquake. When Friday came, I was a mess. The church elders knew about Tyler and that we were living together. They told us we must not have sex anymore until we were married. They said it was sin in God's eyes and I must no longer sin if I wanted to get baptized. If the temptation was too strong, Tyler would have to move out. We had been living together for a year already.

What difference does it make? I wondered. Besides, I had chosen Tyler as my mate, like the woman at the well, whom Jesus told to choose one lover as her "husband." I didn't foresee any problems or sin because we chose to be together for life, but to the church people, evidently, it was a huge difference if we gave in to the temptation. They told me I would lose my salvation and cause a great sin to be upon Ty. I hadn't known better before, but now I did. We didn't have a problem with this rule; that is, until the night before my Friday meeting with their headmaster.

What if he asks about it? I wondered. *Should I lie or tell the truth? God knows what happened. Does the headmaster have to know, too?* I didn't want to die unsaved!

The two young men came to our house Friday morning to encourage us and tell me they were optimistic about the meeting and were praying for me. One of them patted me on my back and said, almost in a whisper, "Just remember to keep knocking until the door opens." I thought his statement was a heads-up for a possible test the headmaster was going to spring on me. I was to meet him at exactly 1:30 in the afternoon. "Do not be late!" they chimed together.

I read so much into their words. By the time Ty and I reached the church, I was a wreck. We arrived at 1:25! Ty waited for me in the car. The front door of the church was locked. The headmaster's office was supposed to be down a long hallway to the north of the main church building. I looked around and saw people going in and out of a side door.

There was construction going on, and I asked a worker which way to the headmaster's office. He pointed to the south end of the hallway. I noticed bathrooms on the way. When I finally reached the door, it was 1:31.

I could see light under the doorway, perhaps from a window. A shadow passed by the crack under the door. Someone was in the office. I knocked. Nothing happened. I knocked again. Nothing happened. I knocked a third time. Nothing happened! I stood back from the door and looked again. A shadow went by again. *This must be some kind of test*, I thought.

I pondered how a holy person would knock to get the door to open. Although I wasn't in that category, I knocked softly yet firmly. I waited and then knocked again. I remembered the young man had said, "Knock until the door opens." This must be a test. It was now 1:45, and the door wasn't opening.

I tried to hold my anger and frustration in check, but with all the stress and guilt, I lost it. I started pounding on the door with all my might. I even kicked it. It still didn't open. I was so embarrassed for giving in to the flesh. I gave up and went to the restroom.

I splashed cold water on my face and wiped wet paper towels on my overheated neck. I stared into the mirror and started to laugh at my situation. *What a nutcase*, I thought. Only God knows my heart, and He knows me better than I know me. I decided to go back to the office and try once more. I knocked, and the door didn't open. It was way past two o'clock. I shrugged and said to God, "Well, I guess You want me to die unsaved. You are in control of all things, and I have been a sinner of sinners. I deserve to die unsaved. I did try." I walked down the hallway, feeling defeated.

Unexpectedly, there was a loud noise behind me and a swooshing wind so strong I fell to the floor. I lay there, filled with fear, thinking God Himself, or maybe the devil, had flown in to get me. As I got up off the floor, I heard someone coming down the hall toward me. I braced myself for anything.

To my surprise, an old, frail-looking man appeared before me. "What are you doing here? Who are you? How did you get in here?"

I told him my name and that I had a 1:30 appointment with the headmaster. He yelled at me again, telling me I was wrong. "The appointment was at two." He knew because he was the headmaster. "I have proof; it's written down right here." He pointed to a tablet in his trembling left hand.

I could tell by the look on his face and his energy that he was lying, but he wouldn't admit it, nor did he show me the proof on the tablet. It was already twenty minutes after two. I figured he was late on purpose, hoping I would give up and leave. Then he wouldn't have to deal with me at all.

He angrily fussed with the keys to open the door. I wondered why he didn't just knock so the person who was in there would open the door. To my surprise, no one was in the two rooms. In fact, the first room was a reception area. There wasn't a window for light to shine in. His office had a window, but the door was closed, so the first room was rather dark. I wondered what was going on.

Suddenly he turned into the sweetest man. In a soft voice, he started asking me questions about my life and what I believed. We discussed many things. I thought we were getting along wonderfully; I was sure I was going to get baptized. Then he asked about Tyler.

I felt the presence of something very powerful behind me. I wasn't sure if it was God or the devil trying to make me tell the truth. Whoever it was pushed down on me like a very heavy weight and pushed me toward the headmaster. At the same time, a voice said, "Tell him!"

I looked over my shoulder to see what it was; it was so strong. The whole room was full of its presence. The headmaster saw me look over my shoulder. He stared at the spot for some time. It seemed like he must have felt or seen something, but he didn't say a word.

I couldn't take it any longer. I told him Ty and I had been doing very well until last night. I was devastated over it. He became Mr. Hyde once more. "That's it! Do you know we get people like you in here all the time? Yep, you're a bunch of borderline schizophrenics looking to get closer to God. You need to go back home, straighten up your life, and stop sinning. Maybe come back in six months or so."

"Okay," was all I could say.

He walked me out to the car. He talked very nicely to Tyler. He didn't accuse or condemn him of any wrongdoing, as if what had happened was all on me.

I now accepted my fate. On Monday, I was going to die in an earthquake. My spirit was not going to spend eternity with God. I was going to spend it in that horrible place Christ had been in when he had taken on all of our sins, when God had turned away from him. In my case, it would be forever. I was numb, resigned.

I had experienced that place for a short time when I had asked God why Christ had sweat blood in the garden when He'd asked for the cup to pass before the soldiers came to get him. I hadn't understood why. After all, more than any of us, He knew He wasn't going to die. He knew He was going to come back. I hadn't taken into account the torture and suffering of His body before it died, setting His spirit free.

God let me experience what Christ had felt at that profound moment in time. I was one with Him and felt the horror of being in a place where God was not. I couldn't feel God anywhere. It was total darkness, full of hopelessness. For the first time in His existence, Jesus had been separated from God!

It's even more terrible of a place when you know you have chosen to be there by forsaking God, love, and goodness (light), and instead choosing self, the flesh, and evil. You are alone for eternity, never to get out of the darkness and hopelessness. Indeed, there will be gnashing of teeth and tearing of clothes. I wouldn't wish it on my worst enemy.

Christ went through both a physical and spiritual death for everyone. He gave us a second chance. How can one not fall in love with this God-man and thank Him and the Father all the days of our lives?

I was sad and angry. I had wasted so much time using my gifts for things not important to anyone except myself and those whose gods were money and power. I mourned what could have been. I smoked a joint and discovered that I had messed up even worse, as I felt God leave me completely. The earthquake definitely was getting stronger and heading straight for me.

I asked for forgiveness. I repented and promised not to smoke pot again. I couldn't stand having God leave me, especially after we had just gotten back together—specifically, before *the* Monday, my final day on Earth. I was resigned to my fate. After all, it was my own doing.

That Sunday, I went to church. I told the young men and elder what had happened with their headmaster. They were surprised. After the service, the two young men and their elder guided me into a classroom. They told me they were going to ask God in Christ's name not to let me die before getting baptized. They asked me if I believed in the Word of God, and I said, "Yes, every word!"

"When two or more are gathered in my name," they said, quoting Scripture, "I am with them. Ask anything in my name, and I will ask the Father to do it for you." The Spirit of God came upon us as they lay hands on me and prayed. I felt the earthquake leave me. Its energy no longer came to me. I told them what I had felt during the prayer. We all thanked and praised God for hearing us. I thanked them, and we went our separate ways.

The next day, *the Monday*, I went to work without fear of an earthquake or dying. As I was getting off my shift, one of my coworkers came running up to me, very excited. "You were right. There was an earthquake today! It came just like you said, from the valley to the mountains to the middle of the lake. But instead of following the fault here, it went the other way!" I smiled and thanked God again for hearing our prayer. I was looking forward to seeing when and where He was going to get me baptized.

Almost everyone thought I had lost my mind. I quit drinking to get drunk, stopped taking drugs, and stopped smoking pot. I used to get high to fill the empty place deep inside. The Holy Spirit lived there now. I was full, complete, and made whole.

Many saw the difference in me and wanted to have it, too. They said I was glowing and started calling me Sunshine. I was always smiling and in a happy mood. Even when I was in a funk, God's Spirit would shine through me to others.

I was timid in the relationship I was renewing with God. I strived for *perfection* and wanted it to be just like when I was a kid, but I still didn't trust myself. God is always constant; He doesn't change. I, when in the flesh, can change from sweet, forgiving me to angry me, demanding justice for myself, when I least expect it. If only John the Baptist were nearby so I could go get baptized right away, before I messed up again.

Catholic doctrine used to teach that a baby had to be baptized immediately because if they died before they were baptized, they wouldn't go to heaven. It was a way to use fear to control the masses. That teaching must have been in my subconscious (and Lucifer was whispering it into my conscious), trying to make me crazy with fear and doubt, making me believe I had to be baptized by a priest or church to be saved.

I was still searching for a church that would baptize me without all the red tape when my younger sister Renée stopped by one day to tell me she had found the perfect church for me. I hadn't realized anyone else was looking. God does work in mysterious and wondrous ways. She was all grown up now, living and working in Tahoe, too.

While driving home earlier that day, she had picked up a hitchhiker because he had looked extremely happy. She was curious to know what had made him so joyful. She asked him, "Why the smiling face?" He told her he had just come from the office of a pastor who had helped him find and accept Christ as his Lord and Savior. Filled with the Holy Spirit, he couldn't stop smiling. He kept praising God. All he could talk about was God, Christ Jesus, and a guy named Brian.

When she dropped him off, she asked him for the church's name and address and Brian's phone number. He not only gave her what she requested, but he also gave her the phone number and address for a Bible study being held that evening. She had felt compelled to give me the information.

I thanked her and told her I would call the numbers later. "NO!" she said. "You have to go check this Brian guy out. I have a strong feeling about this. We are going tonight. I will drive." All I could do was agree with her. We called to get directions. Part of me was excited. The other part was dreading another encounter with zealots who were judgmental and used the Word of God as a whipping stick to get you to submit to their authority.

We arrived at the house and followed others to the door. A young woman was greeting everyone. She seemed to know everyone there. When we stood before her, she said, "You are new faces here. We are so happy you have come! I want to sit with you. Go on in and find a place for us to sit. I have to finish greeting everyone." We followed those in front of us, who had gathered in a large living room.

Everyone smiled and had a soft glow about them. This was a first for me. I hadn't been to a home Bible study. I hadn't even brought my Bible. In the past, I had only seen stern faces in churches. This was refreshing and encouraging.

We found three chairs and sat down to wait for the Bible study to start. At the front of the room, a small group of people had gathered, and they were talking to a man who, we figured, was Brian. He was younger than I thought he would be, and handsome, too. He was filled with the Holy Spirit so strongly that he glowed brighter than the others. I could actually see a halo around his head like on those cards from my Catechism days.

I looked closer at the people in the room. I could see many of them also had halos. Some were brighter than others, but they all glowed with the Spirit. No wonder everyone was smiling. Brian looked at his watch and asked everyone to sit. It was time to get started.

Everyone, including me, sat with expectant faces and hearts to hear the Word of God. Brain welcomed all and was excited to see new faces. He prayed we all would be blessed by hearing God's Word. Someone up front started playing a guitar, and then everyone started singing.

Renée and I looked at each other in surprise. We definitely weren't used to this, but the song was very uplifting. The words made your heart swell with love and joy; it was the same for the next three songs.

During the singing, the young girl who greeted us sat down next to me. She grabbed my right hand and firmly squeezed it. "I am so glad you are here tonight. I sense God is going to bless us all in a special way. I am so excited!"

When the singing stopped, I could feel the presence of God. The hairs of my arms and neck stood on end, and I was filled with a swirling energy from head to toe. I tingled all over. Once again, I was filled with the peace and joy of God. I longed for this to be back in my life for so long.

Brian spoke again. "For those who are new, this is the time when we wait upon the Spirit of the Lord to work and move among us, either in a word, a prophecy, a song, or a testimony. We will just sit here for a few minutes and wait. Open your hearts and minds to the Holy Spirit and then share whatever comes to you."

We all waited. The Spirit was very strong in the room, but no one said or sang anything. Someone quietly started to sing a song of praise, and everyone joined in. I didn't know the song, but somehow I was able to join in. The power of the Holy Spirit was even stronger after the song. I could feel it building; something was going to happen.

Everyone closed their eyes except me. I wanted to see everything. They seemed to be praying or were just in a state of bliss. The whole room was filled with a glowing presence. My heart and mind raced. *What is going on here?* I thought of getting up and leaving. I didn't think I could fit in with this group. (It was the negative voice sneaking in.)

The girl next to me was suddenly filled with so much power that I thought she had been struck by lightning! She sat straight up. She looked like she was being held up by some invisible force; she glowed so powerfully she looked transparent.

She uttered something in a beautiful, powerful voice. I knew it was meant for me, but it was in a language I had never heard before. Renée shoved me with her elbow lightly and said, "That was for you!" Whatever had been spoken had indeed been meant for me, as well as others.

The electricity lasted a good twenty seconds, but I continued to feel it throughout the night. The girl next to me was back to normal. She had tears running down her cheeks. She was very emotional about what had just happened. We all were.

"Our sister in the Lord just spoke in a tongue," Brian explained. "This is the first time it has happened in our group. We must now wait for someone to receive and give us an interpretation. For it is written, when one speaks in a tongue, someone must interpret what was spoken. This is very exciting! Let us pray for an interpreter. If anything comes to your heart and mind over and over, speak out; share it with us."

We all sat quietly, asking for an interpreter for what seemed a long time. I later learned that a tongue is a gift from the Holy Spirit; it is always in an ancient or unknown language and needs to be interpreted.

Brian again asked if anyone had anything come to their mind. A young man sitting on the floor at the front spoke up. "I'm not sure if this is it. I've never done this before. I'm nervous I may be wrong, but these words keep repeating inside my mind and feel right in my heart."

Brian encouraged the young man to speak out in faith. The young man spoke hesitantly at first and then boldly said, "Do not fear, for I am with you always, even by your side!"

Even today, I get chills and tear up when I hear or remember those words because they had been spoken to me as a child. The promise God had given to me so long ago was being given again. My heart overflowed with love and sorrow for having been gone from him for so long. I cried from deep within my spirit for the loss I had endured and the hurt I had caused us both. He knew, before I even had a clue, that I would leave His side. I thanked God for Jesus, for the redemption I would have through Him and the new life awaiting me. We would be one again as soon as I was baptized!

I ate up every word spoken that night. I couldn't get enough of the Word of God or the encouragement, guidance, and love that Brian gave us all. I started going to the church where Brian preached every Sunday and Wednesday nights. He became my spiritual mentor for life. Not everyone there had glowing or smiling faces, though. I wondered at that oddity. I soon got the answer.

The church board didn't want Brian to teach about the Holy Spirit and the gifts He bestows on a believer. If Brian insisted on teaching about the Holy Spirit, he would be fired. During a Bible study in a private home, Brian told us of the church board's ultimatum. We all agreed to follow the Word of God and him wherever the Spirit led.

Meanwhile, I decided to go to Brian's office to ask about being baptized. We had had a few discussions here and there but hadn't gotten into the nitty-gritty of my walk with God. A girlfriend and fellow seeker who also wanted to get baptized went with me; I was uneasy going by myself.

All kinds of thoughts were going through my head, as usual. The enemy was trying to discourage me from getting back with God. He was filling my mind with thoughts of rejection from Brian and God. After all, I was a big sinner, an unforgivable sinner.

The Word of God came to my rescue; the Holy Spirit reminded me, "Do not fear! You will become a new creation. Your sins will be tied to a millstone and thrown into the deepest part of the ocean, never to be brought up again. I am with you always!" These and many more promises of God kept coming to mind, uplifting my spirit and heart. I was ready to take that big jump from the fence once more.

Spiritually I was ready, but my flesh was freaking out. Dread poured out of every pore. It made me nauseous and fearful, but I pushed through it and walked into Brian's office. I sat with my friend and told Brian the short version of my experiences with God, the Spirit, and the dark side.

I told him I had already accepted Jesus as my savior and was ready to get baptized in His name.

He listened quietly. I could see he doubted some of the things I shared. When I was done, he asked me if I really accepted Jesus as my Lord and Savior. I thought I had some time ago. I was caught off guard when he questioned my statement. My flesh was now really freaking out.

Evidently, there is a special prayer of commitment and surrendering to Jesus that everyone in church circles knows. As I had never been in church circles, I knew nothing about this special sinner's prayer. At first, I assumed that my own personal acceptance didn't count.

Brian asked me to repeat after him the special prayer. Basically, I admitted I was a sinner. I affirmed I believed in Christ Jesus as my Savior and Lord and that he had been crucified, had died, and then had risen on the third day. Then I said I believed His blood had been shed to cleanse me of all my sins, giving me life everlasting to become one with the Father, Son, and the Holy Spirit.

As I repeated after Brian, I felt overwhelmed by the Holy Spirit, which showered me with peace. I was cleansed and renewed right there in the office! I saw and felt a huge bright light fall upon my head from the ceiling, completely filling me with its presence and power, bringing my spirit back to full life.

That tiny little spark deep inside came bursting forth as a full flame. I, indeed, became a new creation in Christ, spiritually covered by His blood. I was now purified as white as snow, just like I had read about in Scripture. I smiled. On the inside, I was white! On the outside, I was still a dark-skinned Indian. Would things really change?

I received a new mind and a new heart, too. I only desired the things of God, not the flesh or this world. I had never felt so truly free and alive since entering the world thirty years prior. I felt wonderful, whole, and one with God and creation again; this all aligned with my native belief that we are all one in Spirit.

Brian told me just to sit still and let the Spirit rest upon me.

Meanwhile, he led my friend through the prayer. I listened to her repeat the words and saw the Spirit and a peace fall upon her. It made her glow, too! I was excited for my friend; we were extremely joyful.

Brian told us that the next baptism was going to take place at the church in September. I was once again worried. I wouldn't truly be saved until I was baptized, and September was a long way off. What if I died before then? Would the past prayer by the elder and the two young men still protect me? I started to lose my joy.

I asked Brian if we needed to worry about being fully saved until then. He was surprised by my question. He looked at me as if I were a young, frightened child. "Everything is gonna be alright. Getting baptized does not save you. It is your belief in Christ Jesus that saves you. Don't you remember reading in the Bible where Christ himself said, 'Believe in Me and you will be saved'? He didn't say, 'Be baptized, and you will be saved.'

"Getting baptized is when one publicly shows they believe and are being washed clean and reborn symbolically by water," he continued. "Just like when Jesus was baptized by John the Baptist, the Spirit of God comes upon you. Some people get baptized in the Spirit first and then by water, like on the day of Pentecost, which was when the first time believers spoke in tongues. Either way, to get baptized, one must first believe with their whole being in Christ Jesus."

I was so delighted to hear this good news. I had read much more into the words, "Believe in me, accept me as your Lord and Savior, and then be baptized to show the world who I am." There was nothing about being baptized to be saved. I had heard the other voice harping at me, trying to frighten me and stress me out.

That's how easily the enemy can take the Word of God out of context to hinder a personal relationship with God, Christ, and the Holy Spirit. I was lifted up by Brian's words.

We left Brian's office full of joy and smiling, just like the young man Renée had picked up. The filling of the Holy Spirit made me feel like I wasn't even walking on the ground. I looked forward to publicly expressing my belief in Christ Jesus in September. I planned on walking with Christ Jesus and our Father for the rest of my life.

After that, I learned how to walk in the Spirit, to serve the Lord, and to use my gifts for God. I learned Christianese, church protocol, and how to interact with fellow church members. I learned that my "gifts" were given by the Holy Spirit and I was to allow God to use them through me in Jesus's name.

The church people called it "words of knowledge." They said I also had gifts of discernment, empathy, and compassion to be used along with "laying on of hands" for healing. I had come full circle. My destiny had been revealed. My grandmother had been taken away because God didn't want me to learn the dark ways from her. He wanted to teach me about Himself first.

I love having His Spirit flow through me, just like it had done in the beginning. When I'm in a healing session, God reveals to me the pain or injury of the person I'm touching, and He heals them. He takes the pain away by relaxing their muscles and fascia, clearing all blockages of energy, strengthening their bones, and increasing blood flow.

The world calls this massage or energy bodywork, and some even call it laying on of hands. In most cities and states, you need a license or permit to practice massage. But then again, one does not have to be licensed to do certain kinds of energy work.

I went to school to earn my massage permit. Consequently, I could do healings whenever God sent me or pointed out someone He wanted to contact. Besides showing me physical injuries, God would also show me emotional and spiritual wounds that needed healing. I guess one could say I was a life coach before it became a thing and people started charging big bucks for it.

When I am in a healing session, I don't think about the time it will take for the body to react to the healing energy of the Holy Spirit; it will take as long as it takes, and I do not try to control God or the person being healed.

Emotional and spiritual healings are done on God's time as well. What seems like thirty minutes can actually be two or more hours! Time is nonexistent during a healing session. We are in the presence of God and on His time. The room lights up with His presence. When we are done, the room goes back to its original lighting, and we are glowing, pain-free, happy, and renewed.

Sometimes a person is healed immediately; others may take longer. Some don't heal or accept the healing. Everyone is different. People's injuries are usually caused by overstraining their bodies, accidents, and emotional or spiritual trauma. Everything is connected energetically or spiritually; this is acknowledged by both Yaqui and Christian beliefs.

OVER-FLOWING

After I was saved, I shared my newfound happiness with everyone I knew and met. Many noticed the change in me and thought I had discovered a new drug and wanted in on it. When I told them that I found something better than any drug and reached a higher high than anything I had ever experienced, they really wanted to know what it was and where to get it.

When I told them it was Jesus, they laughed at first. But when I told them my story, and they saw how much I had changed, they wanted to know more. I didn't know it then, but God was building a street ministry. I was privileged to lead others in the sinner's prayer in parking lots, in casinos, in restaurants, on the beach, and in people's homes.

Those people went on their way to follow their own path with Christ. They, too, were saved and were brand new in Christ, starting a new life with a clean slate. Their pride and arrogance changed into humbleness. They became strong in the Lord, overcoming their addictions and shortcomings. They left the places of temptation and began walking with the lord. Some joined Brian's flock, but most of them left the area to avoid temptation and the insanity of being at the lake of spiritual healing for too long.

I was amazed at what the Spirit was doing in my life. He was using me, of all people, to help others come to the Lord. I was new to this Jesus message. I was more comfortable talking about the Father since I knew Him best from my childhood, but Christ is very compelling and important for one's redemption. He embodied God and showed us the way, the truth, and the life. Through Him, we will be able to have a glorious, eternal life. You really can't have God without Jesus and the Holy Spirit.

I was reminded of this during an evening Bible study. Brian used me as an example of the saving grace of God through Christ and the transformation one goes through. He told the story of my coming to his office, looking like death warmed over, one of the living dead.

He told everyone how I had prayed the sinner's prayer, accepting Jesus as my Lord and Savior. He had been amazed at the transformation that had occurred before him. He had seen with his own eyes my transformation from darkness (death) to light (life). I had, indeed, become a new creation in Christ, just as it is promised in the Bible.

I hadn't realized how much evil residue was in my flesh from all those years and how the flesh had wanted to stay in that state of being. I had been concentrating on my spirit, God, and the Holy Spirit being reunited. This could only happen through Christ and my surrendering of self. I didn't think about the flesh and how it looked to others or that I had been holding it inside.

Those on the street saw Christ in me and called me Sunshine because I glowed with His love, but I had been just a tiny light before the sinner's prayer. I was encouraged in my walk when Brian shared that very special moment in both our lives.

Since I had been involved in both the dark and light of this world, many people came to me to know more. God sent people my way everywhere I went. I started to feel overwhelmed by the people seeking my help. I enjoyed it but also needed quiet time in nature to reflect on God's Word and listen to what He had to say to me.

I would sneak away to my special place at the lake to read, meditate on the Word, and talk with God. It was a hidden place, a sanctuary I visited to get renewed so I could continue to help the lost souls looking to be "found." Once more, I was asking questions, and He was answering.

Early one morning, I snuck out to my special place. The lake was very still; not a wave was hitting the shore. There wasn't even a breeze to make the water ripple. It was smooth as glass, reflecting the sky and mountains. I sat there in awe, thanking God for allowing me to experience such beauty and peace. I asked Him for more wisdom and knowledge. I wanted to serve Him and help others the best I could.

As I basked with joy in His love and peace, waiting on a word of knowledge or, perhaps, a vision, I was abruptly distracted by a noisy boat, blaring music, and the loud voices of two men. The boat came closer. I hoped they wouldn't notice me.

When they came into full view, I saw two men with beer cans in their hands, talking, drinking, and listening to the song "Stairway to Heaven." Seeing me, they waved. "Good morning, beautiful," they called out. "Want a beer?"

"Good morning. Thank you, but no. It's too early for me." They laughed and kept going. I overheard one of them say, "She scared the heck out of me. I thought she was a cop."

I laughed to myself, but then I thought about the song "Stairway to Heaven." I remembered the stairway mentioned in the Bible. I asked, "Father, is there really a stairway to heaven?"

Instantly I was high in the sky, looking down at Earth. I saw many stairways to heaven. I noticed the stairways would change now and then for each person. There was only one person per stairway, and they all were at different levels.

Each step was either easy or difficult. Some stairs turned into mountainsides filled with rocky cliffs, which required careful maneuvering. Some people didn't make it and fell all the way to the beginning of the stairway. My heart went out to them. Some would shake themselves off and start over; others gave up and walked away.

The next instant, I was back on Earth, standing at the bottom of my stairway. I looked to the top, and there was Jesus with outstretched arms, smiling, saying, "Come!" I smiled back and headed up the stairway, keeping my eyes on Him.

My climb was going very well until I heard a scream next to me. I looked to my left and saw my friend who had gone with me to Brian's office. She had fallen off her stairway! I was worried for her. Would she brush herself off and keep climbing? Or would she walk away?

I watched in nervous anticipation. To my joy, she started up the stairway again. When I turned back around, the next step in front of me was just over five feet tall. I knew this because I am five feet, two inches tall. Jesus was still inviting me to come. I kept my eyes on Him as I climbed up and over the tall step.

Many different things happened on my stairway. One constant outcome during this climb was that whenever I took my eyes off Jesus, it became harder. My trust and faith in Him helped me over the biggest, scariest obstacles. After those trying times, there would be a plateau, which lasted until I had rested and the Lord knew I was ready to go on. I learned to wait upon the Lord and not try going my own way or in my time.

At one point on my journey, I was carrying a bundle in my arms and dragging a giant bag behind me. Every time I took a step forward, I ended up taking three steps back. I was walking with my head down, using all my strength to make the next step.

Unexpectedly, I saw a pair of sandaled feet on the step in front of me. I looked up. There was Jesus, standing before me! His dark hair was flowing around His face, and His soft brown eyes looked straight into mine. I saw only love and concern.

"Let go of them," He said. "They do not belong to you. They belong to me. Each must walk their own path. You cannot push, drag, or carry them on yours. Let them go."

I didn't quite understand who or what "they" were, but I did as Jesus asked. I gave Him the bundle and the bag. The next step on the stairway instantly opened and was easier to climb. I was no longer going backward. Soon I was elated to have finally made it to the top of my stairway.

I looked all around for Jesus. No one seemed to be home. Before me was a round platform covered in white clouds with a lovely golden glow all around. As I looked closely, I noticed one step was missing—the one just before stepping into heaven, one regular step.

Once more, I heard the two voices in my head. One was saying, "Hey, you can make that step easy. Just take one giant leap like you did at the ranch when you crossed ditches; you can do it." The other voice said, "No, no, do not listen to him. Remember, it is written that anyone who enters in from any other way than Christ is as a thief and shall be cast out!"

I heeded the latter and decided to treat this step as another plateau. I sat down with my back to the temptation. Speaking loudly, I said, "I will wait upon the Lord before taking any more steps." I sat there, looking at the expanse before me and at the Earth below me. The contrast between the two was interesting. Light and darkness were side by side; it was breathtaking. Meteorites zoomed through the sky in front of me.

I was sitting cross-legged on the step, but my legs started to fall asleep. When I stood up to stretch, I felt and heard something whiz past my head. I turned to see where it had come from and saw many tiny meteorites coming my way.

They were just barely hitting me, singeing my hair here and there. I didn't understand what was happening, but I kept saying, "I will wait upon the Lord. I will not fear, for He is with me always, even by my side." As I spoke those words, the step I was sitting on started to crumble away. I tucked my head under my arms and kept repeating words of faith, trusting in God with all my might. The entire step crumbled away. Only one small piece was left, keeping me from falling. It reminded me of Jesus's words, how He is the cornerstone, the rock. I felt safe. He was holding me in his hand.

Suddenly I found myself sitting on the ground under the tree in my hiding place, still saying, "I will wait upon the Lord!" I was in a state of shock. Had I just experienced a vision or a dream? I couldn't wait to tell Brian and get his thoughts on what had just happened.

Brian told me that the people of God can and do get visions, receive words of knowledge, and experience other gifts of the Spirit. Those on the dark side have similar gifts, too. In ancient Egypt, the seers and sorcerers revealed theirs when Moses commanded Aaron to throw down his staff to show the pharaoh a miracle. The staff became a snake. The Egyptian seers and sorcerers threw their staffs down, and they became snakes, too, but God's snake devoured all the Egyptian snakes (Exodus 7:8–13).

My gifts came from God, but when I was on the dark side, I allowed evil to guide and use them. We must thoughtfully discern the source of any gift we have, asking whether they come from God or Lucifer and who is using them.

I had started having many dreams again, but the stairway was my first vision. Looking back, I see how that vision was a short version of my life. I know more troubles are to come, but Christ will be by my side.

Most people who know me know I am a Christian. In fact, some people I hadn't even met knew I was a Christian. I know this because they told me God directed them to me because I was a Christian. One time, in my special hiding place, as I was one with God and Christ in the Holy Spirit, praising and thanking Him for everything, I was brought back to Earth by a loud noise.

Someone was coming toward me through the brush. I heard a man complaining about the tangle of branches. I giggled because I knew what he was going through. I had found my special place the same way, but later I had found a much easier route.

Finally, a man came bursting through the brush. No one knew about my secret place except maybe the two fishermen and God. After catching his breath, he said, "There you are, just like He said you would be."

"Who said I would be?"

"God. Who else? I have been all over the world, trying to get away from Him."

"Away from God?"

"No! Away from Jesus. Ever since I heard of Him, this Jesus, Son of God, Savior, and Lord of all mankind, I've been running. I haven't been willing to accept the story. Everywhere I go, He shows up, or people bring Him up, from huge cities to the wastelands. When I was alone, I would have visions, dreams, and visitations by spirit beings, all telling me to believe, accept, and follow Jesus. Why me? Why doesn't He just leave me alone?"

The Spirit filled me, and I answered, "Because He loves you and has special work for you to do."

"I know," he said angrily. "I have finally given up. I am not running anymore. I asked Him to prove He and Christ are real by sending me to someone who can explain Jesus to me. Someone who isn't school-taught, church-raised, or a famous preacher. I wanted someone unknown, a regular person. Then I would definitely believe in Christ. He sent me to you. He told me you would be here at this lake, hidden in these bushes at this exact time. So, here we are. Now, tell me all about the man named Jesus and what He has to do with me and my life."

At first, I didn't know what to do or say. I was surprised God would use me in this way. I was a newbie to Jesus and churches. I didn't have that kind of knowledge, let alone the authority. Or did I? Then it dawned on me that I had already been doing exactly that: explaining the purpose of Christ to everyone I had met.

I asked him to sit down and get as comfortable as he could; we might be awhile. I held his hands and prayed aloud for God's Spirit to give me discernment, knowledge, and remembrance of His word so I could help the man understand and believe in Christ, our Lord and Savior. I wanted to encourage him to be all God created him to be, here on Earth and beyond. I waited for the Spirit to come forth and guide my words.

It was a wonderful experience to let God's Spirit do all the work. Speaking what was spoken to me and sharing my experiences involving God, Spirit, Jesus, and evil with this stranger was exciting and a blessing.

I explained how the name of Jesus is so powerful that demons fear it and must obey those who use His name without doubt or fear. I'm not sure how long we talked—when God is involved, time seems to stand still while the rest of the world goes by. The man stopped running; he accepted Christ wholeheartedly and left in peace.

When it comes to God and spiritual meetings, I like to call them "divine appointments." I follow the Spirit's lead and do what I'm told. I try to keep myself out of it; I only get in the way. A great example of God doing things when I am clueless happened in a bar where I used to get drunk and played pool for money.

I was talking with someone, sharing how Jesus had made my new-found way of life possible. As I finished witnessing or preaching (whatever one wants to call it), the person wanted to go outside to accept Jesus as their Lord and Savior. There was too much bar noise, so going outside would make it easier for both of us.

As we were leaving, a man who had been sitting at the opposite end of the bar came up to us. He hugged me and said, "Thank God for people like you. I heard every word you spoke to this young person. We need more people like you in this world!" He cried as he returned to his seat. I was excited to know the Lord was using me in a variety of amazing ways.

September finally arrived. I was getting baptized. Technically, it was the second time I'd be baptized, but I didn't remember the Catholic one. I didn't have a choice in that one. This was the first time I would be complete in my designated duties of becoming a full-fledged Christian. I was full of anticipation and worry. Would I be like everyone else? Would I have the same experience as everyone else?

No one had ever expressed the way they felt after being baptized. *Why not?* I wondered. *Is it a big secret?* I assumed it was too personal to talk about, so I never asked anyone.

Everyone was happy for those getting baptized. They slapped us on our backs and said, "Congratulations! Welcome to the family of God. We're so happy for you. You are going to be reborn today, a new creation in Christ!" I was a bit confused with that statement because I thought that had happened when I had said the sinner's prayer.

I was panicking over being dunked underwater. A few near-drowning experiences when I was a teenager and a dream of drowning when a giant wave from the ocean washed me away into darkness had me feeling uneasy. I had always had an instinctive fear of water, but I also loved being near or in it, as long as it didn't go past my chest. I liked listening to it babble and even roar.

I was literally holding my breath to go under the water for God, trusting Him and Brian not to let me drown. I decided I wouldn't fear, because God was with me, even by my side. We both were going under together. I finally relaxed with that knowledge, and under the water, I went, completely calm but with closed eyes and holding my breath and nose.

The water whirled and pressed all around me, roaring in my ears, washing me clean. I was surrounded inside and out with a warm, peaceful feeling that has stayed with me all these years since. It gives me peace to know that God is with me always. I am a Spirit being first and foremost. Nothing can take that away from me, nor separate us ever again.

I had visited many different church Bible studies and Sunday services over the years, led by the Spirit to go to them. My main place, though, was with Brian, his Bible studies, and our new church group.

During this beautiful time of spiritual discovery, my belief that all Christians are the "true church" of God no matter how many of us there are, what building we meet in, or the name we give ourselves ended up being bruised a little. I soon found out, as I had with the Catholic Church, that this isn't the case for some.

Church Dogma vs. Spirituality

Brian was let go by the church and forced to find a new building for us to meet and worship in. Those of us who believed the Holy Spirit was alive and well followed him. We met in people's homes for a time, until we were able to meet in a local school gym on Sunday mornings and evenings.

Those were some of the most amazing years of my life. Together we all learned how the Spirit works and received many gifts of the Spirit, using them to uplift and encourage each other. We especially loved and encouraged those whom the Lord specifically brought into our life's circle to help find Christ and share His love.

During this time, I learned the workings and dogmas of many different denominational and non-denominational churches. Not being part of any other church than the Catholic Church, I had no idea of the terminology, the duties expected, or the protocols of behavior when it came to praying and helping.

Everyone seemed to take for granted that I knew what I was doing, but in reality, I didn't have a clue. I went to many different churches and watched how everyone behaved in and out of church. I learned a lot by trial and error, which meant being embarrassed a lot.

I went to every Bible study offered in the area. I thought I could learn how to live and walk in the Spirit faster by going to as many as possible. I used Brian's lessons as a standard and bounced other teachings off his to ensure I wasn't being led astray. I discovered there were different dogmas, rules, and regulations.

Some differences were minuscule, while others were extreme. All the churches I visited professed to be Bible-believing, Spirit-filled, Christian churches, but they believed different things. I was really getting confused. When I asked questions at some of the studies for clarification or proof of what they were teaching and demanding of us laypeople, I would be reprimanded or ridiculed.

I was told there was a line of command and respect to be given to church leaders. I wasn't to question their knowledge or their teachings. I was a child to them, needing guidance and discipline. I was often patted on the head or back and told I would someday understand it all and shouldn't question any word they spoke, even if I hadn't read it in the Bible.

The Spirit would reveal to me how dark some of them were, not only in word but also in deeds. I believed it to be the gift of discernment. I was being allowed to see both the dark and the light as never before.

There was a Bible study offered by a different church group that was studying in the Old Testament. During one gathering, a participant brought up the subject of sin in the bloodline of people. They quoted Scripture that talked about sin affecting generations in a family.

They believed someone they knew was being troubled by a family curse of sin and asked for prayer. The man leading the study asked if the person had accepted Christ as their Lord and Savior. The participant answered, "Yes, but they are still being tormented by the evil blood curse in the family."

In my naivety in these matters, I spoke up with enthusiasm. "Jesus cleansed the person of all sins, including any sins or curses passed down from ancestors. They are a new creation in Christ. They might be tempted to sin as those before them, but they are no longer doomed by it. They just need to rebuke it, just as any of us who are tempted to sin or go back to our old, fleshly ways must do. We must remember who we are in Christ and, even more, remember what He went through for us."

There was a glimmer of light in her eyes. The man spoke again. "Even though that is true, one can still be cursed."

I disagreed. "All the Scripture I've read says the opposite. If one has not accepted Christ, then, yes, they could have all kinds of problems and curses to battle. If they were to lose their salvation by rejecting Christ, then, yes, they could have horrible repercussions. With Christ, we had victory over such things, and as a Christian, we do battle against evil every day, knowing that we have already won through Christ."

The man disagreed with me. To make his point, he told a story about a Christian man who went to Jamaica. The man didn't believe in voodoo and was witnessing to the people about Christ and salvation. A voodoo priest warned the man that he should stop and leave the people alone. The priest said that if the man didn't, he would put a curse on the man and drive him away.

The Christian man did not listen, nor was he afraid of the voodoo priest. He was confident in his belief and faith in Christ. Soon the Christian man was overtaken by some unexplained affliction; he became zombie-like and was sent back to the States. He never recovered.

The man leading the Bible study alleged that even a saved Christian could be cursed by something they didn't believe in. He said he had seen it with his own eyes. He had been with the man in Jamaica. I didn't see how that related to what we were discussing. The voodoo priest, obviously, had poisoned him by putting some dust or paste in a place the Christian man touched regularly, or maybe even in his food or water; I didn't believe it was a real curse.

I believe in curses. I believe people can be affected by curses, but I also believe that Christians can rebuke them. When it comes to family blood curses, I know the blood of Christ trumps them big time. Otherwise, why bother?

He was really upset with me and treated me like a disobedient child who didn't know better; he might have been right. He told me that someday I would understand. I was polite and thanked them all for the study. I later wrote down many Scriptures to help them understand they were mistaken.

I went to Brian to confirm my findings or find out if I had been acting like a petulant child. To my surprise and relief, Brian agreed with everything. He advised me to go back with love and a humble spirit, definitely not with condemnation or anger. I agreed.

On my way to the next meeting, I felt very secure in my findings and faith, but as I got closer to the church, I started to get nervous, and the voice in my mind told me, "Don't do it. They will just get mad and kick you out. You will be an outcast!" Another voice said, "You must do as the Spirit guides, even if it seems difficult. Remember, God is with you always; do not fear."

Everyone in the group welcomed me. After prayer, the same leader started the Bible study by first asking if there were any questions. I quickly raised my hand and referred to where we had left off in last week's study. I explained how I had found many Scriptures to sustain my point of view and wanted to share them with the group, with his permission, of course.

The leader of the study said politely, but with an undertone of anger, "No, there is no need to go over that subject again." Then he said, "Those who speak ill of our study group by spreading rumors about us should be very careful of what they speak. We are all brothers and sisters in the Lord and shouldn't gossip about each other behind each other's backs, for one may find themselves cursed and unable to speak at all." He stared directly at me as he spoke, and then he added in a spooky voice, "Remember the voodoo incident."

I kept my mouth shut throughout the study, even though I had questions. I had not talked to anyone except Brian. I wondered if the study leader had taken up voodoo after witnessing his Christian friend being "cursed."

I knew of voodoo strategies, but since he didn't know where I lived or where I hung out, I didn't have to worry. I didn't dwell on it because I didn't do anything wrong. I stopped going to that Bible study. Why bang my head against a wall?

One evening, weeks later, I hurried home to change out of my work uniform. I was going to a new Bible study a good distance away. Ty and I had a large walk-in closet that had a window with a wide sill. Below the window was a dresser. To freshen the house, we would frequently open all the windows in the house, including the closet window. I always remembered to lock the closet window, but Ty sometimes forgot. This was one of those times.

Ever since the study leader had threatened me, I was on the alert for any powdery stuff on my doorknobs, windowsills, brooms, or anything that a voodoo powder, gel, or sap could stick to. Rushing in, I flung the closet door open, and a gust of wind from the open window blew a powdery substance at my face! I breathed some of it in before I realized what had just happened.

It was burning my throat and lungs, and I saw the face of the one who had sent it. Old instincts took over. In anger, I grabbed all the energy of the powder out of my lungs and throat and hurled it with a tenfold curse back at the one who had sent it.

As soon as I did, I quickly cried out, "No! Dissipate to nothing harmful. Forgive me, Lord, for giving in to my old ways. I take it back. I wish no one harm, and I forgive this attack." Fear gripped my heart. I could have killed that person by sending a tenfold curse back, possibly losing my salvation.

I quickly closed the window. I grabbed two washcloths, wet them, covered my mouth and nose with one, and cleaned up the rest of the powder with the other one. I even wiped down all the clothes that looked like they might have gotten some of the powder on them. To be sure it was all gone and Ty wouldn't be exposed, I threw the washcloths and clothes into the washing machine.

I was stunned the attacker had used so much powder. The poor soul must have wanted to kill me. I hadn't gossiped about our interactions; I didn't understand why the attack happened. My throat was sore for a week. It was a blessing I didn't breathe in any more than I did. Evil always wants to stop truth from being spoken.

I worked the day shift on Sundays, so I missed morning services. I continued going to other Bible studies and continued to find that each church group had its own teachings, even those who came to teach at our church!

One Sunday night, Brian was gone for a conference. A different pastor led the Bible study. He taught on the gift of tongues and said that every Christian should speak in tongues, hinting something was wrong if you didn't.

I had always been interested in any gift from the Holy Spirit, but I waited upon the Lord to give me what He desires. I noticed at times that God would give me a temporary gift of the Spirit to accomplish what He wanted to be done for someone, but after the task was complete, I wouldn't have the gift anymore.

I have loved hearing others speak in tongues ever since my first Bible study. Hearing a tongue fills me with God's energy or Spirit and makes me feel as if God is speaking to me personally and causes chills to wash over my body. Church people call them Jesus bumps instead of goosebumps. To be honest, I don't covet anyone else's gifts. I already have enough responsibility with the ones I have.

DODGING EVIL

When I was sixteen, a song spiritually came to me while I was riding my horse; I was filled with chills. After singing the song, I spoke in a language that sounded like Chinese. Was that my tongue?

I've had the tongue a very long time, way before I was a baptized Christian. I haven't been overcome by the Spirit to speak in that tongue again, especially in front of anyone but I do speak in it for fun to feel the awesome goosebumps, and I spoke in it when I asked an Asian person if they thought they could interpret it. They thought it sounded like an ancient mountain people dialect, but they could not interpret what I said.

I was told you have complete control of your tongue. You can use it whenever you wish or whenever the Spirit compels you, but there always has to be someone to interpret what you speak. When the guest pastor told us everyone was going to speak in tongues, I was in, even though Spirit was telling me something was wrong. I watched intensely as people lined up at the front to learn how to speak in tongues. The more I saw, the more I doubted the authenticity of what was happening.

I was still a new Christian and was open to whatever was presented in the name of Jesus. Sometimes, though, it just didn't feel right, and the Spirit would tell me, "No, don't do it!" This wasn't one of the two opposing voices I would often hear. It was God's Spirit.

I watched others do what the pastor had told them. They started out by praying, asking the Holy Spirit to give them the gift of tongues because the Bible says the Spirit gives gifts as He sees fit. *If* this was true, then why force it? Anyway, they did and then waited.

After a bit, the pastor told them to start making the sound "da" and repeat it over and over. They were to continue until they became overwhelmed in the Spirit, and from then on, they would speak in tongues. Everyone up front was saying, "Da, da, da, da, da, da, da, da, da, da." Some started saying, "Da, da, dum, dada dum. La, la, la, da, dum."

The pastor said, "Yes, that's it! Keep going. Go sit and practice. Let others come up." The noise they were making wasn't pleasant, and it didn't sound powerful. I didn't get any Jesus bumps.

The pastor laid his hand on the top of some people's heads or foreheads and pushed them down to the floor. He told us they were being slain in the Spirit and would wake up speaking in tongues. I didn't understand the term "slain." Why would the Holy Spirit slay you?

When it was my turn, he asked me if I wanted to speak in tongues. I said, "Yes, if the Spirit so desires me to."

He hesitated for a second and then put his hand on my forehead and told me to say, "Da, da, da." It felt wrong, but I did. I wanted to give it an honest try.

The man started to push hard on my forehead. I had to brace myself to not be pushed on the floor. I looked him in the eyes. He said, "Don't fight the Spirit. Surrender!"

I whispered, "I'm not fighting the Spirit. You are pushing me down, not the Spirit. I'll go down if the Spirit pushes me." His face turned red, and then he told me to go practice in the back. I left.

I drove down to the lake to discuss with God and the Holy Spirit what had just happened. "Why can't I speak in tongues like everyone else?" I asked. "Am I not worthy of this gift?" I waited for an answer but didn't get one. I started to whine about it.

"Why don't I fit in with these church people? I use Your Word to talk with them, and they don't like it. They are not interested in Your Word when I talk. Yet everyone outside of church wants more of Your Word. They love to hear me speak about Jesus and Your promises.

"Your Spirit is strong in and around me. They feel it and want more, but some church people act afraid of You and push me away. There are some, like Brian, who don't. They encourage me to listen to You, to learn Your Word, and share with them what You teach me.

"I don't want to speak in a tongue just because a man tells me I should. I want to speak in a tongue if *You* want me to speak. I will wait upon You to give me the gift of tongues. Holy Spirit, it is Your decision. Whether it be tonight or ten years from now, Your will be done." I sat, basking in God's love, letting everything go. I surrendered all of me to Him.

Unexpectedly, I was filled with the Spirit from within my heart of hearts, and energy bubbled out that I couldn't stop and didn't want to stop. It came up my throat. I opened my mouth, and the most beautiful sounds came out of my voice box, flowing out into the car and to the heavens above.

An interpretation came with the tongue. I was praising God, telling Him I loved and thanked Him for everything. It was such a beautiful sound, nothing like what I had heard in church that night.

Ever since, it has been my secret. I use it when I'm alone and, when the Spirit compels me, under my breath during healings, and it sounds different than my other voice.

The next time Brian was gone, four strangers came into our midst. The first one came while I was ministering at a local bar. A young man who was new to the neighborhood entered the bar with flair. He swirled around the room and went back out as quickly as he had come in.

A few minutes later, he did it again. He looked like Fabio but finer. He had very long blond hair and a six-pack to match the large muscles in his arms and chest. He was a stunning man. He reminded me of what angels might look like without the toga.

He came in a third time, walked right up to me, and said, "You are the one I must talk with." He looked at me like he was going to sweep me up and make mad, passionate love to me right there in front of everyone.

"Talk about what?" I asked nervously as I reached out for Ty to introduce them.

I don't even remember the man's name, but he said he wanted to talk about Jesus, God, and the Holy Spirit. He said he had heard of me and wanted to find out if I really believed in it all. We talked for hours. He knew the Bible and would quote it to me when he thought I was wrong about something. I would then quote another Scripture to explain my position, and I would include my personal experiences, too.

Impressed, he wanted to take me out to dinner to continue our talk. I thanked him, but Ty was going to work, and anyway, this stranger wasn't going to stay. He told me he was headed for the Calaveras County Frog Festival. I wanted to go to a book of Revelation Bible study.

I said goodbye, wished him the best, and encouraged him to follow the Word and Christ. He laughed and said he might come back after Frog Days for more tutoring and to seduce me. "Not happening," I told him firmly.

When I arrived at the school gym for the Bible study, I didn't see Brian. Instead, there were two women and a man who seemed to be in charge of the study. The man was directing people where to sit. I asked someone why Brian wasn't there. They told me he had been called out of town on an emergency.

It was a smaller group than usual. Those who hadn't shown must have known Brian wasn't going to be teaching. Instead of studying Revelation, we were going to have revelations of our own with the help of one of the women, who happened to be a prophetess.

She visited churches and shared her gift of prophecy. The apostle Paul spoke highly of the gift. He said it was the best one to receive. I hadn't met any prophets, so I was excited to hear her words.

They had us sit in a semicircle on the gym chairs. I sat on the very first seat on the left-hand side of the room. I wanted to be first to hear the words from God, good or bad. She told us to pray, to ask God to reveal whatever was hindering our walk with Him.

I looked at her eagerly, inviting her to come to me. I was ready. Instead, she started on the right. That meant I was going to be last. I watched and listened as she went to each person, sharing what God's Spirit spoke for them.

She said things that were very similar to what is written to the churches in Revelation. Christ first spoke of the good they were doing and then encouraged them to continue in their good works. Then He told them where they were lacking and how they needed to change. Finally, He promised them a reward for persevering.

She was doing the same for us. It was a blessing for all of us to hear and see God work through the woman. She didn't know us personally, but the things she said were true and known only to God and close friends. She was incredibly believable.

I was so excited to hear from God. I wanted to know the condition of my spirit. My heart desired to be all God had created me to be and to do all He desired of me. I ached for His love and approval. His saving grace was overwhelming to me. I was extremely grateful.

She came closer, and I prayed hard for revelation about my heart, mind, and spirit. "Please reveal all that is keeping me from serving, loving, and following you, Lord God. Tell me what I need to do to please and serve you for all my days."

When she finally came to me, I spiritually pulled my chest apart so she and God could see inside me completely. I didn't want to hold anything back. She gasped, stepped backward, and grabbed at her heart.

She stuttered, "Oh my! G-God is going t-to use you in a m-mighty way. He has a purpose for you. He is going to use y-your h-hands in a powerful way!" She backed away from me with shock and fear in her eyes.

She didn't touch me or lay hands on me like she did the others. She didn't offer a little pat on the shoulder for encouragement or any words about what I'd been doing or how I could be better. I felt cheated. I needed more information. The flesh took over and hijacked the wonderful news that God was going to use me in a powerful way.

I should have been rejoicing! Instead, I was pouting and questioning why she hadn't told me more like she had the others. I wanted to know if I had been doing all God wanted me to do. I wanted to know how and if God would continue using my hands for healing or something else.

What was going to happen to me? Did I have any promises if I persevered? I also wanted to know what was so shocking to her.

What did she see or hear that had brought her fear? I tried to get her to explain more, but she wouldn't look me in the eyes and kept moving away from me to talk with others. I kept following her around to try to find out what she meant.

That's when I smelled pot and noticed someone outside the gym's back door. I shook my head, knowing the person was smoking there on purpose to shock the Christians inside. *What an arrogant hippie*, I thought.

A few minutes later, in sauntered the Mr. Fabio look-alike from the bar. He was higher than a kite, full of mischief, and grinning from ear to ear.

The prophetess went berserk. "I know you!" she screamed. "I know who you are. You don't belong here. I rebuke you in the name of Jesus. Get out of here now!" She even started hitting him with her hands. "Get out!" She was fuming, and then she became afraid when he didn't listen to her.

He got very close, inches from her face, looked her in the eyes, and said, "I know Jesus. Who are you?"

She looked around at all of us for help. We all were frozen in shock. She bowed her head and began to pray earnestly. I wasn't afraid of him or angry, but I was saddened that he thought his actions would be a funny joke.

A group of men surrounded him and tried to direct him out the door. He was friendly and apologetic, but then he told them he had come to see a sister in the Lord. He had to talk to her about his salvation because he was a sinner. He told them he coveted his neighbor's wife. He wanted to make love to her.

"There she is!" he yelled at the top of his lungs, pointing at me. "I love you! I want you! I want to hold you and kiss you all over. Come to me, save me." I walked over to them and apologized for his bad behavior. He was trying to shock everyone and embarrass me. He wasn't harmful; he wasn't going to hurt me if they let go of him.

I said a prayer, laid hands on him to heal his mind and heart, and turned down his offer of sex. He made a smart remark under his breath about my hands as he left our little church. The men made sure I got safely to my car. I never saw the prophetess or him again.

The next time Brian was gone, a team of exorcists came to our church. They offered to cleanse all of us Christians of demons or other evil spirits.

How can this be? I thought in disbelief. *How can a person saved by the blood sacrifice of Christ have an evil spirit inside of them?* I could see how oppression would be possible, but not possession.

It just didn't feel right, even though they reported to have done a lot of exorcising in many churches across America. Of course, they asked for an offering when they were through.

I watched them closely. To me, they seemed to be just like occult people. Their energy was the same as those in the occult. When they laid hands on people, they asked them if they felt anything strange in their bodies.

Did they have to cough? That was an evil spirit coming out! Sometimes people would throw up bile or have to blow their nose, hiccup, or even laugh. Maybe a muscle twitched, or they sneezed. They said those were all signs of possession. I couldn't believe they were getting away with that stuff.

The blood of Christ means nothing if a demon can get into a bona fide saved Christian. A pretend Christian or non-believer, however, can surely have one or two, but true believers, no way. If so, then how can anyone ever trust in Christ or someone who professes to be Christian? They would be pro-God one minute and pro-Lucifer the next. Chaos would reign.

Wanting to test their claims, I asked them to go with me to see an acquaintance whom I believed was possessed by a demon, maybe two. I told them I had never seen an exorcism by professionals and I would really like to learn from them. They put very pious looks on their faces, rocked back and forth, and then said, "If it's God's will, we will go. Let's finish here first."

Among us that night was a person I thought was evil. He pretended to be Christian in many ways, but I seemed to be the only one who saw through him. Maybe it's because people raised in a church tend to be more trusting. They didn't know the world as I did. They were innocent concerning evil and how it actually deceives the world, just as I was innocent about the workings of churches.

I watched the exorcists as they approached that particular man. He was very nervous when they began checking him for demons. They talked briefly and then laid hands on him. He fell to the floor like a ton of bricks, supposedly slain in the spirit, but he would peek with one eye or the other to see if anyone was watching him.

They knelt down, telling him he must rebuke the demon of sexual perversion. I was impressed with that diagnosis because I had known he was a pervert from the moment I met him. He tried to kiss me on the mouth and grope me right away.

A holy kiss, he called it. When I pushed him away, he backed off, but he tried again every once in a while. I watched him do the same with the other women and girls of the church. They would giggle and roll their eyes about it, but no one said anything about his yucky behavior publicly.

I told the people who were hosting him at their house that he was an evil man and a sexual pervert. They wouldn't believe me. They said no one would believe such a thing.

I had run into that statement before when I tried to tell someone their son was a physical and sexual abuser. I asked them, "What if someone came to you and said your son did terrible things to them?" They laughed and said, "We wouldn't believe it, even if you were the one to say it. Our son would never hurt a woman. We raised him right."

I had a hard time trusting God to make it all right "someday." I didn't understand. Why not now? In the years to come, I would learn why not now. The pervert stopped coming around, as did the exorcism team. They made excuses not to go with me to do a real exorcism. They only wanted to do Christian ones. They were paid offerings to do those.

The next teaching when Brian was gone was the "name it and claim it" movement, where the guest pastor taught that whatever you want (money, healing, or forgiveness), all you need to do is just name it and claim it, and it will come to you. He also hinted that the more you give in tithes, the more you get in return. He used Luke 6:38 and Psalm 37:4 to encourage us to give more money to God in the tithe basket because the Bible says God will give tenfold back to you! I do believe Psalm 37:4, which says that if you delight in the Lord, He will give you the desires of your heart, but not in the way this man meant. To prove that tithing would return what you gave tenfold, the man claimed $500 would be raised that night in the collection box. God would answer our prayers, he said. He continued his sales pitch by telling us we just needed to claim the authority God gave us through Christ, and we would have all our hearts' desires.

At the end of the service, the money in the collection box was counted. Lo and behold, there was $550 in it, more than ten times the number of people there.

At the next meeting, others claimed they, too, had received money needed for this or that. There were very few healings, but a lot of cash was being claimed and delivered. Not in my case. Those of us who didn't receive cash assumed it was because none of us had money to invest or items to sell. Perhaps the old saying "It takes money to make money" is true after all.

Anyway, we were content with what we had; our needs were met. If God wanted us to claim a bunch of money just to have it, we were sure He would make it happen whether or not we named it and claimed it.

I am still amazed by how Lucifer uses the Word to manipulate and divide God's people. Lucifer is so subtle, and it is maddening to me how people don't see right through it all. Some people won't stand firmly against it, even if they do recognize it.

After all, this is America, and everyone has the right to believe what they want and worship how they want. There's no more shame or persecution for not following the status quo. Even so, some hate others and want to destroy those who don't believe the same as they do. They use the Bible or other religious books to condemn, judge, and even kill.

Since religions became institutionalized, many souls have been lost. Many people have turned away from God, Christ, Spirit, and church because of religious dogma, hypocrisy, and fear. True freedom is about a personal relationship, not a set of rules.

I call myself a Relationist Christian. I'm not religious, nor do I belong to a specific denomination. I do believe the Bible is the living Word of God and a training manual for Christians. I have a very personal relationship with God and Christ Jesus in Spirit. I speak to them every day, not just Sundays and Wednesday nights.

I learned from and follow the examples given in the Bible. I let the Holy Spirit teach and guide me. I learned to know the wisdom, love, and power of God. I do believe the Bible is from God, even though men wrote it, translated it, and canonized it. Remember, the Holy Spirit, not man or woman, is our teacher. The Bible is a great example of how life is with and without God as a daily personal companion. A Relationist Christian is like having a good friend who gives you advice, supports you, and shares their wisdom and love, all without condemnation or judgment.

The problem with blindly following a teaching of a church or religious leader has been recorded in history and even seen on TV. The leaders can position themselves as a type of god, prophet, apostle, or even Christ Himself. Antichrists, of which we are warned to beware, are abundant.

Unfortunately, it is the same with evil spirits. They seduce you with thoughts, and when you allow them to hang around, they creep into you slowly but surely until they take over. Some will wait for a weak moment to jump right in, like when one is drunk or high on drugs.

It was exciting for me to read that before Christ left this world, He prayed we would come to know the height, width, and depth of God's love so we would be able to become *one* with the Father as He and the Father are one, meaning in Spirit.

Evil spirits are skilled in leading people away from God. They lie, pretending to be pious and loving until they get you to trust them to the point of denouncing God or Christ from your life. They want to lead you down the smooth, wide road that ends with destruction.

People forget that demons also know Scripture and are very manipulative. They can appear as angels, but they actually are fallen ones. We humans, on our own, can cause much chaos without the help of demons. We need to have discernment of spiritual activity and discipline to stop the chaos.

We have to accept the fact that we are not perfect. We are weak when it comes to emotions, gossip, egos, and being judgmental. Sadly, I found out that this is true even within church groups. Some groups I met were adamant that a dress code be observed. No pants, pantsuits, slacks, jeans, or shorts were to be worn by any female at any time. Dresses were to be below the knee or to the ankle. Women were required to keep their head covered by a hat, cap, or scarf, and they could never show any cleavage.

I was once confronted by one of the pastors as to why I didn't comply. He asked me, "Do you want a closer walk with Jesus?"

"Yes."

"Then start wearing dresses. You are sinning when you wear men's clothes!"

"I'm not wearing men's clothes. I'm wearing women's pants. They are made differently. Just like in biblical times, men and women wore tunics, *dresses* designed for each sex. I am very uncomfortable wearing dresses; I feel exposed."

"What do you mean?"

"Every Sunday, I've watched the women and girls going into the building in their dresses. The men stand together and watch them walk in. I was surprised to notice that from where they all stood, the men could see through those dresses because the sun was behind the women. This is especially true with white or light-colored dresses. Their bodies have been exposed to the eyes of others. You could see everything under the dress."

He blushed and spoke no more about it.

Another pastor once asked me why I didn't speak in tongues with the others during service. He wanted to know if I ever spoke in tongues. I told him, "Yes, I can and do, but I choose not to. The Bible says only one or two shall speak in tongues, not all at once, and only if there is an interpreter." I continued, explaining, "When all of you speak at once, it hurts my ears and gives me a headache, and I haven't yet heard an interpretation."

"You women are the hardest to make obedient!" he said loudly, almost yelling.

Later in the afternoon, he brought up a topic that wasn't scriptural. He really didn't have a leg to stand on, and when I confronted him a second time, he got frustrated with me. I just sighed and shook my head in wonder at his arrogance and pride. Suddenly his chair collapsed under him. Everyone looked at me like I had something to do with it. I didn't. I thought God was humbling him.

Once, I was asked to go to a woman-led church. It was a church where the men were in the submissive role. It was interesting to observe and learn their dogma. A woman taught from the Bible, but she was the Paul or Peter of the group.

She recruited college girls and independent professional women who weren't interested in being controlled by men. I overheard one of the young girls tell another that she couldn't wait to get married so she could command her husband around, making him serve her every wish.

The leader was in complete control. From what I was told, she ruled the group with an iron fist. She would take over a member's home and even live there as long as she wanted. She would commandeer a vehicle or anything else and use it as long as she wanted. She would even walk into your home and take your food.

The one thing I really liked was the music. They sang so beautifully, like how you would think the angels in heaven might sound. I haven't heard any other singing similar to it. It reminded me of the mythical story of the sirens who would lure ship crewmen to captivity and death by their singing, not that I witnessed or heard of anyone dying.

I didn't go back or inquire about that group after my short time visiting. The leader was arrogant. The men seemed very timid and quiet. They actually looked afraid of her, and even some of the women were, too.

One church I visited was close to where I was moving, though still a distance away. It was similar to Brian's church. I thought it could be my future church home. They professed to believe the Bible is the living Word of God, that the Holy Spirit is alive and active today, just as He was in the past, and that worship should be a large part of services.

It was a good thirty-minute drive from our new home. I left early so I wouldn't be late. I dislike being late for anything because my parents always made us late when I was a kid. I was the third car in the parking lot. It was my first time visiting, and I was a bit apprehensive.

I walked into the building and sat in a pew to wait. No one was there. Then I heard voices, so I decided to search for them. The voices were coming from a hallway. I walked until I heard them loud and clear in what seemed to be a classroom.

I started to enter when I heard the pastor say, "My sermon tonight is about obedience, and I want you, George, to speak in a tongue during worship. Do it toward the end and then interpret it to match my sermon topic." George halfheartedly agreed.

I couldn't believe my ears. They were planning to deceive the congregation. I quickly turned around and headed back to the main door to leave. By then, many people had arrived. When they saw me, they came over and welcomed me, insisting I sit with them.

They knew nothing about what had happened behind the scenes. I wanted to see how it all worked out, so I stayed. The pastor gave a beautiful sermon, very strong and biblical. There was no need to set the stage during worship with the false tongue interpretation. It was clear the Holy Spirit was in him and God was using him to teach his Word to the flock, despite his doubt and deceit.

One Sunday, my grandparents asked me to take them to a healing Mass at their Catholic church. Since I've always been the black sheep of the family concerning the Church, I was surprised they asked. They thought I understood the new charismatic movement that was going on in the Church world at that time and could explain it to them.

I had heard the Catholic Church was losing parishioners to the movement, so they were changing with the times. I was intrigued and agreed to take them. I was taken aback at how the priest was different than those back in the day. He dressed in the same clothing, but his demeanor had changed. He talked and walked like a Baptist televangelist but prayed to Mary and Joseph for help.

"Someone in this section has stomach problems, and someone in this here section has back problems or a terrible headache; God is telling me He wants to heal you!" I watched the people in the sections. No one raised a hand to confirm. There was a long silence. After a bit, he encouraged someone to speak up, to not be embarrassed or afraid.

Finally, a woman raised her hand and confessed she did have a small tummy ache, but nothing enough to bother God for a healing.

"God wants to bless you with a healing!" He excitedly walked to her, laid hands on her head and stomach, and asked Mother Mary to help him.

I had to bite my tongue. He prayed and laid hands on people for headaches, backaches, and stomach problems that, sadly, didn't seem to be healed. He then invited anyone who wanted to come up to the altar, single file, and he would pray with each one for whatever their need might be.

I felt sad for him. I was reminded of how Jesus couldn't do many miracles in His hometown because those who knew Him as the carpenter's son lacked faith. It was too hard for them to believe in Him.

My grandparents went up. When they returned, Grandmother confessed, "Nothing happened. I don't feel any different. Am I supposed to feel different? Will it happen later?"

I told her that sometimes healing takes time and sometimes it is instant. "It depends on what God's will is for you and your faith in Him," I explained. She wasn't the only parishioner who looked perplexed.

The priest ended the healing service with a long oratory of thanksgiving to God. I was pleased to hear him thanking God instead of Mary and Joseph for a change. My bubble was burst when he said, "Thank you, Father, for sending me those Baptist preachers who gave me the gift of healing and taught me the ways of the Spirit!"

It took everything I had to not jump up and yell at him for saying such a thing. How could he not know that the Spirit gives gifts, not Baptist preachers?

I waited for all the people to leave the church. I walked up the aisle to talk with this poor, confused priest. I hadn't gotten far when he turned to look at me. His face turned red; it was almost purple. He glared at the Bible in my left hand. Foam started coming out of his mouth.

With eyes filled with rage, he yelled, "You people who believe in the Bible make me sick! Don't you know the Bible is nothing? What is written in there has nothing to do with today. It is the Church that is real. The Church is everything, all-powerful, the truth. You are out on a limb with that book!" Foam dripped down his chin, onto his clothes, and then the floor. He was definitely possessed by an evil spirit.

"I'd rather be out on a limb with God and the Bible than in your church!" I walked out.

I often wondered whether I should have cast the demon out of the poor man. At that time, though, I was still under the impression that only men could do exorcisms.

I was invited to give a talk (or, as they say in church circles, a testimony) about my experiences with the dark side and how God, Christ Jesus, and the Holy Spirit had set me free from its influence. A group from the local women's shelter, which also doubled as a rehab center, came to hear me share that night. Since they were not allowed to leave the building until the end of the service, they were literally a captive audience.

I was nervous to talk in front of so many people on that topic. It was a dark hole from which I had been lifted. Talking about it, to me, was embarrassing. Yet it also showed the love, faithfulness, compassion, and power of the Father, Son, and Holy Spirit.

Looking over the crowd, I noticed a woman with a demon in her. It had her rocking back and forth and running to the bathroom throughout my testimony. She tried to get the guard to let her leave because she was sick, but he made her sit back down.

I was surprised the demon was even in the church building. I wondered how that could be, but I kept on with my talk. I let everyone know they, too, could rebuke and cast out demons by using the name of Yesu, short for Yeshua, which literary means "to deliver" or "to rescue" in Hebrew. In English, it translates to Joshua, but for some reason, it was changed to Jesus. I prefer to use Yesu, but Jesus is best known. Every believer has the authority to cast out demons, with the caveat that one must not doubt.

After my talk, most everyone went into the kitchen area to indulge in snacks and drinks. Others stayed to talk with me and ask questions. The possessed woman once more ran to the bathroom. She came back just as the last person was leaving.

She grabbed my hands in hers. "Please, help me! I think I have a demon in me. Please, get it out of me. It has been trying to get me out of here ever since you saw it." She started crying loudly, "I want it out. Get it out! I need an exorcism!"

Since I was a guest in the church, I felt I should have the pastor come and pray with me. We both prayed in the name of Jesus, demanding the demon leave her and not return. I asked God to fill the now empty space with His Spirit, love, and peace so the demon couldn't move back in.

While we were praying, the demon came out of her. She cried out with both fear and joy, "Did you see it? I saw it!" She was in shock. I was surprised to see a reptile-looking being come out of her. I had never seen one like it before, and I haven't since. The pastor didn't see anything.

She told us she had seen a giant, ugly, black and green lizard come out of her. She felt free and much lighter than ever in her whole life. After the woman described what she had seen to us, the pastor was happy he hadn't seen it.

Everything seemed to make sense to her now. She was going to change her life for the better; she accepted Christ as her Savior. No more drinking or drugs. In fact, she didn't even crave or desire them anymore. Most importantly, she didn't want that horrible creature to ever come back.

Another church group I visited worshipped pretty similarly to Calvary Chapel. The main difference, though, was that the people were not joyous or happy. In fact, they looked like dead, dry bones sitting in the pews. The Holy Spirit told me to stay. I did my best to fit in, despite some doctrine of men issues.

I gently questioned them when the Holy Spirit urged me. Some people didn't like it, but others did. On more than one occasion, someone would secretly come up to me and say, "Thank God you asked that question. I've been coming here for over twenty years and wanted to ask but was afraid."

The Holy Spirit gave me insight or words of knowledge concerning certain people. He would give me words of encouragement for them, which I repeated to each person in private. They thanked me but were usually suspicious as to how I knew their situations. The more I did as the Spirit asked, the more members distanced themselves from me.

One Sunday, a woman came up to me after church service. Pulling me to the side, she confided, "I had made up my mind I wasn't going to have anything to do with you, especially after I heard your testimony and heard others talking about you. I have been watching you for some time, though, and have come to the conclusion that anyone who worships like you must love God. I want to get to know you better." I felt blessed and encouraged to hear those words.

As time passed, I kept hearing the same request from the area's church pastors: "Pray for a revival! Pray that many will come to the Lord and be saved." This would also bring forth the return of our Lord Jesus. I dutifully prayed along with the others, but to no avail.

One Sunday morning, after a year of praying for a revival, I asked God why nothing was happening. This is what the Lord said:

"There will be no revival until my people humble themselves before me. Again, I say, humble themselves before me. They must put far from them their pride and arrogance. They must stop judging one another and start loving one another. They must stop hindering my Spirit from moving amongst them!

"Again, I say, my people must humble themselves before me. Look! I am reaching out to you. Take hold of my hand and let me lift you up! Now, go tell the pastor what I have told you, and he must tell the congregation. If he doesn't, then ask his permission to let you tell the congregation."

I didn't like getting up in front of a crowd of people to talk about anything, let alone an exhortation from God. I trembled all the way to church. "Why do you do this to me, Lord? Why do you make little nobody me go up against the men of a church?" I prayed. "I am a woman, not white; they don't like it when a woman speaks or, Lord forbid, questions them. Even so, I am humbled and glad to do Your will no matter the outcome.

"The worst-case scenario is that I'll be kicked out of the church and shunned. I don't fear, as I have You and the Holy Spirit with me always. I'm never alone. I know this, so why do I doubt myself?" I wished I was still at Calvary and could talk it over with Brian.

I bravely walked into the church, this time with Ty and the Holy Spirit supporting me as I looked for the pastor. He was nowhere to be seen. I asked if anyone knew where he was. No one knew. I was relieved. I didn't have to tell him if I couldn't find him. I would tell him later.

It was getting closer to the start of service, but all the deacons were missing, too. The Holy Spirit pressed me to find the pastor. Finally, I saw someone who knew where he was. He was having a special meeting with all the deacons in his office. I was filled with anxiety and excitement.

How is he going to react to what God told me? I walked down a hall to the pastor's office. Their voices paused when I knocked on the door.

My knees were wobbling, my hands were shaking, and my mouth was dry, but the Spirit strengthened me. The door opened. Everyone was surprised to see me. They looked kind of guilty, like when a child is caught with their hand in the cookie jar.

"What do *you* want?" questioned the pastor. I asked him to come outside so I could talk with him in private. I didn't want to embarrass him in case he should deny God's request. He refused and said I could speak in front of everyone.

I told him all that God had spoken. To my surprise, the pastor said he had received the same revelation and had been preaching it to the congregation for the past few months. That was true, but I told him God wanted him to tell the congregation what He had told us *today*. The pastor firmly refused. So, I did as God told me. I asked for permission to recite God's urgent message to the congregation myself.

My heart pounded as I thought about speaking before such a large group of people. The pastor sternly said, "No, you cannot. It wouldn't be coming from God if *you* say it!" Surprised to hear those words come from his mouth, I started to object, but Spirit stopped me.

Spirit told me it was okay; I was done there. I was free to move on to another church. Not only was I tested in obedience that day, but so was the pastor.

I was then led to go to the local paper and submit God's message in a letter to the editor for the religious section. At first, he agreed to publish it, but then he reneged, thinking it too controversial. I wondered whether it would have been too controversial if a white person had submitted it. I haven't heard of any revival—yet.

One evening, I went to a church potluck dinner. I took a peach cobbler, and I was hoping people would at least taste it this time. My food always seemed to be rejected by everyone at church get-togethers, no matter which church I attended.

I took home many untouched dishes. When it *was* touched, it was by me. I didn't know why no one would even try it. The only time people ate the food I brought was when I was too busy to cook and brought tubs of KFC. It was gone so fast that I didn't even get a piece.

My feelings were a bit wounded. I figured there was so much food the other times that no one was able to eat anything more. I had noticed that desserts were always eaten and people complained there was never enough. So, this time, I made a dessert.

At the end of the night, the only dish left on the table untouched was my peach cobbler. I picked it up and started to leave. One of the women saw me. "Oh, that is *your* dish!" she exclaimed. "We were wondering who had brought it. No one knew. What is it?"

"Peach cobbler."

"I thought it was something like that. It hasn't been touched, though. You can't leave here without someone eating some." Concerned, she ran back into the kitchen. She returned with a fork and plunged it into the cobbler. "Yum, that is good! Too bad others didn't get a chance to have some. There, now you can leave." She quickly walked back into the kitchen.

I stood there in mild shock, thinking, *How strange is that?* I pondered all the prior potlucks. I thought about the personal interactions I had had with people at each church I had visited. They would ask, "Hi, how are you?" but they had never stopped to hear what I had to say.

It seemed like I was being patronized and not truly accepted into the groups. Only a few accepted me and made me feel welcome. I thought my race might have been the main factor since they were primarily all-white churches. By the time I made it home, I was drowning in self-pity.

Tyler asked me what had happened. I burst into tears and told him how no one wanted to eat my food and no one wanted to talk or hang out with me. He told me to stop going to church. I didn't deserve to be treated that way by anyone, let alone Christians. I ran to the bedroom and cried my heart out.

"Lord, why does this keep happening to me? What am I doing wrong? Why are they refusing my offerings of food? I want to share my testimony and your blessings with them, but they don't want either.

"In my culture, refusing a food offering is a great insult. Brian and a few others are the only ones who have taken the time to talk and share with me, but that is Brian's job as a pastor. He treats everyone as if they are special, and he uplifts us all. Why am I even going to churches? What am I supposed to do?" I cried until I couldn't cry anymore.

In the silence, I heard God's voice. "What is a root?" I didn't answer. He asked once more. "*What is a root?*"

I thought about the odd question. "It's the part of a plant that searches in the earth to find water and nutrients to feed the plant," I answered, "but what does that have to do with me?"

The Lord said, "*You are a root of the vine.*"

I didn't get it at all. *How can I be a root of a vine? I'm a human being, not a plant.* I continued to think about His statement.

Then it dawned on me. The "vine" had been used to describe Christ. As a root of Christ, I would search through the earth, wherever I might be, and find people to become one with Christ. I would be drawn to them like a root is drawn to water.

I was to work underground as an undercover agent for the Lord. Hidden from others, quietly working, unseen, unnoticed. Suddenly I had my job, my purpose, my place in this world.

I was here to help others find their way back to God through Christ's teachings and be an example of His love. I was to teach them how to surrender to the Holy Spirit so they, too, could be one with God and Christ. To help them cross the gap between darkness and light to fulfill their spiritual destiny. From that moment on, I didn't worry about fitting in with any specific group, church, or the world at large.

Spirit reminded me of a story in the Bible that pertains to a similar situation. It was when John the apostle approached Christ. "Master," said John, "we saw someone driving out demons in your name and we tried to stop him, because he is not one of us."

"Do not stop him," Jesus said, "for whoever is not against you is for you" (Luke 9:49–50 NIV).

I would do whatever the Holy Spirit told me. Sometimes that meant not going to church on a Sunday or a Bible study. Spirit would lead me to someone's home to talk and share. Other times, I would be led to speak with someone in a market or mall, on the street, on the beach, or in a parking lot. Spirit would give me knowledge of what the person needed to overcome to be made whole. It was easier for me to be led by the Holy Spirit than to use my intuition.

I didn't care what people thought about me. I knew God was being honored and praised by the works being done through me, by His Spirit, in the power of Christ's name.

One Monday afternoon, while driving from Nevada into California, I was thinking about the sermon Brian had given on Sunday. He had told the congregation we wouldn't die until we completed our purpose here on Earth. I was conflicted by the truth of that statement. Many children die at birth or are killed by unloving parents or strangers. What was their purpose? Was it to cause pain and suffering or shame to those who had done them harm?

Was Lucifer trying to take away the faith and belief in God of not only the parents but also many others? Was Lucifer trying to get us to blame God or deny His existence for allowing bad things to happen, just like my dad had done?

I maneuvered my car around the sharp curves of the road, some so tight only one car could make it through. I had driven the road so often that I was on autopilot. Around the next curve, I came face to face with a stretch limo. Neither one of us had anywhere to go.

The limo driver and I looked at each other. "Oh my, we are gonna die!" I cried out. "Oh Lord, this is it!" We hit head on. I was braced for a collision, but instead, we turned into particles, just like in Star Trek.

We floated through each other. It tickled me as the limo, driver, and unsuspecting passengers passed through me. I looked in my side-view mirror and could see the driver's eyes bugged out, probably just like mine, full of surprise and asking, "What the *$*# just happened?" Neither of us stopped. I was excited because I knew my purpose wasn't finished.

My purpose is to accept those who come to me or whom God sends to me for healing of their physical, emotional, and spiritual traumas. Also, to give encouragement, guidance, and even exhortation. But the teachings or dogma taught by churches, Paul's writings, evil thoughts, half-truths, and lies of Lucifer had me thinking that women were not to be involved in certain areas of the church.

It seemed that men were in charge; the order was God first, Jesus second, men third, and women and children last. The apostle Paul taught that women were to be submissive, obedient, and silent in church unless their head was covered, and even then, they could teach only women and children. The apostle Paul also wrote that this was his own thinking, not a command from God concerning what role women had in the church. The impression I got was that women were a threat to men's relationship with God. It had all started with Eve and her disobedience to God. She had listened to Lucifer, who had seduced her mind and corrupted her innocence. She had trusted that the snake was telling her the truth, despite God's command. No one had ever lied to her or Adam before, so she didn't know the difference between good and evil until after she had eaten the fruit. Adam, knowing the command and having free will, chose to make up his own mind. Then he blamed Eve and God for his choice. Women obviously distract men from godly things. It seems they bring unholy thoughts to their minds and hearts. Why don't they just come out and admit that they don't have control of their sexual desires?

The Catholic Church forbids marriage of their priests and nuns, but that doctrine has brought carnage upon innocents throughout time. Babies have been murdered immediately after birth and later buried in the basements and walls of convents. Priests have molested and raped both male and female parishioners. Religious leaders have told the people they must be obedient to them because then they are being obedient to God.

Women are hated by some cultures and are beaten, tortured, raped, and mutilated just because they make men weak. All men can think of is sex. In some religions, they think about how many virgins they can acquire in their heaven. Typical ungodly male thinking.

In God's eyes, there is neither male nor female. Marriage doesn't exist in heaven. I had a lot to think about and learn.

More Spiritual Lessons

As time went on, I experienced many dreams and visions, which helped me to learn more and understand the Father, Christ Jesus, and the Holy Spirit. I became convinced I could always count on them to be there for every circumstance, even though I didn't always understand the why and how. I knew they would reveal to me everything I needed to know when I needed to know it.

One example of this occurred when I was at a Bible study. Just before leaving, I noticed a black cloud floating in through the door when someone left. It floated to and hovered over the teacher and then entered his head. It slowly moved down into his legs and stayed there.

I knew it wasn't anything good. It gave me a headache and a thick, heavy feeling in my whole body, especially my legs. The person didn't act like he felt anything, although he did look like he didn't feel well.

As I was leaving, I stopped and asked him if he was okay. He thought he was coming down with something. The flu was going around. I laid hands on his head and shoulder and silently prayed for the headache and the flu to be taken away. It troubled me. *What did it mean? Was I supposed to do more than I did? Should I have told him what I saw?*

A few days later, I heard through the grapevine that the Bible study leader was in the hospital. I felt awful. Perhaps I was supposed to have stopped it from happening. Why else had I seen it? Spirit didn't say anything.

I was so used to keeping quiet about things I could see. Many Christians were frightened of me, thinking I wasn't of God and Spirit but a psychic of the devil himself. I receive the same reactions to this day. It gives me just a little taste of what Jesus went through with the religious groups of his day. Even those who heard everything he taught and who witnessed him heal, cast out demons, and raise the dead still turned against him.

Seducing spirits are everywhere, working hard to deceive us and lead us away from God. We all are susceptible. That is why we should be knowledgeable of His Word, have discernment, and be filled with the Holy Spirit. Ask the Spirit of God to teach you.

Speaking of Spirit, I was being urged to go to the hospital and tell the person what I had seen, touch his legs, and pray for healing. The Lord told me it was going to be a slow healing, not an instant one. Still, I did as the Spirit told me.

On the way there, condemning thoughts came to mind, making me feel worse than I already did. The voice was telling me I was a terrible person for not speaking up earlier. Everyone could have prayed together and cast it away. The poor guy would now be paralyzed forever, and it was all my fault.

I almost didn't go into the hospital. I was embarrassed, and I was scared that he and his wife would chase me out for not speaking up in the first place or that they wouldn't believe my incredible story. I don't know what I must have looked like that afternoon, apologizing for not saying anything about a dark floating cloud that night.

I asked if he would let me lay hands on his legs and pray for healing.

I felt flushed, and my hands were sweaty and shaking. After all, it was the first time I had revealed one of my gifts and the first time laying on of hands for someone in my church family alone.

He and his wife were polite, although they looked a bit incredulous and didn't know what to make of it all. God was preparing them both for something in the future, and only time would reveal what, where, and how. I was surprised when they told others about what I had seen and done. I thought it would be kept between God and us.

Soon brethren were coming up to me and asking me to please tell them if I were to see any black clouds over them or going into them. I promised I would. In time, the man was able to walk and lead worship again, and he even became our assistant pastor. He and his wife now have a ministry of their own in another country.

Another frustrating demon experience occurred when a man who had a demon attacking him asked for healing or an exorcism. "Just please, somebody, get rid of it," he begged. The demon was causing seizures, and the man asked for help at Sunday services and Bible studies.

Many people had laid hands on and prayed for him, but nothing seemed to work. It was a Sunday afternoon when I was first asked to be a part of helping the person. I didn't feel or see any presence of a demon.

I asked him what would happen when he was attacked. He said it usually snuck up on him, but lately, he could feel it coming from a distance. Then it would go into him and take over his body.

"Good!" I said. Those present looked astonished at my outburst. I continued: "Then you can stop it from getting into you. When you feel it coming, start rebuking it in the name of Jesus. Cover yourself, the house, and room you are in with the blood of Christ Jesus and proclaim your faith. You belong to Jesus. Nothing can take you away from Him nor possess you. Stand firm on the Word of God." He promised to do it the next time it came.

He reported the next Sunday that it had worked; he praised the Lord. A few days later, he called and told me it was coming more often than before.

"Did it get in?" I asked.

"Almost!"

He told me it was coming at that moment and he was afraid. I told him not to be afraid and to command it to go away as he had done before. I prayed for and with him, asking God to rebuke it in the name of Jesus. It was a long battle, but it didn't get in. He told me he was tired, getting a headache, and wanted to go to bed, but he wanted me to continue to pray against the demon.

I agreed to pray often. This went on for some time. The man would tell us that God had saved him and then that He hadn't. It was back and forth. There wasn't a real victory. The Holy Spirit led me to concentrate on the entity only, leaving the person out of my prayers. I had touched its energy or life force when it tried to enter him during the phone battle. I knew when it was around. I felt rage from the demon when I prayed in Jesus's name, directly commanding it to end its oppression and possession.

The man began acting differently. He had suddenly accepted his fate, saying he was never going to be unfettered from the demon. He was going to have to keep looking for the certain someone God had told him would someday set him free. Sadly, he said that someone wasn't at that church, so he said he must move on.

"What?" I blurted out.

He told me to stop praying, that the demon was furious and attacking more often than before.

"Don't give up," I told him. "This is good news. It means we are making progress. We must continue to rebuke it together." He declined. I was confused but did as he asked.

One night sometime later, he called me in distress. "Pray for me!" he insisted. I did immediately. As I was praying in Jesus's name, asking and sending God's love, protection, and power to get rid of the demon, "it" suddenly appeared before me.

It was a most unexpected-looking creature. It looked like a big wad of pink bubblegum, slimy, with spit dripping from it. "Leave us alone!" it screamed. "We have a pact. He doesn't want to be freed any more than I. Stop praying. You are wasting your time and energy. He will never let me go."

"Even so, I command you to leave him and my house in Jesus's name and never come back."

It turned red like the Catholic priest's face. As it left, it yelled, "You don't understand! We can't be separated. Stop, STOP!" It disappeared just like the man. He moved away shortly after that night's spiritual battle. I don't know what happened to him.

As I came across others like him, I discovered I didn't have to "do" anything except pray for God's will to be done concerning any person or situation. I also learned that epilepsy and seizures aren't always a demon. They are caused by actual medical issues, too.

༄ ♦ ༄

A profound revelation happened on a trip to Sedona, Arizona. A friend wanted me to see a psychic there, but I didn't. She kept insisting that the "best of the best" psychics were there. I told her most were not of God's Spirit and it would be a waste of time and money.

God advises us not to go to anyone who claims to talk with dead people or tell fortunes. He said, "Let no one be found among you who sacrifices his son or daughter in the fire, who practices divination or sorcery, interprets omens, engages in witchcraft, or casts spells, or is a medium or spiritist who consults the dead" (Deuteronomy 18:10–11 NIV). There are too many Scriptures to list here, but I hope you get my point.

While driving through a deep canyon, I happened to catch a glimpse of a giant spirit being standing on a mountaintop. He looked like a warrior angel. There was a huge sword in his hand. I'm not sure if he knew I could see him, but he suddenly flew into the air and came down the mountainside and into the canyon like a wind devil (a small twister). He crossed the road in front of our car, hit a tree with his sword, and knocked it across the road, blocking all traffic!

My friend slammed on the brakes when I yelled, "STOP!" The tree would have hit us if she had kept going. I told her what I had seen. She thought she had seen it, too, when it had crossed the road before the tree had come down. Both lanes of the road were blocked. Everyone just sat in their vehicles, looking at the tree. I thought that someone didn't want me to see a psychic, either, but which side?

I left the car and walked up to the tree. I noticed it was perfectly balanced over the guardrail, making it possible to push the tree sideways and off the road. I pushed. My friend got out of the car to help me. Then some men came to help push, too. Before long, the tree was out of the way, and traffic in both lanes began moving.

I jokingly told her I wasn't supposed to see a psychic. An angel and a tree had been sent to block the way. Despite my negative ranting, she continued to the psychic center.

She and I picked one that we felt looked real. I went upstairs to his room. He was pleasant and asked what he could do for me. I told him I didn't know. After all, he was the psychic, not me.

He was taken aback but accepted my challenge. He held my hands and closed his eyes. To my surprise, he prayed to God, asking for knowledge of me. He opened his eyes and then told me I had been stuck in my walk with God. I wanted to know where to go from here concerning our relationship. I wasn't sure what I was supposed to do.

At that particular time, those words were true. With a knowing smile, he said, "You made a deal with the elders, and they are calling in their marker."

"What elders? What deal?"

"You know who and what it is. I'm not going to tell you. I will say you have to take better care of your physical health. You must be able to do what you're supposed to do concerning the elders." He laughed, gave me a big hug, and said, "Good luck!"

This new startling information put me in a soul-searching, mind-bending state of being. Over and over, I asked God about the deal. Who was it with? When did I make it? He was silent. I didn't receive an answer until weeks after I got back home.

One night, after I prayed again, asking what the deal was all about, I had a dream or traveled back in time. I was a young spirit, observing a group of older spirit beings. I realized I was the younger, prideful, judgmental spirit who was going to show everyone how easy it was to be both human and spirit.

Yep, no problem. HA! What a mess I had made in my life, both spiritually and physically, but by the grace and power of God, I was making progress. It hadn't been easy. Wow, what an adventure! How reassuring it has been to have the memory of why I have come here.

I began this life filled with boundless love and wonder, and then evil and the world stripped it all away. I became filled with hate, revenge, pride, and arrogance. I became self-centered and judgmental...even evil. I was then forgiven, renewed, and reborn into spirit and love. I now can live and walk with God through Christ Jesus, the One Who Knows, in Spirit, even though the whole universe may turn against me.

I again learned that anyone who believes and surrenders to God, Christ, and the Holy Spirit is truly free indeed. Lucifer had to put in his two cents' worth, too. I was feeling so safe that I had forgotten how sneaky he is in worming his way into my thoughts. Before I knew it, I was free to do *anything* as long as it didn't take God's place in my life or have control over me.

For instance, I was invited to play in a women's poker tournament. I liked playing poker. In the past, I hadn't had enough free time or money to play as often as I would have liked. The entry fee wasn't expensive. I could afford to play, and even lose. I knew it would be a lot of fun.

In Christ, I was free to play because gambling had no hold on me. That particular week, I had nothing else to do. I was on vacation. The tournament started Thursday night and finished on Saturday, so I wouldn't miss church. No one would know outside of the casino workers and other players. No harm, no foul. I did pretty well. I ended up on the final table of five and ultimately came in fourth place. Payouts only went through third place, but I had a blast and didn't mind losing.

Little did I know, but my picture ended up in the local Sunday newspaper! It let the whole world know I had participated in a poker tournament. I knew I hadn't done anything wrong. I wasn't worried or embarrassed, but "my freedom" caused a young man from my church to misunderstand and stumble.

The young man came up to me at church that Sunday. He was happy and grateful for my showing him a Christian could gamble, that it wasn't sinful. I was surprised he knew of it until he showed me my picture in the paper. There I was, the queen of spades!

He confessed his addiction to gambling, how it had destroyed his life and how guilty and depressed he felt whenever he thought about or went gambling. He was trying hard to stop, and then he saw I did it, too. It was a relief to him to know he didn't have to feel guilty or alone.

I shared my past temptation with gambling and how God had helped me to not be obsessed with gambling. I told him I had asked God outright, "Father, is it a sin for me to gamble?" God had answered, "It is to Me as if you are going to another god."

I had been shocked and ashamed by God's answer. To make God feel or think I was going to some other god broke my heart. In my mind and heart, I thought God had been allowing me to win. When I lost, Lucifer took advantage of my greed and told me to keep playing to get it back plus more. It was a vicious circle. But it was easy for me to quit being tempted or obsessive about gambling after that eye-opening conversation with God.

Scripture tells us we all have our own measure of faith. I now have the faith to know gambling is not a sin to me because I was set free from that bondage. I have discipline now. Even so, my actions shouldn't cause a brother or sister to stumble because of their lack of faith or understanding.

If anything takes the place of God in my life, it is sin. If I have doubt or am just not sure it is sin, then it is sin. The apostle Paul wrote to the Corinthian church, "I have the right to do anything, but not everything is beneficial" (1 Corinthians 6:12 NIV). Moderation is the key; the alternative is abstinence. If it is troublesome or keeps me from being closer to God, I stay away from it. Nothing this world offers is worth losing my spiritual relationship of peace, joy, hope, and love, which only God can give for eternity, not just here and now.

The young man listened and seemed to understand. He decided to leave the area and the temptation. I do not know what happened with him. Only God knows the hearts and minds of man. I hope and pray he made his peace with God and became victorious over his weakness.

I continued having dreams and visions. I would share them with Brian, who would occasionally ask me to share one with the church during a Sunday night service. I ran everything I experienced past him to make sure I wasn't wandering off the path into unbiblical areas.

I didn't want to be fooled into serving the other side. Because of my past experiences in being led astray, I didn't trust myself. I was afraid instead of having faith. I had to figure it out. Brian told me I couldn't stay on that merry-go-round of doubt. I had to reach for the golden ring of faith, grab it, and hold on tight.

True Love and Marriage

Ty and I married in a chapel on the Nevada side of the lake. It was the first ceremony ever to start and end on time. My parents and grandparents missed it. They were late, as usual. We passed them on the highway as we were headed for the reception, which was supposed to be an intimate affair of family and close friends.

The word had gotten out that we had married and the reception was being held at a nearby public park. We didn't know so many people knew of us. The park was overrun by people we knew but hadn't invited. We had to get more food and drinks to feed all who came. We didn't have the heart to turn them away; besides, it was a public park.

God provided the money, drinks, and food. It was like the story of a wedding feast in the Bible but in reverse. Instead of no one showing up who *was* invited, we had everyone showing up who wasn't invited. We all had a wonderful time and were blessed by all who came to wish us well.

Some people didn't think our marriage would last. And since we lived in a gambling area, some even bet on it. The odds were two to one we wouldn't make it past a year. I was saddened, but I remembered the discussion my mom and I had had.

When I told her about my true feelings for Ty and how there might be some red flags for us to deal with down the road, she was glad, but confided, "What's more important, though, are the things you don't like." She told me to consider the things that bothered me about him because I would have to live with them for the rest of my life.

"Those things," she insisted, "will never change. Especially the little things, like leaving the toilet seat up, leaving the cap off the toothpaste tube, or leaving peanut butter and jelly to harden on a knife. Does he leave shoes and clothes lying on the floor? Does he walk in front of you or behind instead of with you? Does he eat noisily, fart, burp, or talk loudly? If you can forgive all those aggravations for a lifetime, then all the rest is gravy. If you can't, then you will be resentful toward him for the rest of your life. How can either of you be happy or last?"

I pondered and prayed on those things. Some were very hurtful to me, but the hurt could have been my baggage from past relationships. The worst one for me was how he wouldn't tell me where he was going or what he was going to do but I had to tell him everything. That brought flashbacks to the days of David. I wondered if it was a white man thing. I didn't know any native men with whom to compare this behavior.

Tyler's mood changes were also hard to handle, but I thought I knew where they were coming from and why. I felt confident we could get through them with God's help.

Being told I could never have children again meant it would be just the two of us dealing with the ups and downs of life and our red-flag behaviors. God told me to love him through everything and to stay with him no matter what. I thought it would be easy to do with God's help, and it was until, at times, it wasn't.

DODGING EVIL

In our fourth year of marriage, we discovered Ty was bipolar. He had been having manic episodes, not just being a weird, irrational, sometimes mean jerk. In year five, we became pregnant. A miracle! This brought an unanticipated dynamic.

Being pregnant, I decided not to work in the casino. Then Ty lost his job, and we decided to move to the ranch. We sold our motorcycles and packed up our belongings and the dogs; it was time to leave the lake. We had overstayed our time for spiritual healing. The baby was due sometime in late April to mid-May. We left the lake mid-September, hopefully in time to get enough wood stored for the winter. We would drive to Brian's church, which had been named Calvary Chapel of Truckee, every other week.

I was terrified to go through the same horrible pain and suffering I'd had with my first child. I prayed not to have to go through it again. As the time came closer, I threw myself at the mercy of God. I trusted that whatever was coming, God would get me through it. I tried not to dwell on it.

As the due date neared, I was told to go in for a checkup on a Saturday afternoon. To my surprise, the doctor on duty was the same one who had stood at the window and looked for the three wise men long ago. I wasn't having any pain or contractions, but when the doctor checked me, he told me I was in labor and it might be breech.

They called my new doctor and hooked me up to a machine to keep track of the contractions. My sister Renée had delivered a breech baby, and she advised, "NEVER do it. Get a cesarean!" So, when my new, young doctor asked whether it was okay for him to do a cesarean, I said, "Sure. Let's do it!" Under my breath, I said, "Thank you, Father, for answering my prayer." I didn't have to go through another horrendous, painful experience.

This brings us back to where we began.

I don't know how long I was out, but I woke up because I felt the baby being pulled out of me. I was afraid they would take him away like the first time. I panicked. I spiritually opened my eyes. I saw him being pulled out and whisked away by someone. I feared I would never see him again. My heart was broken, and darkness enveloped me once more.

I woke up alone. A nurse came into my room. "Good, you're awake. Would you like to try nursing your son?"

"YES!" I could barely control myself as I anxiously waited for her to return with our son. She laid him in my arms and showed me how to nurse him. Then she made sure we were connected and left us alone.

I wondered where Ty was, but then I noticed it was two in the morning. He must have gone home to get things ready for the baby. I had gone into the operating room around six at night. Wow! I had been out for a long time. Ty must have held our son before me.

Overwhelming emotions came boiling up from the depths of my soul as I held our son in my arms, against my breast. They were both amazing and horrible. The feelings overflowed into waves of unbearable love so strong I thought I would burst into a million pieces. At the same time, it brought up the loss of never having the chance to touch or bond with my firstborn. It hurt as much as the love I was feeling. The feelings of overwhelming love and devastating loss caused me to break down. I cried my heart out for both.

I was sobbing and wailing so much that the nurse came in, worried something horrible had happened. She asked me what was wrong, but I was embarrassed to tell her about the lost love of my firstborn. She kept asking, telling me she wouldn't tell anyone. I told her I was joyous for my newborn son, but I was also mourning my firstborn son. I had never gotten the chance to mourn his loss. I had stuffed all the emotions down deep in my soul, and now they were coming out.

I had to face them now to be able to go forward and love our son completely. No more hidden guilt and shame. I was being cleansed and healed by love. She said she empathized with me, but it wasn't good to nurse when so upset. She took my son back to the nursery, making me cry even more. I couldn't stop the deep-soul, gut-wrenching crying.

I was making so much noise that a doctor asked the nurse what was wrong. She told him! (Another liar!) He crudely said, "What the hell is wrong with her? Why cry about the past when she has one now? Give her a sedative so we all can get some sleep." They just didn't have a clue what it felt like to lose a child.

Even more amazing, two years later, when our son Aaron (which means miracle) was talking, he said, "I wuv you, Mommy! Remember when I was bornded? When I looked down and saw you, I was sad. I thought I would never see you again." He ran to me and gave me a big hug and kiss! His words revealed to me that he, indeed, had the family gifts.

Our marriage was and still is a roller coaster ride of emotions, commitment, loyalty, forgiveness, and pure, unconditional love. We are at this moment enjoying our forty-third year of marriage. As I look back over the years, I remember the first prayer I lifted up to God. I asked Him to give me the ability to love and forgive as He does. I asked for it because I really wanted to be like Him.

I discovered that for me to be able to love and forgive as God does, I would have to go through many gut-wrenching moments of betrayals and disappointments. I would have to be tested to my core and experience something like birth pains before coming out on the other side and being able to love and forgive just like God.

I would never have been able to do it without the power of the Holy Spirit and the encouragement of Brian and God's Word to hang in there and just love. I had a hard time forgiving others, let alone my husband. It was difficult for me to forgive Ty because he self-medicated with drugs and alcohol. He would treat me with disrespect as a wife and a woman. He would call and say he was on his way home but then forget to come home.

Worried, I would go looking for him and find him in the arms of another woman, dancing, drinking, and gambling. When I would ask him anything, he would say, "Why? You writing a book? Leave this chapter out." He constantly accused me of being too honest.

The others I had a hard time forgiving were neighbors, coworkers, family, the person who cut me off and caused me to go off the road, and even so-called Christians. They were mean, dishonest, selfish, abusive, and liars.

My heart ached with the sorrow I felt for *myself*. I asked God to make Ty and the others realize they were wrong in their thinking and deeds.

God answered me by saying, "You must forgive them."

"I just can't on my own, Lord. I give Tyler and them to You to forgive. I just can't right now."

"Yes, you can. See them as I see them."

I was surprised by what God showed me. Tyler and the others suddenly all looked sad, lonely, and fearful. Poor, lost souls, my heart went out to them all.

"See! They do not know or have not been shown love. They don't have me. How can you expect them to be any different? Forgive and love them as yourself." That revealed another problem. I didn't love myself. I hadn't forgiven myself.

I learned to be careful for what I asked. For instance, if you want to learn patience, don't ask for it unless you are willing to have it tested every moment of every day until you have it. I learned not to expect God to take away the things that made me impatient, but instead to be prepared for God to allow situations to happen that would teach me to overcome my impatience. All choices have good or bad consequences to pay and a lesson to learn.

One night, while reading the Bible, I came to a story about Christ exorcising a demon. To my surprise, it was a simple procedure. He didn't yell loudly nor make a big fuss. He simply told it to leave the person.

He even taught the disciples how to do it, too, but for some reason, the steps on how to do it had been left out of the Bible. Yet there are many examples of Jesus and the disciples casting out demons throughout the New Testament.

Jesus commanded, and they left. Jesus said, "Be healed," and they were healed. He said, "Rise!" and Lazarus rose from death. Christ Jesus spoke, and all things, trees, demons, people, and even the wind, obeyed him. This was just like what God had told me when I was three about what He had done when He created everything.

Amazingly, it is written that we, as believers, can do all Christ did and more—if we believe without doubt. I was so excited to read those words. I wanted to share with Ty what I had learned. I looked up, and Ty was watching TV. I also saw a demon looking at me with hate in its eyes and a sneer on its face. Then a wonderful, unexpected thing happened. I saw fear in its eyes as it realized that I could see it. Calmly, with authority, I said, "In the name of Jesus, leave him. Do not return."

It looked at me with disbelief and wailed, "Noooo!" as it left Tyler forever.

Ty quickly looked over at me and asked, "What did you do to me?"

"What makes you think I did anything?"

"I'm not sure, but all of a sudden, a heavy weight lifted off of me. I feel different."

Joyfully, I told him what I had done in the name of Jesus. That night, he started reading the Bible for himself. He read it at work and would talk about it, too. He was seriously thinking about accepting Christ as his Lord and Savior and getting re-baptized.

◆

During those first five years of marriage and being a new Christian, I experienced many lessons that helped me grow stronger in the Spirit of God. I continued to have dreams and visions about spiritual matters.

Some of the dreams and visions were about my own personal and spiritual struggles with Ty.

I refused to get high or drunk. In one dream or vision, Ty asked me to go for a ride. He turned off the highway, onto a dirt road, drove a few miles, and then pulled over and turned off the engine. Ty pulled out a joint and asked me to share it with him. I was polite but told him no. He called me a party pooper, jumped out of the truck, walked briskly down the dirt road, and disappeared around a bend.

I thought he was being considerate by smoking the joint outside and away from me. Every time Ty asked me to get high, I reminded him that I had promised God I wouldn't smoke pot or get high ever again. I didn't need or want to anymore.

I waited for some time, but Ty didn't come back. I worried something had happened to him. In my dream, the Holy Spirit told me something was wrong. I followed Ty's tracks in the dirt. I walked around the bend and came upon a large campground picnic area. Many people were drinking, smoking, and doing all sorts of drugs. Some were making out, even having sex in plain view, while others were eating wonderful-smelling grilled food. I couldn't see Ty and was relieved he hadn't joined in.

When I passed a camp trailer on my way out of the park, I heard men laughing and girls giggling. I froze. I recognized Ty's voice and laugh. I walked up to the open doorway to look inside. Ty was sitting on a barstool, naked, with two naked women fondling and kissing him all over. *Not again!* I thought, remembering David and my so-called friend. I fought off the idea of beating them all up and kicking naked Ty out of the trailer and all the way back to the truck.

Instead, I walked in and asked the women to stop. "He's my husband," I told them. One of the women apologized, said she didn't know he was married, and walked away. The other defied me. "No! I want him. If you want him, you will have to fight me for him!"

I was surprised and hurt as Ty thought it was funny and encouraged a fight. The flesh was saying, "Yes! You could whoop her good. You have Marine skills and one heck of a right punch. Heck, just wrestling her down and choking her out would be easy."

The Spirit, on the other hand, said, "You are now a Christian. You cannot fight her. You are to try and reason with her and forgive her. Turn the other cheek. Be like Christ."

I tried to reason with her, but she got nastier and started poking me in my chest and getting up in my face. The trailer was too small. I couldn't get away. I asked her to let me go outside to pray to God and my Lord Jesus for help. I didn't want to fight.

She laughed hysterically. "Sure, go outside and pray to your God and Lord Jesus. They can't help you, because they aren't real!"

She followed me onto the grassy park area, still naked and unashamed. She mocked me and told everyone to gather around to watch her beat up a dumb Christian. I knelt down to pray, and she stood in front of me. Behind her was a multitude of people, laughing and mocking, waiting to see what was going to happen next. I was both angry and full of compassion toward her and the crowd of people.

God allowed me to see them as He saw them: poor, lost spirits who didn't know Him or Jesus. They knew not love. "Lord, help me!" I cried quietly in my mind. "I don't want to fight her, yet she is going to attack me. What am I to do?"

As I prayed, a sword came out of my chest. It was followed by a helmet and then a man in full armor and with a breastplate and a shield: the full armor of God. The man was Jesus.

He came out of me and stood facing the woman and the crowd. He then said, "Follow me! I go before you in all battles." I felt a great peace fall upon me as I watched Him go forth, and I followed. At that point in the dream, I was like a third person watching everything unfold before me.

The woman fell flat on the ground. She started crying, and with great joy, she loudly proclaimed, "HE IS REAL! JESUS IS REAL! Don't you all see him?" Jumping up, she ran all around the park, telling everyone, "JESUS IS REAL!" She had seen him with her very own eyes.

I was shown that Christ goes before me in all battles. All I needed to do was follow Him wherever He leads. When one believes and knows Christ, they are indeed truly free—free from fear of everything. That dream and other dreams and visions showed me that no matter what was going on in my life, all would be well spiritually as long as I kept my eyes, heart, and mind on Jesus. I just needed to remember His command to love and forgive.

Physically, not so much. I could still get injured, stub my toe, have a car wreck, or get the flu. Most of these things were caused by choices I made, not to mention my body was getting older and failing. We all know our bodies are going to die. Because of Christ, we have hope of getting a new body, incorruptible and immortal. Praise His name!

Not long after Ty was freed from the demon, his spiritual miracle, we bought a used Chevy Blazer. During fishing season, we would go on fishing trips on our days off. The dirt roads were rough on our car, and it was difficult to sleep in, so the Blazer was a blessing.

One late afternoon, we drove to a nearby lake to test out the Blazer's four-wheel drive and to find spots to camp. We were four-wheeling in a meadow, following some tire tracks. It was springtime, and there were patches of snow and ice still scattered throughout the meadow.

The ground started to get mushy. I suggested we back up the way we came. Ty decided to turn around where he thought it looked solid. We sank down to the axles and had no shovel, wood, or rocks to put under the tires. The jack was useless. We were stuck, and no one would be out there anytime soon, if ever. Ty became angry.

He didn't want to spend the night in the middle of nowhere. He didn't want to miss his favorite TV show, either. He mockingly asked, "Why don't you go pray to God to get us out of here?" I wondered why he didn't ask me to pray with him. Praying was new to him, and as a man, maybe he saw it as a sign of weakness. He didn't want to be seen as weak, especially since his machismo had gotten us into this predicament.

I found a dry spot near a big rock, knelt, and prayed, "Father God, please hear this prayer, not for me but for Ty so he will believe in you even more. I give you praise and thanksgiving for what you are about to do. In Jesus's name, amen."

I was still kneeling when the Lord spoke to me: "Get into the Blazer and put it in neutral. I'll do the rest." Tyler also spoke to me, saying, "Get in, put it in reverse, and punch it. I'll push from the front." I did as the Lord and Ty told me. I got in the Blazer, started up the engine, put it in neutral, and hit the gas.

To my amazement, the Blazer lifted in the air, flew back to the firm, dry road, and came to rest facing out toward the main dirt road. I held on for dear life and still had my foot on the gas pedal.

"Get off the gas!" God and Ty both told me. I was shaking from head to toe. Even Ty looked surprised, but he tried to hide it.

"Let's get outta here," he said with relief, glad he would be getting back in time for his TV show.

After seventeen years of marriage, Tyler decided to move our little family back to his Midwest hometown in the spring of 1994. I didn't want to move. I wouldn't have family, church family, or friends nearby. I would have to start all over in a strange place with a climate I didn't like.

I asked Brian if there were any loopholes in the Bible that I could use to get out of going. He laughed and then seriously told me he felt God had a plan for me. I should go. I went kicking and complaining all the way. I was having another full-blown pity party. I forgot God dislikes complainers. But, gee, I had a lot to complain about!

We wanted a house; we got a house trailer. It sat on the only hill in a trailer park…in tornado country! I didn't want gas anywhere except in a car; the heat was gas. At least there was an electric cooking stove, but then I was worried the gas pilot light would go out and, when I turned on the stove, it might blow up the trailer. I was extremely upset. I was being a big crybaby, ungrateful for what *was* being provided.

If that wasn't enough, I had been injured both in a car accident, when someone had run a stop sign and T-boned my car, and a strong-arm robbery when I'd been at work at a video store in the winter of 1993, four months before we moved to the Midwest. I hadn't been able to work for some time. I couldn't use my right arm because of a rotator cuff injury. I also had dislocated ribs and whiplash from the car accident, more reasons for me to feel sorry for myself.

When we moved in 1994, I still couldn't work, but my father-in-law would come over every morning to tell me about jobs I should check out. I was feeling pressured and cornered. I wanted to go back home to the Sierras. I didn't want or need a new set of parents hovering over me, telling me what to do. I was a full-grown woman, and if I got pushed anymore, I was afraid I would blow up at my poor father-in-law, who, I'm sure, was only trying to help. I was in pain, exceptionally frustrated, and feeling totally harassed.

One day, while Ty was at work and Aaron was in school, I drove down to the local lake. I parked under a tree and began to petition the Lord. I missed going to my special secret place in Tahoe. I needed to find a new special place. It was a much smaller lake, but I soon felt comfortable enough to let go, and boy, did I. I cried and complained for some time. Finally, I ran out of things to cry about.

As usual, only when one is silent can one hear God speak. To my astonishment, He spoke these words:

"Do you really believe in me?"

"Yes, of course I do."

"Then you trust in me?"

"Yes, I trust in you."

"Do you love me?"

"Yes, Lord, you know I love you!" I was in tears.

There was silence. In a gentle yet firm voice, He said, "Then what is your problem?"

I laughed at myself, shaking my head, and said, "Wow! You got me, Lord. You must shake your head at me all the time. My problem is me!"

I then heard, "Oh ye of little faith."

I completely surrendered everything to God once more. I complained no more about what was happening in my new world. Well, until the next big trial or tribulation came along. After all, I am only human, not perfect yet. I was reminded once again of something God had told me when I was troubled: "Things of the flesh are not lasting, but the things of the Spirit are everlasting."

Through many supernatural occurrences, I discovered I actually had power over evil, especially when I used the name of Yeshua, or Jesus. When Aaron was one week old, I was sound asleep when I felt a strange presence. I didn't sense evil per se, but I felt a mild fear. Was it evil? God never felt like fear to me before.

Searching the room, I saw an entity floating in the air above Aaron. It had a round body that glowed and pulsated like a jellyfish. I felt and heard a loud heartbeat. Eyeballs with all the colors of eyes were in its body. Its jellyfish-like tentacles floated up and down in the same rhythm as the heartbeat. Two tentacles were already in Aaron's nostrils. It was both beautiful and horrific.

I reached out energetically to learn what it was doing. Looking into all those eyes was hypnotic. Our breathing and heartbeats matched. We were connected as one, but it was in control. It was both soothing and frightening, and I started to drift away. I looked down at Aaron. He was having difficulty breathing. The two tentacles were still in each nostril, so I panicked.

I said firmly, "If you are not from God, I rebuke you in the name of

Christ Jesus. I command you to leave us." At first, it stayed floating in the air. Its tentacles were still in Aaron's nostrils, and it just stared at me with all those eyes. I stood firm and told it to leave with more authority in my voice. "We belong to Christ. His blood covers us. You have no authority here. Leave!"

It still just stared at me, stubbornly not removing the tentacles. I thought maybe the being was from God and I was interrupting something important. Not sure, I moved toward it to knock it away from Aaron, but it stopped me.

I couldn't withdraw myself from it, and I could no longer move or talk out loud. I could still talk with my mind, and again I firmly commanded it to leave us. I couldn't read all those eyes like I could one set of human eyes. I couldn't concentrate and was confused. I didn't know what it wanted or what it was doing to Aaron.

I watched the tentacles leave Aaron's nostrils. He squirmed and whimpered as he pushed them away with his tiny hands. The entity stared at me with complete indifference and floated straight toward me. My heartbeat and breathing were still in sync with the strange creature. It reminded me of the same breathing and heartbeat I had experienced on mescaline. I was conflicted as to which side the creature belonged. I still couldn't move, but I didn't show fear as it slowly floated toward me, through me, and then released me.

I ran to Aaron, picked him up, and checked him out closely. He seemed to be fine. I pondered if the creature's purpose had been to cause sudden infant death syndrome (SIDS). I moved the cradle closer to my bed just in case it decided to come back. I was so protective of our son that some thought I was being paranoid. Even Ty, who slept through the whole incident, found it hard to believe.

Through the years, Ty and Aaron were harassed by evil spirits. I fought the battles for them in Jesus's name, teaching them how to do the same for when I wasn't around. Our son encountered evil spirits in the form of flies, bats, and even in the image of the Count from Sesame Street, who would tickle him until he couldn't breathe. He would wake me with his loud laughter. I would wake him and chase the Count away in the name of Jesus. Other times, Aaron would come into our bedroom and ask me to go into his room to chase the spirits away.

Aaron would stay with Ty in our bed because he felt he wasn't as strong in faith as I was yet. His saying "yet" made me happy. That meant Aaron wasn't giving up. Someday he would be able to ward off evil himself. He had inherited the same family gifts. I was teaching him how to use them for good and not to fear or abuse them.

One encounter made me scream in fright. A bat had come into Aaron's room through the closed window, and it flew at his head. He came running to our room, telling us, "The Count turned into a real bat!" I figured it was just a dream and went to chase the "real bat" away. I told him real bats couldn't fly through closed windows.

I settled into his bed, waiting to see or hear a bat. To my surprise, I saw a large bat flying outside the closed window. It hovered for a moment and then flew right through the window without breaking the glass. It flew toward the bed. My head was partially covered by the blanket and sheet. I hoped it would think I was Aaron. I would surprise it by hitting it away and demanding in the name of Jesus that it leave. I thought it was in spirit form. I hit it, expecting my hand to go through it. Instead, I hit a soft, pliable wing and furry body. I screamed and hid under the covers.

Still, in Jesus's name, I loudly told it to leave our house and never come back. It never returned, but from then on, I checked outside the window whenever I put Aaron to bed.

During this time, I discovered one doesn't have to be a man to stand against evil. I had been trying to dodge evil by calling upon my Father to save me. Through Calvary Chapel and Brian, I learned I have the freedom, power, and authority in Christ to partake in things I had thought to be only a man's domain.

I learned the Holy Spirit chooses to give to whomever, male or female, whatever He wills. Through the Holy Spirit and Christ, I have the power to cast out demons, heal, counsel, and encourage others. I have the ability to love unconditionally, to forgive, and the really important ability to not fear.

As the Apostle Paul wrote, we can only do so by Spirit. We can be one with the Father and Christ. Like all things, to become good at it, one must practice, practice, practice. The life of a true Christian is hard, yet it is tempered with the knowledge of God's promises.

Many evil spirits influence the minds and hearts of people; they test us every day. Just when it seems there is no relief and all is lost, I'll meet another person who is walking in the Spirit. It is uplifting and encouraging. I cry with joy every time. It's more proof that the Yaqui and Christian beliefs are compatible in the sense of being "one in Spirit."

EVERYTHING TAKES TIME

TIME. I've always had an aversion toward time. First, there doesn't seem to be enough. There's the "wait a minute; give me a second, an hour, or even a day or two" excuse. Then there's the "let's wait a year or two" defense.

We are told, "It takes time to do or learn this or that; be patient." Then we are also told, "Hurry up! You're wasting time. You're taking too long; we don't have time for this. What is wrong with you? Get moving!" Time frustrates me. On the one hand, it is forever, and on the other, it is running out.

Then those in high places decide to give and take an hour every spring and fall. Some people don't participate; they get up when the sun rises and go to bed when the sun sets. It's a simple life of doing whatever you want or need to do between sunrises and sunsets.

When I am in a healing session, I don't worry about time. It will take as long as it takes. I wait for the body to react to the healing energy of the Holy Spirit. When an area is healed, I'm guided to another area until the whole body reaches its maximum healing potential for that particular moment in time. Sometimes it is an instant healing. I would love to have instant ones all the time.

Someone once told me, "You can't have instant gratification all the time."

"Why not?"

"Because you wouldn't appreciate nor be grateful for anything. You would be a spoiled, self-centered brat without respect or compassion for anything or anyone else."

I guess I had never really thought about how destructive it would be to instantly get what you wanted all the time. Kind of like socialism. It sounds good until you start living it and find you have less freedom and wealth than you were told you'd have. Seems only those in charge reap the benefits.

I opened my own business in 1986. As a business owner, I control the time, conditions, and prices of my services. The Lord provides for all my income and expenses.

I must admit, I was skeptical about charging for my services. I knew it was God working through me. "Freely you have received; freely give" (Matthew 10:8 NIV) came to my mind often. I wanted to do what God wanted me to do, so I asked Him, "Should I charge for your blessings of healing?"

"The worker deserves his wages" (1 Timothy 5:18 NIV) came to me. Then the Lord added, "Those who will come will be blessed." That is what I wanted, whether I made money or not. I trusted in Him. I put myself in the hands of the Lord so He could use my hands.

My purpose is to help those who come into my circle of influence, to share their physical and spiritual burdens, to give them guidance, and, most importantly, to introduce them to the presence of God, Christ, and the Holy Spirit. I want to help people cross the gap between flesh and spirit, light and darkness, so they may be able to stand firm in the face of evil in its many forms.

After a while, I questioned my relevance and debated whether I should continue or quit, retire or get back on fire with the work of the Lord. My answer came from an unexpected source. I received a timely invitation in the mail from a man who promised to give a word of knowledge or a prophecy from the Lord. I wanted to find out if this person was legit or a con man.

I took a client with me to hear what the man would tell her. I already knew what was going on with her. I didn't intend to get a word or a prophecy for myself. As always, God knows my thoughts, needs, and heart's desire.

The man told the person with me what I had known to be true. I was convinced he was filled with the Holy Spirit. He did have the gifts of knowledge and prophecy. My client was a bit skeptical, too, but was convinced by his words and the filling of the Holy Spirit in her. Later he came up to me to tell me he had a word for me! I was surprised and glad to hear what the Lord had to say.

He told me, "This is what the Lord says to you concerning your walk with Him. 'I have given you hind's feet. Again, I say, hind's feet so you may climb higher than anyone else can climb, so you can stand firm when others will slip, stumble, or fall. You will stand strong and firm in the gap. Someone must stand in the gap to help those who desire to cross over to righteousness. I have given you hind's feet so you can do the work I have sent you to do. Go forth, stand firm, do not fear. You have hind's feet!'" I was blessed to hear those words and the command.

I wasn't sure what a hind was, so I looked it up. A hind is a female deer. She can place her back feet exactly where her front feet stepped. They never lose their footing. She's mentioned in poetical parts of Scripture to describe activities such as gentleness, feminine modesty, earnest longing for truth, maternal affection, and steadfastness. She is also timid and shy, and she prefers to stay away from the haunts of men. Wow! That last part sounded just like me! Although some of the others did as well since I had become a Christian.

I was to continue my work with the Lord. I know He does the work through me. I am just an extension of His hands, love, and power. I speak the words He desires to give to those He sends, to bless and help them find their way back to Him, to cross the gap between them.

Through the years, I've had teachers of the Holy Spirit, who also used the gifts of the Holy Spirit, ask me with concern and sadness, "How do you handle all the rejection you've endured?"

I always smile and say, "I don't take it personally. They're not rejecting me. They are rejecting Christ Himself, which causes me to have great compassion toward them. I pray for them to see the light and the error of their way, to someday be reunited with God, whether with my help or someone else's."

God is always reaching out to us. He wants to have a personal relationship with each of us. We must be Spirit-minded, Spirit-walking, and Spirit-proficient. To be proficient, one has to practice being in Spirit, as with anything in which one wants to excel.

With practice, in time, you will become Spirit-wise. You will become fearless to the threats of evil, whether from people or demons. You will recognize which thoughts in your mind are from the Spirit of God and which are from evil because you will know that you know God *IS*.

You will know you are a spirit being and will return to God when the physical body falls away, and thus you no longer have to fear death. Scripture says we will get a new body just as Christ did when He rose from the grave. Remember, He told His disciples not to touch Him, as His new body was not ready. It wasn't *time*…

TIME. God's time, government time, job time, your time, my time, a time to live, a time to die, all valuable, yet much is wasted. We are given a certain amount of time to be here. Each person's time is predestined.

The moment we are brought into this realm, the clock of our time here starts ticking away. We all should be spending this time doing good, loving, helping, sharing, and encouraging others to live a full, happy, rewarding life in the Spirit. The flesh is never satisfied or in complete, lasting peace.

In this realm of fleshly, selfish, evil influences, it is not easy to live and walk in Spirit. There are many distractions, and others object to it. If you can do it, they have no excuse to not live it, too. They just don't want to be held accountable for their choices and don't want to give up anything accumulated in this realm, no matter how they achieved their power, fame, or fortune. I am amazed that they even say, "Well, you can't take it with you when you die!" So, why cling to it so tenaciously while you are here?

The resentment of the world is the reason those who have lived and walked in Spirit—who have put themselves out there to show the way—have been persecuted, ridiculed, tortured, imprisoned, and murdered. Those who rebel against God and His teachings of love, compassion, and forgiveness hate—yes, hate—those who walk with God. They want to destroy them, usually by lies aimed at character assassination, but sometimes they will demand death.

The world calls believers judgmental, cold-hearted, or mentally ill. They think only sane, well-educated people know all things and know what is best for everyone else. They think there is no God, devil, demons, angels, or life after death.

They think there is no good or evil, or they switch the meaning, calling evil good and good evil. They say we are here only to experience this world physically. Why do they bother to obtain fame, fortune, or power? Why ask for (or in some cases demand) admiration for themselves or their accomplishments from those they deem of less value?

That way of living doesn't make any sense. It isn't logical or beneficial to anyone but self. Self is its own god. We become our own judge, jury, and executioner when we are prideful and arrogant. Self puts itself above the laws of God, nature, and mankind.

Then there are others who try to take care of everyone they meet and get dragged into terrible situations while they are lost themselves. It causes much torment to one's soul. Besides burdening others around them, they get stuck, like in quicksand, with no way out.

I remind them there is only one God, telling them, "It ain't you, and it ain't me." Most importantly, God is faithful to us even when we are not faithful to Him. I learned this the hard way. God's faithfulness is revealed in *time*, in God's time, in the time one takes to surrender all of self to Him. It takes time to learn to be Christ-like, to walk in the Spirit instead of the flesh. It takes time for us to be perfected, to become what God created us to be. This is one of the reasons He promises eternity.

I'm sure I will need eternity to be perfected, to live it twenty-four-seven, every day. I've had seventy-plus years to live and learn. I know I need more time. I haven't reached the excellence I strive to reach on Earth, to fulfill my reason for being here. I'm still in the race, heading for the finish line, while also standing in the gap.

Only God knows when my time is up. Until then, I will live and walk in Spirit and fight the good fight against the flesh and evil. No more dodging evil. Now I stand firm against it, rebuke it, or cast it out. There is no fear to hinder me. I have God, my Father, Christ, my Savior, and the Holy Spirit, who unites us all as one and reminds me of those words spoken to me as a child and again Forty-three years ago. Those words stand true to this day and beyond…not only for me, but also for you! "DO NOT FEAR, FOR I AM WITH YOU ALWAYS, EVEN BY YOUR SIDE."

Epilogue

For the last thirty years to the present, I continue to walk in Spirit with God and Christ. I work in my business, That Special Touch Healing Center, under the guidance of God, serving those who come for healing. Sadly, because a texting driver ran a red light and crashed into my car, I received injuries that have caused me to be semi-retired.

Both Mom and Dad have passed over, as well as my grandparents, godmother, older sister Allie, and my father-in-law. My sisters are scattered in different states and are doing well. Aaron is all grown up, single, and running his own business.

Throughout the years, I have tried to contact Yaqui relatives and join the tribe in Arizona, but they have made it very difficult for me to join or even talk to anyone who is a relative, even though those in charge of the tribe have the same last names as my grandmother and grandfather on my mom's side and even my dad's family's last names are on the tribal membership rolls. Perhaps they know of my grandmother's reputation and feel they must shun anyone related so closely to her.

The only knowledge I have is that they believe we all are spiritually tied together with our Creator and all creation. This, I have known from my inception. God is with me, in me, and in all things because He created everyone and everything. I think this is why they, as I, have accepted the Christian faith; we believe the same about spiritual things, which comes naturally to native peoples.

I hope *Dodging Evil* enlightens all who read it. May it give them hope and peace for the future through all that will come their way in this life, especially by letting them know they are Spirit beings, alien to Earth, just passing through…on their way to our true home. I hope to see you all there!

About the Author

P C Field lives in the Wisconsin countryside with her husband of forty-three years and their two dogs, Blu and Trouble. She is an energy-based bodyworker and has been performing mind, body, and spiritual healings for over forty-three years. She also gives spiritual counsel, as she has been an ordained minister of the ULC (Universal Life Church) for over fifteen years. She is a wife, mother, and nature lover. Fishing has been a lifelong pastime that always leads to conversations with God, and she has always loved telling, reading, and writing stories. P C Field has another book pending publication, *When His Love Comes Trickling Down: Little Miracles*, book two in the Dodging Evil series. It is a sampling of the spiritual and physical healings God used her to facilitate. He also allowed her to see the spiritual change in her mother before she died. These healings occurred during the last thirty-plus-years to the present.

PC Field has two other books on the writing board. One is a story about her dream horse and is titled *The Wasp: A Love Story*. It is full of adventures she shared and lived through by the grace of God. Finishing the Dodging Evil series is book three, *The Things I Have Seen: Short Stories of Spiritual Events*. It is a compilation of the supernatural and spiritual events that have occurred in her life so far that she wasn't able to fit into *Dodging Evil*. (All coming soon to a book store near you!)

For questions or comments, you can reach P C Field at the following:

E: specialenergy2touch@yahoo.com

Website: https://pcfieldbooks.com

FB: P C Field – Memoir Writer Pregnant with Author-hood

Author: *Dodging Evil, A Yaqui Girl's Shocking Education from Society, Religion, and Spirituality*

Author: *Natural Mescaline vs Man-made Mescaline-What a Trip!* Online Magazine, The Closed Eye Open, Issue 2 Oct/Nov 2020

www.ingramcontent.com/pod-product-compliance
Lightning Source LLC
Chambersburg PA
CBHW021056080526
44587CB00010B/264